John G. O

# FINANCIAL ANALYSIS FOR MARKETING DECISIONS

# Financial Analysis for Marketing Decisions

**SAM R. GOODMAN**

**DOW JONES-IRWIN**  Homewood, Illinois  60430

Previously published under the title, *The Marketing Controller*

ISBN  0-87094-158-5
Library of Congress Catalog Card No. 77-171670

*Printed in the United States of America*

*This book is dedicated to my mother*
VIRGINIA GOODMAN
*who still refers to me as "my son the author."*

# Table of Contents

    Profit vs. Profitability . . Capital Budgeting, The Cost of Capital, and Marketing Decisions . . The Return on Investment . . Product Life Cycles . . Marketing and the Controller . . Marketing and the Research and Development Function . . Marketing and Management Sciences . . Marketing and Production Planning . . More About the Marketing and Finance Face-off . . Marketing and the Marketing Department . . Ideas to be Explored . .

## CHAPTER II

    Are Marketing Controllers Really Needed? . . Can the Areas Ever Integrate? . . Postwar Emergence of the Marketing Concept . . Need for Increased Accounting Dynamism . . Marketing Area Has a Quantitative Financial Void . . Marketing's Training to Understand Finance's Statements . . The Adequacy of Marketing/Financial Communication . . Training Programs and Training Attitudes . . Controllership in Marketing . .

## CHAPTER III

    Recognition by Various Authorities . . What is Marketing? . . What is Finance? . .

## CHAPTER IV

    Centralization Versus Decentralization in Marketing . . The Product Manager Dilemma . . Profit Responsibility Through the Product Manager System . . Centralization Versus Decentralization in Finance . . Marketing Organization Specifically for Planning and Control . . Finance's Role in Services for Marketing . . The Role of the Controller in Decision Making . . The Existence of Marketing Strategy and Decision Committees . .

# CHAPTER V

# CHAPTER VI

# CHAPTER VII

# CHAPTER VIII

# List of Exhibits

# Preface

It has been my pleasure to work closely with Dr. Sam Goodman for a half-dozen years. I can, without difficulty, appreciate the concerns expressed in this work and also agree with the principles involved in the proposed solutions.

In writing this preface, it is my assumption that the preponderance of readers will be executives with a financial or management control orientation. My comments are made from the other side of the mirror. From this side of the glass, it is clear that the control function can and must make a greater contribution to decision making.

Certainly, we must have records of the past if only to satisfy the legal requirements of the corporation. Additionally, past performance, be it success or failure, frequently provides a meaningful guide to future action if properly analyzed by people with a true understanding of the initial situation.

Fortunately, Dr. Goodman's point of view reaches beyond the past into an area which should be of even more interest to marketing organizations. This is the matter of evaluating alternatives and predicting the profit result of future actions. To these predictions, we must apply the discipline of probability and do so continually, whether these are committed to paper or handled through the mental gymnastics commonly labeled judgment.

I am familiar with the dilemmas presently facing many product or marketing managers and have had some experience which indicates that the availability of a financial man "on the inside looking in" can be of immense assistance.

In summary, one essential characteristic of good marketing is a keen interest in the past, coupled with an obsession about the future.

DOUGLAS B. WELLS
*President*
Libby McNeill & Libby, Inc.

# Author's Preface

The purpose of this book is twofold: to lay bare what the author believes is a critical problem existing in today's marketing environment and, after having accomplished this, to present a program for practical applications which will help to salve the abrasions in the marketing/financial relationship within contemporary companies. The book is designed so that two threads wind continuously through the presentation. The first thread is that of specific research findings based upon a comprehensive look at the marketing decision practices of twenty of the largest companies in the world. The second thread is the discussion of networks of techniques which should help the small, the medium, and the large company avoid the pitfalls exposed by the research.

## Background of the Study

The concept of instituting a new position such as that of "marketing controller," is far too broad in its ramifications to theorize its application in a simple manner. A prerequisite to the implementation of the concept and the assessment of its validity was a survey of the current state of the marketing decision-making process. Consequently, an attempt was made to learn something about the financial and marketing relationship in selected large consumer organizations. A research outline was prepared which proposed an inquiry into the "marketing controller" concept.

The outline envisioned a series of personal interviews with senior executives at twenty domestic consumer-oriented companies. The approach taken consisted of an interview which probed the nature of the marketing function as practiced within each concern. Questions also probed the financial area and its workings. Both marketing and financial personnel were separately asked for their opinions about the adequacy of decision-impelling information emanating from the financial area, and for their views of a proposed new corporate position, the "marketing controller."

The selective aproach was preferred over one which would seek a broad sampling of replies, as in the "in-depth" nature of the inquiry mandated personal interviews. Contacts were established with the Marketing Science Institute and the Financial Executives Institute. It was felt that cooperation from these two groups would facilitate the writer in gaining entry into large companies at the senior executive level. The author is extremely grateful to Mr. Jean Pumroy, Associate Director of M.S.I., and Mr. James Rutherford, Managing Director, and Mr. George Hobgood, Director of Research, of F.E.I. for arranging interviews with their members.

For the most part the companies were located in New York City; a few were located in areas of Pennsylvania, New Jersey and Connecticut. Senior marketing and financial personnel were interviewed. Each meeting averaged between two and three consecutive hours in length; additional correspondence clarified any points in doubt and confirmed the notes taken. Definitions of all uncertain terms were reviewed with persons interviewed, and every attempt was made to record faithfully the substance of each answer.

Where companies engaged in both consumer and industrial products, questions were directed to the consumer area. Personnel of selected divisions of decentralized companies were also interviewed.

## Construction of Research Questions

An interview guide was prepared.[1] It consisted of an ordered grouping of questions designed to elicit open-end responses to questions.

Section One of the guide was designed to enable the positioning of the respondents relative to the range of products produced, the definition of marketing and finance employed by the company, and the company's status as a conglomerate.

Section Two asked for objective measures of size expressed in terms of sales volume, number of employees, principal marketing divisions, and mainline products other than flavor or size variants.

Section Three positioned the interviewee in terms of the company's customer mix.

Section Four probed in depth the organization of the marketing and financial functions, particularly in regard to the impact of centralization or decentralization, and analyzed internal reporting relationships.

Section Five inquired into the marketing organization, especially as it relates to profit responsibility, the product manager system, adequacy of accounting measure of profit, and the planning and control functions. This section was directed towards marketing personnel only.

Section Six is similar to Section Five, but was addressed to financial executives. It inquired into the role of the corporate or division controller, the use of sophisticated analytical techniques, the competency of marketing personnel, and the value of accounting services available to marketing.

Section Seven probed the horizons for marketing analysis, the influence of EDP on decision-making, and the presence of an organization for evaluation of market strategy.

Many ideas will be put forth in the material which follows. No idea, however, is worth anything unless a definite conclusion and a practical application can be found relative to its certain thesis. The ideas that follow are presented in conjunction with the conclusions drawn from the material. Each of these ideas, and the justifications for the conclusions are thoroughly discussed in the balance of the book.

√IDEA No. 1:

The basic structure of marketing is becoming increasingly oriented toward quantitative methods and techniques of management sciences. Research into the awareness of and need for the marketing controller concept will yield information usable in evaluating current corporate organization structures and their ability to meet modern marketing requirements.

Conclusion:

Marketing is becoming increasingly oriented toward quantitative techniques. Research has shown that the marketing and financial functions have thus far failed to organize properly to take advantage of the potential benefits to be derived from management science techniques. Research results have demonstrated that a need and awareness are present relative to the marketing controller concept.

IDEA NO. 2:

The time may have arrived to change the conventional segmentation of professions; individuals trained in both the accounting area and the marketing area will be required to assist the marketing function. Greater quantitative inputs highlight imperfections in reporting relationships and make mandatory a more precisely defined linkage between marketing management and its financial counterparts.

Conclusion:

Unquestionably, the unanimously favorable response demonstrates an awareness and a need for a marketing-oriented financial specialist. The research implied that it may be desirable to change the conventional segmenting of professions but it by no means confirmed the hypothesis. Respondents seemed to posit the individual *either* in finance or marketing, per se, not in a consortium of the two functions as a joint decision-aider.

IDEA NO. 3:

The age of specialization may be rendering obsolete formerly held conceptions of the conventional controller's position. Whereas current controllership practice emphasizes the function of reporting to management, owners, and government, and the specific control of most nonmarketing expenditures, future requirements based on marketing needs will be oriented toward marketing decision-making and the control and evaluation of marketing costs.

Conclusion:

This hypothesis has been amply confirmed by the running thread of replies implying that finance needs decision inputs for promotional efficiency studies, simulation, customer/geographic profitability studies, etc. In addition, the consensus of observations by the respondents emphasized that the marketing controller should be freed from reporting disciplines.

IDEA No. 4:

The conceptual evolution of a marketing controller is a natural development following the birth of the field of accounting, and traces a course leading from functional bookkeeping, fractionalized manufacturing controllership (plants), and reporting responsibilities, to other specialized decision-making areas such as taxes and capital decisions.

Conclusion:

The confirmation of this hypothesis certainly must be subjective. In the light of the earler Controllership Foundation study and respondents' replies in the research implying the need for financial specialists (one suggested that there should also be a production controller), it is the opinion of the author that the marketing controller concept is a further step in the continuing evolution of financial specialization.

IDEA No. 5:

The marketing controller is likely to be an active, decision-making participant in such marketing-oriented areas as new product venture analysis, sales incentive planning, and media and promotional profitability planning, as well as ancillary corporate functions such as acquisition and purchasing policy determination.

Conclusion:

From the research data and conversations with the participants in the study, numerous qualities which might characterize a marketing controller were evaluated. Sufficient information was obtained to formulate a position guide for the marketing controller.

# Chapter I

# Introduction

The traditional marketing concept views the marketing function as being entrusted with the task of finding customers for the products that companies sell. This outlook is becoming obsolete and dated. In its place has been substituted a somewhat newer viewpoint, more typical of highly industrialized industries. The substitution is the recognition that marketing's task is to sell products in response to the customer's wants. Make no mistake: this is an innovative marketing concept. Companies which have failed to grasp this idea have gone the way of the dinosaur while their products litter the pages of marketing textbooks as case studies.

Although I will get more specific in later stages of the book, for our immediate purposes, I shall define marketing as the analysis, the organization, the planning, and the controlling of those resources of a firm which are directed toward satisfying the various needs and wants of customer groups . . . and at a profit. This definition of marketing is quasi-synonymous with a firm's objectives and one might be tempted to take the extreme position that the chief marketing officer should direct the entire company operation.

A somewhat more detailed expostulation of this position was made by the author in his book, *Techniques of Profitability Analysis*.[1] In it, a statement was made to the effect that, "In essence, marketing may be the motivation which provides for the continuity of all other corporate services. The conception of a functional organization can best be described as taking the form of a wheel in which marketing is placed at the center, akin to a hub, while the ancillary services of administration, controller, purchasing, engineering, data processing, and distribution, all rim the wheel." A shift to this type of philosophy from the more traditional and wholly deficient organizational charts might force company employees to admit, perhaps for the first time, that they are all working for the same company. That this is not presently the case is amply demonstrated by the plethora of behavioral science papers dealing with the problem of sub-optimization in corporate behavior.

This book will deal with the modern-day marketing function and its interaction with other corporate disciplines. That these interactions are at present normative rather than descriptive in the majority of American companies is a sad tribute to the power of corporate inertia. The book will begin by reviewing certain basic but very powerful tools that are critical to the full comprehension of subsequent material. These tools, however, can be understood and applied in the light of the earlier research findings. The technique used will be the study of the interaction of marketing with other disciplines on a one-to-one basis. In all of these studies, extensive use will be made of the basic tools which are available for application with each discipline.

A great deal of emphasis in the book has been placed upon the definition by Clarence Eldridge of modern marketing, which he describes as, "ascertaining, creating, and satisfying the wants of the consumer . . . at a profit."[2] The modern marketing environment exists in that organization which adheres to and lives up to this encompassing definition. Emphasis must be placed on organizational response. For it *is* and *must be* a total corporate effort that will provide this environment. The purpose and objective of the environment must necessarily dovetail with that of the corporation. It is marketing and its environment that provide the final service vehicle for implementing the corporate philosophy of being. An understanding of the environment requires an understanding that all functional efforts lead to the same objective.

The result of the generation of this environment will be a departure from precepts of the past that regarded each department or function in an organization as separate and doing "only its thing." In the past, meeting this criteria has been tantamount to saying that the little box on the organization chart is living up to its standard of performance. This is an antiquated administrative and corporate concept; yet, in too many instances, it remains in place.

The common thread running throughout all functions and departments in an organization should be a corporate objective of satisfying people. As this is a common charge for all functions and the primary charge for the marketing function, it follows that all functions are either directly or indirectly providing the marketing service. It is essential to understand that this is a concept of being and operating, not just a form of organization with marketing at the head. All corporate functions should continue to "do their own thing." The common understanding required is that there is this unified goal and that through improved communications with the marketing function, the direct or indirect marketing services of all other corporate functions will be provided and used in the most effective manner.

Earlier in the discussion it was noted that marketing would be confronted with problems emanating from other disciplines. The discussion which follows attempts to highlight these abrasions in terms of an overview of topics to be covered in the substance of the book.

### Profit vs. Profitability

Profit is a residual concept which is far better adapted to reporting than to decision-making. Profit is owner-oriented, static and historical. It can be manipulated by using combinations of "generally accepted accounting principles." This includes methods of depreciation, methods for valuing inventories, the subjective employment of capitalizing vs. expensing techniques, uses of accounting for the investment credit, or through the use of acquisition accounting in merger negotions. By contrast, profitability connotes dynamism and tends to result in more rational decision-making. The use of relevant costs (costs that would cease to exist if the product ceased to exist) is the essence of profitability. Relevant Costs can be quantitively defined as a rate of change of profit based upon changes in the physical volume of sales. It allows for charges or for expenses to be separated into direct costs (costs that are directly attributable to the existence of a product) and indirect, or period costs. This latter category contains types of costs which change over periods of time, and thus have a closer correlation with the temporal dimension than with rates of change of physical volume.

The need for analytical decision-making tools in the present day environment hardly needs belaboring; product life times are shrinking. The development and introduction costs of new products are skyrocketing; the penalities for introducing worthless products or for failing to introduce new products, are staggering. In these terms, all available analytical techniques must be placed at the disposition of businessmen to allow them to supplement or formulate alternatives to their hunches or intuitions. Only by doing this can out-of-pocket dollars be saved or productively utilized. Profitability analysis is one of the more important of the techniques.

### Capital Budgeting, the Cost of Capital, and Marketing Decisions

Every capital planning decision is a marketing decision. The decision as to whether to build a new plant in order to make a new product is not an isolated manufacturing consideration nor is it an academic capital budgeting problem. The quantitative root cause for the evaluation is the development of a new product. The final solution to the capital budgeting problem may well be that the company would be better served if the product were not made in a new company plant, but perhaps made by another company with manufacturing facilities already in existence. In this respect, it is not so much a capital investment problem as it is a make or buy problem. In all of this, the undercurrents of a marketing consideration are very evident. In the discussion dealing with capital budgeting, reference will be made to the four traditional approaches of evaluating capital proposals:

1. The average rate of return
2. The payback method

3. The internal rate of return method
4. The present value method

From a marketing point of view, number three will be demonstrated to be superior. The internal rate of return approach implies that funds generated from the results of the proposal are reinvested at the internal rate of return for opportunities available to the firm. This latter rate is far more realistic and hence the discounted cash flow technique will be used in our discussion of return on investment evaluations.

The cost of various forms of capitalization will be discussed. The relationship of these costs, and their weighted averages, to the minimum rate of return on investment projects, will be emphasized.

### The Return on Investment

This is another financial technique which is used by businessmen to crystallize their intuition. It serves both to evaluate progress and to help make a decision between alternatives. Succinctly, the cash inflow from a project, discounted to its present value, is divided by the investment required to achieve this inflow. In essence, and in its most crude semantic form, return on investment expresses the question of "What am I giving for what I am getting?"

Just as the earlier discussion distinguished profit from profitability, there is here the need to differentiate short-run ROI and long-run ROI. The former deals only with the past period's results, while the latter attempts to project future considerations. In essence, the long-run ROI expresses the future results of present day actions. It is almost synonymous with managerial efficiency. The emphasis in the book will be upon the use of long-term ROI. Historically, an overemphasis on short-run ROI has led only to the focusing by the manager of his attention on "beating the system" and upon improving personal showing. This hardly qualifies the technique as a good accounting tool or as a good marketing tool. The use of the long-run ROI method results instead in coordinating individual and corporate goals.

## Product Life Cycles

American business has traditionally thought of profit only in terms of its quantity. It is probably inconceivable on the surface that a company with a pattern of steadily increasing earnings may in reality be a very sick company. It is rare that anyone asks the question which will probe into how long the stream of earnings will last and from what specific sources do the earnings derive? This book will attempt to provide a singular look at corporate profit as measured in terms of the "quality of profit." The concept of product life cycles will be discussed with particular reference to its impact on corporate planning and the need for a firm to use different marketing techniques to create, alter, or reverse the various stages of a life cycle will be explored. Reference will also be made to the recent Nielsen study of consumer product life cycles and the various techniques for regeneration of a product. The importance of this particular discussion lies in the Nielsen finding that on an average, a product has a life only of about 2.9 years. This is a supreme tragedy for American business, because in that short span of 2.9 years, the product must run the gamut of the development of the prototype, formula or packaging improvements, the introductory phase, test marketing and national distribution, a huge marketing investment spending program and hopefully, either a recoupment or the generation of incremental profit. This subject and its relationship to marketing decision-making thus begins to take on tones of urgency.

## Marketing and the Controller

The finance function has traditionally viewed marketing from without, as if it were under a magnifying glass. Numerous functions and techniques within the financial area are unknowingly marketing-oriented. These techniques can be directly related to assisting the marketing decision-making process in areas such as new product introduction, the pricing of new products in new markets, evaluation of new market areas, evaluation of salesman performance or even the value of research and development expenditures. Through the use of these methods in a marketing area, a greater sense of financial profit responsibility is combined with a creative optimism in the marketing function. Rather than finance telling marketing what the minimal project earnings requirements are, marketing may have an opportunity for an honest understanding of what these requirements entail and mean. Marketing can exercise greater discretion in examination of the impact of price/volume/cost decisions, new product decisions, media and promotional expense strategies, etc. This approach must certainly lead to a greater understanding and appreciation of the accounting concept of the balance sheet and its relationship to the somewhat overworked profit and loss statement.

The control and accounting function has also been too far removed from the marketing process. The control function has too often viewed marketing not necessarily as a decision-making function, but as a sales area requiring considerable and continual monitoring of expenses. This is a misconception, but nevertheless it exists in many companies. Unfortunately, marketing has not made much effort to improve the mutual working environment. The controller's area, while traditionally supplying historical "what happened" information, is in perhaps the strongest position to provide "what will happen" information, based upon the choice of alternative marketing strategies.

The controller, by virtue of his overwhelming concern with profit, has been primarily attuned to the past. This is not to fault him; rather it is an attempt to recognize the traditional view of the firm's structure and of the marketing concept. The new marketing concept and resulting corporate structure, which were discussed earlier, lead to an enlargement in the traditional controller's job. Being a technical expert in cost analysis, he must use all of the analytical tools that are at his disposal to serve all departments, and most particularly the markting department. It is his responsibility to be certain that the manager is guided by relevant data that will lead him to the best decisions. Historical data may be helpful in the formulation of predictions, but past figures in themselves are irrelevant because they are not the expected future data that managers must use in intelligent decision-making.

Out of this analysis naturally grows the concept of the *market-*

*ing controller.* In the early portions of this book, a survey of current practices in this area, as well as a job description for such a position will be discussed. Such a man should have a broad training in the financial area, coupled with an intensive marketing exposure. With many firms the marketing controller may already be an existing person or function. Aside from providing the quantitative expertise in the areas of conflict enumerated in the research, his primary function will, or should be, to stimulate an evolutionary change in the constitution of the modern marketing environment. His emphasis should be providing a decision framework that focuses on tomorrow. He should draw upon the specialized disciplines to achieve this focus. Today's business schools are concentrating heavily on the quantitative techniques required by such a specialized analyst. The principal block in his way toward a more receptive understanding of the modern marketing environment is probably contemporary upper management. It will take, therefore, an evolutionary time period before the internal conflicts are removed and the new marketing concept and the concept of the marketing controller are more fully accepted. The required go-between types will necessarily have to understand this and live with this situation while the the change takes place.

## Marketing and the Research and Development Function

This is perhaps the area where the greatest antagonism to marketing exists. A research and development scientist's major quality is creativity. A marketing man's principal focus is satisfying customer's needs. Only secondarily is he necessarily interested in creating new products. This leads to a conflict between the scientist who says to the marketing men, "I've developed a fantastic little widget, how many of them can you sell?" and the marketing man who in return responds to the scientist, "I've got a $10 million market for green blobs, can you make them for less than $1.00 per pound?"

This difficulty is further compounded by the fact that, when a scientist comes up with a multimillion dollar product, it is still the man who sells the millions of dollars of product who gets most of the credit. The solution to this dilemma lies in better communication. The scientist should make available to the marketing man the list of attributes of the proposed product, while the marketer should provide the scientist with the characteristics for all of the markets that they can penetrate. Formerly, with the traditional organization shart showing marketing and R&D on a parallel and same level, this was an improbable course. With new hub-like marketing concept, a more meaningful market/R&D interaction is possible. Furthermore, marketing, through the marketing controller, would be able to assist R&D in more carefully evaluating their projects from an investment viewpoint. A partnership rather than a competition may be in the offing. This would immeasurably strengthen both departments.

## *Marketing and Management Sciences*

The business sciences, recently developed in the post war years, are beginning to make an impact on the corporation. The behavioral sciences, developed by men like Drucker, Levitt, Mazlow and others, have opened many doors into the motivation of employees and groups, and have influenced the theory and practice of management. If only a handfull of these theories and methods were understood and effectively employed, the communication lines necessary to the modern marketing environment, could easily be opened and maintained. In turn an even better understanding of the concept and operation of the marketing environment could be achieved. Thus far the behavioral sciences as a part of management sciences have been explored and applied in an almost experimental case-by-case procedure. While they may have improved the operations of a part of a corporate function, they have not yet brought seemingly diverse functions together behind the common goal in the marketing environment. Management sciences or quantitative techniques have and are demonstrating their worth in such areas as inventory control, forecasting and other specialized quantitative decision areas. Their worth can be judged by their ability to enhance managerial judgment and awareness in decision problems. The fact that they are used in specialized areas within separate functions tends only to further separate the functions and maintain the separate department-separate function concept. A successful technique which enhances or improves the operation in one area should not be restricted to that area alone. The impact of the improved operation should be extended to the operations of other functions. Management science, as well as finance, has tended to develop areas of acute specialization. Too often these special capabilities are kept within the area of their development and use, rather than shared. In today's marketing environment, operating centers within the marketing function are held responsible for total profitability. The special abilities of the finance and control functions should work *within* the marketing function rather than without. The special abilities of the marketing man in areas such as product life cycle analysis, should be employed by the finance department during acquisition programs. Too often these special abilities are not used or traded on an internal basis; hence, the historical concept of operation is maintained.

Operations research, or that specialized section of the corporation which applies management science techniques can, in conjunction with the control function, develop and use various quantitative methods to assist the marketing decision-making process. Specifically, probability analysis can be applied to the areas of optimum alternative selection problems. These techniques can also be applied to sales forecasting problems. Plant or distribution location analysis can be optimized by the use of the simplex algorithms of linear programming as can the determination of optimal product sales mixes and/or production mixes. Simulation exercises can be developed to predict new product successes. Product and market life cycles can be related to the quality of the profit dollar, as well as to the quantity of dollars. The point is that, if these techniques are used with care, the judgment of the marketing decision maker can be enhanced and the input to his decision-making process greatly refined. Too often these marketing-oriented techniques lie dormant in the towers of the operations research center. The existence of these techniques may be known by other personnel within the corporation but they are not truly understood by the practicing professions.

Of extreme interest has been the development of *mathematical models* for marketing decision-making. Models are constructed as an aid to understanding and controlling real world events. With the increasingly high costs of preparing and introducing new products as well as rapidly decreasing product life times, it is becoming imperative to spend research, advertising, promotional and test marketing investment funds in as optimal a manner as is possible. Some hopeful approaches towards product introduction optimization have been offered by David Learner's DEMON model and Glen Urban's SPRINTER model. On the buyer's side, John Howard and Jagdesh Sheth have published *The Theory of Buying Behavior*.[3]

Consumer behavior problems differ from production/inventory distribution problems in that behavioral relationships are critical rather than merely peripheral or incidental. The fact that human behavior is the key element in most marketing models implies a second distinctive feature: the relationships to be represented are very difficult to observe. For the same reason, however, mathematical models may well contribute more to the understanding of marketing than of any other area, simply because they provide a badly needed framework for defining and measuring relevent factors. Ultimately, the identification and measurement of these relevant factors will permit useful generalizations about the factors to be created. This is precisely what Howard and Sheth have attempted to do in their book. Although all of their variables are operationally defined, the interaction between these variables is actually quantified. This is not the case, however, in their factor/analytic model of brand loyalty. It is designed to replace the currently inadequate Markov chain representations of buyer behavior. Their model provides a single number for each buyer which summarizes his pattern of purchase behavior over a period of time. This is the first step towards quantifying the extraordinarily complex consumption behavior of man.

Our discussion so far has ignored that element which by itself determines the success or failure of the mathematical model: the willingness of management to accept the concept of a model. As sophistication, accuracy, and correspondingly, management's confidence in models have increased, models have become acceptable and accepted. However, they should not be used indiscriminately. It is an old axiom that the value of information should always be more than the cost of obtaining it. Good models, being very complex, require the use of, and access to, large computers. Hence, only large companies in the highly competitive consumer market can use the newer models with a high degree of efficiency. Middle-size and smaller companies must rely on prepackaged programs for consumer models which may be run on a time-sharing basis. Under the appropriate circumstances, the marketing man should rapidly espouse his opportunity to quantify his hunches and inspirations and, accordingly, to reduce major new product failures. It is rare that any marketing man attempts to place a dollar sign on the cost of making a wrong decision.

## Marketing and Production Planning

With the evolution of the new marketing concept has come a parallel modification in the traditional view of the product manager. Profit has again yielded to profitability. As stated earlier in our discussion of return on investment, no accounting method should be used which primarily focuses the manager's attention on "beating the system." Any measure of performance used to evaluate a manager must help him to harmonize his objectives with the overall organization goals. Specifically, the measurements must not overemphasize one facet of the total operation, must not encourage short-run gains at present to the detriment of long-run results, must not fail to delineate responsibility, must not fail to distinguish between controllable and uncontrollable factors, must not encourage false record keeping, and, most certainly, must not create or engender faulty cost analysis.

The new product managers should be judged on a profitability basis with all of the attention concentrated on the *direct profit* resulting from his product. Even in so doing, a word of caution is in order. Any product may have several managers. This results in the product manager only being a major *influence* in the determination of product profitability rather than being its sole *determinant*. The marketing departments of the newer organizations significantly assist in the decision-making processes of the product managers. Specifically, these departments aid in product development, sales forecasting, objective development, budget determination, as well as advertising, media and promotional planning. The interaction between the marketers and the product managers in this context will be discussed in greater detail at a later point.

Formal production planning must not be permitted to remain oblivious to its effect upon the working capital position required to support a product. The wise use within the company of the financial function or of the marketing controller, where he exists, will establish the quantitative trade-off between the carrying costs of inventories of a product and the savings which might result from level manufacturing production. There is often a prejudice in the minds of administrative, non-manufacturing management against overtime operations under the theory that overtime operations are always more non-productive in terms of marginal costs. If measured in terms of the financial impact upon profits, it can quite often be demonstrated that overtime is a much more inexpensive way to accelerate production. If it precludes a company from hiring additional workers for regular time production, the out-of-pocket savings begin with the elimination of additional fringe benefits. Additionally, there is the sometimes forgotten consideration of learning curve efficiency. When a man continues to do a repetitive operation, he becomes more efficient as he progresses up to a point. Overtime should cease at the fatigue point.

Product managers as well as administrative managers should always be kept fully informed of the "months of coverage" or stock supply for products. The "months of coverage" is an expression derived from comparing the physical stocks of a product at a given date with the sales expectations for the same product. A further extension of that computation can be made by taking the excess of inventory over sales expectation and valuing it at an annualized interest rate. The resulting figure indicates the annualized dollar cost impact of carrying excess inventories.

### *More about the Marketing and Finance Interface*

History suggests that if financial managers are to bring their desires for growth to fruition, they should have a rather broad conception of their company's product line. Few successful companies have continued to produce the same type of products throughout their life time. Successful companies are usually market-oriented rather than product-oriented and the type of product demanded by the relevant market tends to undergo radical changes as time passes. Unless a company's product mix is restructured to meet the market's changing demands, growth will be impeded, if not prevented.

Numerous examples can be cited of corporations which have fallen into serious difficulty because diversification was permitted to run rampant. Twelve years ago for instance, Olin Industries and Mathieson Chemical Corporation merged to form the giant Olin Mathieson Chemical Corporation. The product lines of the new firm were among the broadest in American industry. They included, industrial chemicals, agricultural chemicals, brass, aluminum, cellophane, batteries, firearms, lumber, tools, fuels and drugs. After twelve years, it still is not clear whether this multiple of parts has been coordinated into an efficient whole.

There are many valid reasons for negotiating a merger. For example, a company may be underutilizing its plant capacity and the merger may provide a convenient way of adding product lines that can be produced by the idle plant. Frequently, the new and existing products have complementary seasonal patterns. Similarly, the products added by a merger may be sold through the same channels as the company's existing products, thus making a more efficient use of the markting facilities. Another reason may be that the products of the merging companies serve as raw materials or as end-products of the merged companies.

All these reasons are marketing oriented. It can probably be stated without exaggeration that most unsuccessful mergers are occasioned by a failure to contemplate the marketing factors. Here again, changing the organizational position of the marketing department so that it will be at the center of a hub will lead to more effective acquisition programs. The marketing department will help provide the finance department with sharper corporate goals, with more extensive marketing expertise and with product life cycle information. Alternatively, in some instances the marketing department may even point out to the financial people the increase in the span of corporate activities that would result from the purchase of the company by an industrial giant.

## Marketing and the Marketing Department

The worth of the techniques of modern marketing must be measured against traditional marketing activities and the tradeoff established. The previously introduced concept of product life cycles can be extended to analyze the optimal product mix. Even though corporate earnings may be at a record high, the product line may be long on yesterday's bread winners and short on tomorrow's hopefuls. Use of the life cycle analysis allows the categorizing of the firm's products into four groups for deciding on the optimal strategy to be followed.

Firstly, products may be classified into those which currently enjoy a high market share but a low acceleration of growth. Their satisfactory earnings may be sometimes used inappropriately to justify continued investment in that product, where the proper objective might be to maximize the cash flow, consistent with maintaining the present high market share. Another type of product may be identified with high market shares and rapid growth. These are the future high dollar earners and, as such, must be paid the maximum attention. Heavy cash and earnings investment are prerequisites to reaching that stage. If instead, one attempts to extract higher earnings during the growth stage, the products may instead land in the last category of products that we will be discussing, that is, those with low market share and slow growth. Other products may have low market shares and rapid growth. These require a heavy cash investment to move them into a dominant market position before the saturation stage of the life cycle becomes apparent.

Lastly, products that have a low market share and slow growth must be identified readily because, on a marginal basis, they may be draining funds from the corporation. Programs for phasing out these weak products must be established in conjunction with marketing and finance.

A conclusion can be reached, based upon the above, that very careful planning is required with respect to the timing of new product introductions and product regeneration. This can be greatly facilitated by use of the life cycle worksheet, described in a later chapter in some detail. The present plight of many an industry, including the aircraft industry, can be explained by a lack of a similar planning effort.

The high rate of failure of new product ideas and of new products, the ever shortening life time of new products and the ever increasing cost of new product development, all mandate that extraordinarily careful attention be focused upon new product decisions. In this context, new product ROI analysis and the product improvement decision guide are both critically important. Examples of both these techniques will be discussed. The use of models in this connection will also be investigated, as they are particularly useful in determining the optimal marketing mix for new products.

The use of ROI in setting prices for new products will be contrasted to the outdated and unanalytical technique of cost-oriented mark-up and going rate pricing. The use of models for initiating and responding to price changes in products will also be reviewed.

Excellent tools of logic cannot serve as an erstaz for creativity, particularly in marketing. They can only hope to eliminate some of the grosser potential errors and to provide the decision makers with an intelligent compilation of all of the available data. At this point, human creativity and ingenuity must enter being. The enterpreneurial spirit has not been superseded. Rather, it has been equipped with the necessary armament to cope with the increasingly complex modern day world.

# Chapter II

# The Marketing Controller: An Emerging Function

Companies continuously innovate in product marketing and technical areas involving manufacturing and research and development. It is interesting, therefore, to note the relatively new trend of innovation which has begun to invade the skeletal structure of corporate organizational patterns. The job of the chief operating officer is slowly being reshaped as a consequence of the immense complexity of the decision making requirements of the position.

In recent years the concept of the troika has been injected into the business world and, indeed, the expression, "office of the president" has become an accepted part of organizational structure.

It is therefore not too far afield to take a critical look at the financial function in order to examine its relevance to current responsibilities. As a discipline, finance was born in Italy, weaned in Scotland, matured in the United States and, there, has entered a stage in life suggesting flaccid middle age.

Accounting (finance) has become a series of specializations developed to meet defined needs. The controller evolved from the accountant who, in turn, evolved from the bookkeeper. This was a vertical process of evolution. Horizontally, the controller separated his function when the age of organizational decentralization came into being. When manufacturing plants required specialized assistance, the concept of a plant controller was born.

Now, companies are beginning to recognize that marketing may impose a set of different requirements upon the financial staff. Companies such as General Foods, duPont, American Cyanamid, Trans World Airlines have all recently created organizational positions of Advertising Controllers, individuals who are quantitatively trained but who share a marketing empathy. Publishing houses such as John Wiley & Sons have installed financial specialists *within* the operating divisions. Johnson & Johnson has completed a partial transition to the use of divisional *marketing* controllers. As will be discussed subsequently, the Nestlé Company pioneered the formal adoption of this concept in 1965. Other companies such as British Overseas Airways Corporation and Heublien have, in the past, structured themselves to recognize a position of *marketing* controller.

As a formalized concept, therefore, it is new. The marketing controller concept was conceived out of a recognition that marketing and its related functions are in immediate need of *creative* assistance for planning and control. Under this proposal the primary thrust of the marketing controller will be to exercise free form and creativity in assisting the decision-making process. An illustration of a possible direction for activity lies in the common corporate problem of committing and spending media funds prior to the time that benefits presumably derived from the media source will be recognized in the books of account. The normal procedure is to expense this type of item in the year of commitment; for television advertising this usually occurs in the fall of the year. Thus, costs associated with benefits to be recognized in 1971 and 1972 will have been expensed in 1970. In addition to severely straining an accounting guideline dictum of "attempting to match revenues with expenses", a great deal of the credibility of the operating statement for both 1970 and 1971 is open for questioning. Indeed, it may be that for decision-making purposes an annual operating statement is specious and misleading. Very recently, the power of advertising recall was visibly demonstrated with the modest sucess of Ipana toothpaste, now no longer being manufactured or marketed by Bristol Myers.

The marketing controller would not be subjected to formalized reporting constraints. Rather, his role in this situation could easily be the creation of pro-forma operating statements based upon a media year instead of the rigid calendar year requirement for external reporting purposes.

## Are Marketing Controllers Really Needed?

The marketing area can no longer afford the luxury of making decisions in isolation which have quantitative implications. Most marketing decisions have a quantitative end product which, in turn, will affect the operating statement. Therefore, marketing must seek out individuals who are quantitatively trained but who possess the broad ability to integrate *into* the marketing function.

Secondly, the marketing controller function can serve to counterbalance the preoccupation of the financial function with what happened yesterday. As a result of training and experience, accountants, when entering a room, walk backwards. All of the generally accepted accounting principles are oriented to the reporting requirements of the profession. These reporting requirements, regretfully, may have no relevance to a decision today that will affect an outcome tomorrow.

## Can the Areas Ever Integrate?

Acceptance of the premise that much of the lack of dialogue and goodwill between finance and marketing stems from personality traits ingrained in each of the two disciplines will enable one to take steps towards the integration of functions, attitudes, and objectives.

Organization charts are self defeating; they encourage individuals to consider their little "box" as their private kingdom, and woe to the man in the box across the chart who tries to intrude. In addition, subordinates are constantly looking at other subordinates' boxes to see if they are higher in level than their own.

A preferable view is that which depicts organizational life as a wagon wheel, with marketing at the hub and ancillary services rimming the wheel. Lines of communication from the nucleus to service areas distribute information and receive appropriate feedback. In addition lines of communication feed back and forth

between the supporting services. This depiction of corporate relationships has the virtue of recognizing that the *raison d'etre* of
the corporation is marketing and that all concerned are working
for the same company.

*Postwar Emergence of the Marketing Concept*

Marketing is being defined in a new environment. The Committee on Definitions of the American Marketing Association
defines marketing as "The performance of business activities that
direct the flow of goods and services from producer to consumer
or user."[1] Staudt and Taylor criticize the definition because it
"places emphasis on the economic role of marketing and does
not clearly portray the scope of executive responsibilities for
marketing."[2] In the context of the above definition the role of
marketing has been changing rapidly, giving credence to the
characterization of the decade of the 1960's as "the decade of
marketing."[3]

Marketing is a vast panorama of activity which defies specific
definition. Through the years, especially since 1952 when Ralph
Cordiner, the president and chairman of the General Electric
Company, popularized the term *marketing concept,* the function
has undergone an evolution precipitated mainly by the Second
World War. Prior to that period marketing was thought of mainly
as a selling and distribution function. The role of the marketing
group was to bring the product to the buyer and induce purchase.
The impetus for action was derived from the producing company.

Gradually, the "in" word became *consumer.* The corporate
dialogues taking place in the mid-fifties began to respond to consumption patterns created by a constantly prospering consumer.
Corporate organization underwent changes that would permit
response to actions not of the producing company, but of the
consumer.

Attempts were made to redefine marketing. Five years ago,
Remus Harris sought to broaden the scope of marketing by defining it as "the total procedure of creating customers efficiently."[4]
By broadening the concept of marketing, Harris encompassed the
immense world of all corporate functions. By telescoping his per-

spective, Harris has recognized that the conventional corporate controller is a member of the marketing team. In 1966, Clarence Eldridge compiled a revealing set of essays entitled "The Management of the Marketing Function." In this series, Eldridge advanced the definition of marketing a step further in sophistication. He characterizes the function as "ascertaining, creating and satisfying the wants of people; *and doing it at a profit*" (italics supplied).

The hypothesis that branches of a corporation work together as a team to achieve a common marketing objective is far more realistic than are the traditional approaches that view the dynamism of a firm as a series of unrelated but coordinated functions.

### Need For Increased Accounting Dynamism

As this turbulence began to increase, accountants themselves began to look inwardly and question their roles in the marketing sphere.

H. Jackson Hendricks established the link between the accountant and the marketing sphere as an outside looking-in relationship.[5] His accountant probes marketing as a devil's advocate probes potential candidates for canonization. The accountant, in this role, asks the sales manager pointed questions about his sales force. These questions embrace an area covering "Do you need a sales force at all?" "How do you design territories?" "How many customers do you want?" The worth of this approach, in Hendricks' view, lies in the process of self-examination and self-rationalization. One of the potentially poor relationship-building aspects of this approach is the probability that the accountant, in this role, will be regarded as an "expert from out of town." Nowhere does Hendricks expand his thesis by suggesting that the accountant could just as well be *inside* looking in.

In another essay, Clark Sloat discusses "What the Accountant Can Do for the Marketing Executive."[6] His conceptual relationship sees the accountant as a "financial adviser to the marketing executive." Although he still positions the accountant as an outside adviser, his conclusions are interesting because he questions the term *profit,* and interchangeably uses the term *profitability:*

The accountant's contributon to marketing can be classified into two general categories. The first . . . is missionary in character. It involved education of marketing executives in the intricacies of finance and the real meaning of . . . financial analysis. In many cases this education has to begin at the most elemetary level. What is profit? What expenses are deducted from income to determine profit? Why are expenses written off against income currently when some part of them relate to efforts to secure future business . . . ?

The second contributon—and still of great importance—is the providing of data which are of value to marketing management. Not technical analyses which please the accountant, but data which give marketing executives the required figures for the important decisions they must make. And these decisions are of major importance. How much should be spent for advertising? For sales promotion? How many sales territories should we have? How many salesmen? These decisions control the *profitabilty* of the company . . .[7]

When the marketing and the accounting functions maintain dialogues, invariably the results reveal that there are gaps existing which pervent a symbiosis between the two fields. Sloat found that "it would almost seem that, in some cases, accountants have deliberately set out to confound and confuse marketing executives through use of technical accounting devices and language without any explanation in 'English.' "[8]

In the dialogue between the Schiff brothers, Michael Schiff contended that:

I don't think the accounting departments have fully comprehended the marketing task and they have the ancient notion that marketing is nothing but selling. They don't understand the marketing concept. Their orientation is manufacturing and since they have done so well for manufacturing—developing systems and controlling costs to the point where they can almost force a decision and predict results—they feel marketing has the same attribute as does manufacturing.[9]

Dr. Schiff has touched upon the basic weakness of management accounting relative to its role in the "Marketing Opportunity Concept." The concept has been defined as "a particular way of looking at the market opportunity problem—that is, perceiving, defining, evaluating, and selecting market opportunities for implementation—which is the first phase of achieving corporate viability, and profitable growth."[10]

In his essay, Clewitt maintains that "profits, costs, and risks need necessarily be analyzed in detail to determine which market opportunities will contribute to profitable corporate growth and to what extent."[11]

### Marketing Area Has a Quantitative Financial Void

Much of the foregoing discussion gives evidence of serious concern about the accountant's role in the marketing function. New concepts in marketing planning and management are emerging which give preeminence to decision-making techniques, and management accountants are sitting up and taking notice. There is a reasonable question which may be asked concerning the identity of the individual who is equipped to speak with confidence about such subjects as input-output, value analysis, new product venture analysis, and management information systems. The age of specialization exemplified by the above decision-making techniques may be rendering obsolete formerly held conceptions of the conventional controller's position. Current controllership practice emphasizes the function of reporting to management, owners, government and the specific control of most nonmarketing expenditures. The accounting profession cannot slip back into its tent of manufacturing orientation and close the flap. Because of its timidity, the profession was "naturally reluctant to enter the marketing sphere."[12] Yet there is an apparent missing link between the implementation of new techniques by marketing and the dissemination of the output by accounting. One solution to the problem is to fill the void by changing the traditional pattern of organizational structure, permitting quantitatively trained and oriented individuals from the financial function to serve in staff capacities *within* the marketing function. "The accountant often is qualified to aid the top marketing executive to make strategic decisions which have heretofore been made with less than sufficient information and analysis."[13]

It is extremely unfortunate that, in the past, controllers have traditionally shied away from participation in marketing activities. There are few individuals in a firm who have the degree of sophistication and breadth of exposure to overall corporate activity that the controller has. "No profession I know of is more important than financial management."[14]

## Training Marketing to Understand Finance's Statements

In an effort to ascertain the degree of expertise of various lower echelon marketing executives, senior executives in selected corporations were interviewed and asked, "Are marketing personnel trained to understand the implications of financial data?" Surprisingly, in the range of answers, only one company, that has a comprehensive training program in all management areas, was able to claim that its marketing planners had formal financial training. The balance of replies centered mainly on training by exposure and experience, and reliance on staff or division financial personnel. Most attended seminars at times both off the job and within job confines.

Company B admitted that, historically, marketing people were not trained in financial areas. In the future, however, they will be trained by working with financial personnel. It is also intended that they will learn by "doing" and by attending financial seminars.

Company H gave an interesting reply, stressing the fact that they recuited MBA's from selected graduate schools:

> The controller's group periodically puts on a one-day seminar for the marketing group, designed to acquaint them with financial techniques. It is questionable as to whether it is truly necessary for marketing personnel to be trained in the financial areas. Within a product group, the individual's initial experience deals with numbers. In addition to this, the man probably already has an MBA degree and has been exposed to managerial accounting and economics. "He'll know that a P&L is—the difference between an actionable cost and an allocated cost." The company tends to rely more on the education that marketing personnel have already had. Our function is to capitalize on that.

Company I stated that they continuously hold orientation courses for nonfinancial personnel. The courses are conducted by the financial area and thus far have proved to be highly successful.

Company P admitted that such training comes only by chance. They still feel that there is a great deal of internal development needed. Further, many of their younger product men are "MBA holders and have B school experience." Their point is that financial assessment is not strictly a requirement of the job but it is a "demand of the job."

Company S spoke openly of its weaknesses:

> The marketing area is weak in the understanding of financial data. There is a current effort underway to try to improve this understanding. It derives from the fact that the company attempts to promote from within and frequently men are brought in from the field with no knowledge of finance and find themselves in a headquarters situation where they are expected to understand these concepts. "It is unfortunate that these men can't get the exposure before they do; their efficiency is impaired for a pretty long time."

The above replies are disturbing in view of the abundance of quality financial training available to nonfinancial executives if the true will were present to take advantage of it. Many graduate schools now offer quantitative courses in their marketing programs dealing with marketing models, Fortran training for marketing and courses in marketing decisions based on financial inputs. It is difficult, therefore, to sympathize completely with the complaint of Company S that their personnel do not receive a financial exposure until a late date.

## The Adequacy of Marketing/Financial Communications

Participants in the study were asked, "Have there been significant instances where closer financial/marketing communication linkage would have improved marketing decision-making?" The question deliberately asked for *significant* instances because in daily operations of business there are always momentary gaps in communications.

Only eight of the twenty companies felt secure enough to reply in the negative. Comments from the others proved to be extremely frank and showed that this is a prime area for corporate interest.

Company B lost a great deal of money because of such communications lapses. The tea beverage operation of the company is about $20 million annually and appeared to generate a satisfactory gross profit; however, there was no pack size data available. At the insistence of the new marketing vice president such data was produced and it was found that the company was losing $1 million annually on one size of their instant tea.

A somewhat related problem was referred to by Company K which, because of irrelevant data, at one time dropped products from their lines. They admitted that if they had the sophistication then that they possess now they would have evaluated products on a marginal basis and as long as a product contributed to period costs they would have retained it. "Unfortunately, it's too late now."

Company T laid bare, in its reply, the problem in a decentralized organization of corporate staff people acting as final filters for divisional data:

> Within the division, no; because relationships are close. Between the corporate analysis area and division personnel, improvement is needed. A better definition is needed which will clarify to what degree a division should have accountability to a corporate group when the implementation of the plan is within approved strategies. "The corporate group should not ask how profits are obtained as long as they are within the framework of the plan. They *should* be concerned, though, as to whether the divisional system of checks and balances is working." Just as the division controller is the conscience of the division head, the corporate financial group should be a cross check on the division head."

Company M gave an interesting reply, referring to old line management attitudes toward the incremental concept:

Yes, there have been instances when marketing has decided to abandon new product concepts solely because they showed a loss at the net profit level after allocated expenses were applied. I realize that the accounting boys have hit very hard at that point and have tried to teach us that new products should only be evaluated on an incremental basis. However, the problem stems with our top management who are somewhat old fashioned and believe that if a cost exists, it must be allocated somewhere. Really, it is strict heresy to suggest that, for decision purposes, not all costs have to be considered. Even though we have agreed to a reporting system which uses modern concepts, such as relevant costs, the financial area is still asked to allocate corporate period charges to products. In practice we try very hard to ignore any reporting below the direct profit level.

The sensitive area touched upon here is that of the education of entrenched older managements who have been weaned on accounting relationships that may not be standing the test of time. "The use of older ideas places a tremendous stress on the magical significance of something called 'gross profit.' " It is certainly a useless vehicle for short-term decision-making if plant period costs are still retained in the number. Moreover, it prevents managers from gaining an insight into the nature of period costs.

Many controllers insist on allocating all costs known or estimated, before giving their approval to future projects. But the smart decision-maker knows there is no virtue in this, unless a given decision relates to a long-term project, or deals with changes in production capacity or cost-plus pricing considerations.

That is, in the long run, all costs are variable. By their very nature, they change in relation to time, not in relation to units of production. This means that decisions on short-term or intermediate projects do not usually require allocated costing. Or, if they do require it, then only those costs that will be incremental to the decision should be allocated. Incremental costs are costs that exist because a product exists, not those—such as overhead costs—that exist anyway.

Moreover, concern with allocated costing prevents top managers from gaining a real insight into overhead costs. It should

be understood that overhead costs are a penalty incurred by a
decision-maker for going into business in the first place.

Once he is in business, of course, he may be faced with further
incremental costs, and these can be critical to decision-making.
But no one should fail to realize that overhead costs are really
just a big bag of money; it is not necesary to allocate them to
divisions or to products, especially if they will have little to do
with go and no-go decisions.

This point can best be illustrated by recounting a pathetically
humorous incident which occurred some years ago. The head
of a small specialty publishing house, which was a subsidiary of
a larger concern, was boasting of his ability to spot books that
were unprofitable. In fact, he proffered a list of books—with their
dollar return in sales, their profit return, their manufacturing
costs, their administrative costs, and, of course, their corporately
allocated overhead costs.

On this basis, one of the books was plainly losing money, and
he planned to delist it. Asked if delisting it would result in any
change in the amount of corporate overhead, he said it would not.
The suggestion was made that he take the corporate overhead
that had been allocated to it and assign it to the other books on
his list.

As a result, another book on the list became, as he put it,
unprofitable. So it was suggested that it also be delisted. All of a
sudden, a light bulb went on in his head. He realized that ultimately his list would contain only one book. In short, the world
of product charges and allocated overhead charges had upset his
world of logic.

The answer to allocated costing is *relevant* costing. Relevant
costing is a much greater aid to decision-making. It involves taking all the costs that pertain to a given situation, throwing them
up in the air, catching only those costs that are directly traceable
to the situation, and ignoring those that would exist anyway.

To put the matter another way, the concept of relevant costing
involves asking this question: "If I didn't have this product (division, factory), would I still have the cost (income)?" If the
answer to the question is no, the cost is a relevant one and should
be considered in any decision. Relevant costing will be discussed
in detail later in the book.

One company that did something to improve communications was Company P. They added an assistant controller to the marketing staff in an attempt to improve communications and he has already proved himself valuable in the area of inventory adjustments. In addition, monthly meetings that include the controller, the vice president, consumer products division and the director of marketing have been initiated. The assistant controller, marketing accountants and the group vice president also attend.

This latter course is commendable. Each side has a unique contribution to make to the the marketing effort and the forum of a monthly meeting gives ample opportunity for concentrated dialogue. One could question, though, why purchasing and distribution are not represented.

### Training Programs and Training Attitudes

Participants were asked whether formal programs exist to provide:

    a. In-house seminars by outside experts
    b. Off-location education
    c. Interdepartmental training

None of the participants have any formal programs bringing in outside experts other than IBM personnel who speak about their equipment.

All companies replied that their policy was to encourage personnel to attend off-location seminars. Participants volunteered that, by far, the bulk of their training efforts are interdepartmental.

Participants were additionally asked, "Is it desirable for marketing and financial personnel to be formally trained in each other's respective functional area?" Representative replies are shown below:

> No, it is a nice thing, but it is not necessary. It would probably be more desirable to have personnel as experts in finance, but merely knowledgeable in the marketing area. On the other side

of the coil, financial training is probably highly desirable for the marketing area.

They have to have an understanding of each other's respective areas. Marketing personnel can't get out of financial people what they're capable of giving unless they understand them.

It is terribly important for marketing people to have a good understanding of basic accounting and what the company's economics are.

It is highly desirable for marketing and financial personnel to be formally trained in each other's respective areas. This need not imply that each should become expert. Rather, it implies that they have a reasonable knowledge of day to day operating requirements.

### Controllership in Marketing

The role of controllership as it relates particularly to functions of planning and control for marketing as described by Schiff is:

1. To establish, coordinate and administer as an integral part of management, an adequate plan for the control of operations. Such a plan would provide, to the extent required by the business, profit planning, programs for capital investing and for financing, sales forecasts, expense budgets and cost standards, together with the necessary procedures to effectuate the plan.
2. To compare performance with operating plans and standards, and to report and interpret the results of operations to all levels of management and to the owners of the business. This function includes . . . . the preparation of operating data and of special reports as required.
3. To consult with all segments of management responsible for policy or action, concerning any phase of the operation of the business as it relates to attainment of objectives and the effectiveness of policies, organization structure and procedures.
4. To continuously appraise economic and social forces and

government influences, and to interpret their effect upon the business.[15]

The above is essentially a restatement of the definition of controllership advanced by the Financial Executives Institute. A refinement of the definition as it applies to the marketing function can be added:

5. To utilize creativity in establishing alternative reporting methods designed to measure the effectiveness of performance responsibility under the marketing concept by measuring the fiscal implications of media and promotion policy and profit responsibility under the product manager system.

Changes in the field of accounting and marketing in the last two decades have created profound conceptual problems for the two professions and it is somewhat surprising that in that interim, the professions have not conceived of an amalgamation of part of their common functions. Yet, each is vitally concerned with profitability and with responsibility.

# Chapter III

# Marketing and Finance

## Recognition by Various Authorities

In the dialogue between the Schiff brothers, Michael Schiff commented on a rhetorical question that implied that marketing people do not understand the financial operation and, moreover, probably do not know what to ask for or from whom to make the request. His comments follow:

> A marketing man develops a plan and talks to the finance man who puts the numbers down. It's dangerous. You won't find a factory superintendent doing this. What I've urged—and this has been done in several companies—is to have an in-house accountant in the marketing department. I've used several titles for this man. He's called a profit manager or a marketing cost consultant. Actually he's on the staff of the marketing operation—a business manager, so to speak. He's knowledgeable in accounting and he has ties with the accounting department, knows what's available and knows the accounting language. He becomes the resource man for the VP of marketing. This has met with some degree of success. But there's no substitute for a continuing education program, of getting people in marketing to understand the financial implications of decisions they made and plans they formulate.[1]

The significance of the Schiffs' dialogue bypassed many of the writers who followed up the marketing orientation of the

35

article by writing further about the accounting/marketing relationship. The important point raised by Michael Schiff is that
*his* accountant was no longer an "expert from out of town." His
conception posited the man as a member of a marketing team—
divorced from a staff accounting identity. In his 1966 article,[2]
Thomas Kelley, Jr., restates the thought that marketing management must rely heavily upon the accounting department for services and vital data. Although his article adds little additional
knowledge to the subject (his accountant provides conventional
reports like customer billing, sales activity, stock availability,
etc.) it is noteworthy in two respects:

1. Its publication was not in a financial magazine but rather,
   in the *Journal of Marketing*.
2. Despite the earlier Schiff article (1965), Kelley's accountant is still a servicer in an outside-looking-in position.

Somewhat later, John Barry inquired into the accountant's relationship with marketing and observed that he was, in essence, a
"bridge builder."[3] He called for creativity on the part of the accountant in training sales forces and in analyzing territorial profitability. Barry's accountant analyzed commissions and physical
distribution, computed profitability (the author does not define
the term and used it interchangeably with "profit") for product-
groups and classes of trade. Importantly, however, his man is
still on the outside of the marketing circle.

Perhaps the problem is in the use of the term *accountant*. It is
an honorable profession but inevitably is derided because it is
symbolized by the poor soul on a high stool using a quill pen,
wearing a green eyeshade and keeping his sleeve tight with a
rubber band. It is not uncommon for parents and youths to rank
the profession of accounting consistently low in terms of prestige
and desirability: teaching, law and banking consistently outpace
accounting. If the writers could have visualized the man as "de-
cision-information creator," they might have more fluidly moved
the man *into* the marketing circle.

An expansion of the Schiff concept came in 1968 in this
writer's article which appeared in *Budgeting*.[4] In a reference to
the concept of "marketing controller," the article stated:

The pride of the profession and its traditional adherence to conservatism has prevented it from planning for its survival or recognizing its own evolutionary processes. The decison-making world has been thrust upon us and the profession is still mainly concerned with reporting what has happened. For a discipline which owes its precepts to the teachings of economics, accounting, as a student entity, has learned poorly. In economics, a sunk cost, because of its prior existence, cannot affect a future decison. The profession, though, is still interested in reporting yesterday.

In a similar vein, the conventional controller's position is becoming obsolete because it is more geared to the reporting function than it is to the decision-making function. Viewed in perspective, the positon of "marketing controller" is a step further along the ladder of evolution which has seen the accounting family tree send off shoots from the main branch of bookkeeping to accounting, per se, to tax accounting, plant controllership, cost accounting, etc. The "marketing controller" should participate directly in marketing decision-making as it is affected by acquisition policy, new product venture analyses, value analysis, purchasing policy, and management information systems. The divorcement from the reporting function should be essential. This man must utilize creativity in perhaps establishing alternative reporting methods showing the fiscal implications of media and promotion policy.

The television season runs primarily from fall to fall. Media commitments, as a result, tend to follow, thus distorting calendar year operating results as they affect the profitabilty of various programs. Likewise, promotional planning is highly seasonal and the profitability affect of many year-end promotions is masked by the calendar cut-off requirements. The "marketing controller" would be subject to no such artificial constraints.

The above is an expansion of thoughts expressed in a letter written to the editor of *Financial Executive* in 1967.[5] The problems of media distortions resulting from accounting conventions were recognized even earlier by Richard Feder.[6]

## What Is Marketing?

The art of marketing has never been easily defined. "Marketing is accepted as a business discipline, but there is no one universally accepted definition of it in the broadest sense, much less one for its multitude of parts."[7] Many authors and teachers have ascribed much of the existing lack of uniform definitions to a gap in communications. The definitional failure takes the techniques of marketing a step further away from statements of objectives. Without clarifying statements of objectives, the state of the art must remain intensely personal—defined in the eyes of the individual policy makers. While there is little current doubt that the essence of marketing is a recognition of response to consumer demand, there is doubt that the means of implementing the marketing concept are fully understood or practiced.[8]

In his initial essay in the series, Clarence Eldridge does not equivocate in saying that the totality of marketing is encompassing and, in addition to its major functions of advertising, selling and promotion, it must include supporting activities, such as marketing research, pricing, packaging and so on. His unique contribution to the field is his thought that the "sole activity of the business (under the 'total marketing concept') . . . is therefore marketing."[9]

Many large companies do not ascribe to Mr. Eldridge's encompassing concept of marketing. Five of the companies interviewed for the research study excluded distribution from their definition of marketing, two excluded the function of sales, and one excluded market research.

Significantly, though, in the responses to the question of definition, five companies showed an acute awareness of consumer orientation:

Company A replied:

> The marketing function is defined as encompassing everything that exists between the shipment of a product from the warehouse to the purchase by the consumer. It would include diverse functions such as, advertising, market research, sales and distribution.

Company F answered:

> The company employs a broad concept of the marketing function. It includes the merchandising, promotion and selling functions. Distribution control, however, is excluded from the defini-

ton. Other than this exception, marketing consists of the system which enables the product from inception to reach the ultimate consumer of the company.

Contrast the replies above with the following reply, which demonstrates an awareness of creativity and the economic concept of value:

Company J talked in terms of the marketing mix:

> Marketing encompasses the creative function specifically attributable to the control of the prime elements of the marketing mix—price, advertising, media, promotion and packaging. A centralized sales force, market research, production, and quality control are excluded from the definition of the marketing function.

The pressure of competition and the pride of quality of product were very apparent in the reply by Company S. The spokesman for the company spoke of marketing in terms of satisfying value levels in the minds of the consumer. He indicated also that their basic marketing goal was not to proliferate "me too" lines, but to make genuine contributions to product development.

The most sophisticated answer came from Company K. The answer demonstrated a complete awareness of the marketing mix and listed the elements of the corporate marketing policy:

Sales and Sales Management
Market Research
Profit Planning and Pricing
Credit
Advertising and Sales Promotion
Customer, Trade and Public Relations
Transportation, Warehousing and Distribution
Product Development and Packaging
Production Scheduling
Economic Forecasting

This company's aggressiveness was demonstrated in the closing portion of the answer where the Vice President, Marketing, said: "We are a highly marketing oriented company and the principle purpose of this company is not to manufacture but to sell."

One of the more interesting aspects of the above is the implication that credit policy is a marketing tool. The more recent textbooks on corporate finance devote a great deal of writing to the ramifications, to both the issuer and the recipient, of credit policy.[10]

Although not in direct response to the question, the executive referred to above said:

> In properly organizing our marketing function today, we are aware that we are in the people business. It was research that gave us the Edsel and one man directing a team effort gave us the Mustang. In this company, the idea of adapting _____ Liquid into a spray has been tested and rejected. When I joined the company, years ago, we took a second look at the product, rethemed it, test marketed it, then marketed it nationally . . . today we have won the dominate share of the _____ market at well over 30%.

He is obviously referring to the marketing requisites of creativity and definition of objective; together, these two characteristics stand as a synonym for the marketing plan. Interestingly, Company P answered the same question in terms of a marketing plan. They stressed that the basic function of marketing is the establishment of a marketing plan, a course espoused by most marketing writers who have positioned the function of modern marketing management in terms of the marketing concept. The reply further cited the ingredients of the plan including advertising, promotion, packaging, market research, etc. They felt that the execution of the plan is dependent upon the sales function. This latter point can be philosophically argued: if marketing is viewed in its broadest sense, certainly the execution of a plan requires the additional cooperation of the purchasing, distribution, manufacturing and financial function. In their reply, there is an indication of a throw-back to the old concept of marketing which saw the function in a sales-oriented light.

From the above replies, it is obvious that there is no unanimity of definition of the marketing function. Considering that the marketing field is highly creative and largely staffed by strong personalities, it is hardly surprising that there is a lack of agreement. No firm patterns emerged from the responses relative to sizes of companies or line of business. It did appear, however, that the smaller, aggressive companies or units of companies offered the most comprehensive view of the marketing function. The impression is that the hungrier, aggressive units must work harder to overcome the lack of size.

### What Is Finance?

The meaning of the term *finance* is being considerably broadened today to include accounting and analytical functions whereas formerly it was used almost as a synonym for corporate finance. A new breed of workers is being trained and recruited, and entitled "financial analysts." In this capacity, they are being given assignments which are akin to product profitability analysis. This trend is especially evident in high multi-product companies, such as the General Foods Corporation and the Nestlé Company, Inc.

It is somewhat surprising, therefore, that replies to the question concerning a definition of finance were conventional, and that they concentrated mainly on the schism between the treasurer's function and the controller's function. Most important, though, was the *complete omission* by *all* respondents of a discussion of their role in the marketing concept. Generally speaking, the descriptions of the functions performed correlated rather closely with the findings of the Controllership Foundation, a decade and a half earlier.[11] That study found that in addition to accounting functions, there was some participation in policy-making and decision-making processes.[12]

A close correlation was also found in the interviews with a *Harvard Business Review* survey[13] of the role of the controller relative to computer responsibility. In that survey, which covered 108 companies, it was found that the senior computer executive reported to the financial officer in 59% of the companies surveyed. The present research study, which covered 20 large companies, found that half of the financial officers replied that the senior computer executive reported to him.

Replies to the question dealing with the definition of the financial function varied in scope.

Company S replied:

> The financial function of the Consumer Products Division, as centered in the Control Manager's Department, is involved more with the management reporting aspects of finance than with custodial accounting. Its basic job is to plan and to control. However, a close, though "broken line," relationship is maintained with division sales and production accounting groups to assure that custodial accounting requirements of the corporation, as established by corporate accounting policy, are being complied with. (Periodic audits by the corporate Internal Audit Department and the corporation's Public Accountants provide further control in this area.) In essence, the Control Manager's Department is a communication center for interpretation and transmission of financial information between division and corporate management and to the various business and functional areas of management with the division. Routine monthly accounting data, such as sales summaries, cost of shipment and plant balance sheet reports, are fed directly into the corporate accounting structure from the division accounting locations, with information copies to the Control Manager's Department. A "broken line" relationship exists between the Division Control Manager and the Corporate Controller.

Company T replied that its financial organization consists of the following:

> Internal Auditing
> Corporate Accounting
> Accounts Receivable and Payable
> Profit Planning
> Data Processing
> Computer Planning
> Office Services
> Systems and Procedures

Company A reported that its financial staff was centralized within the corporate staff area but that the controller was able to service various marketing divisions through financial analysts who acted as liaisons to the divisions. Their financial responsibilities included general and cost accounting, auditing, taxes and data processing. They did make a strong point that the controller function was distinct from that of the treasurer, whose main responsibility lay in cash control, investment management and banking relationships.

In that same connection, Company D made plain the fact that their controller, at times, was subservient to the treasurer. They split the controller's duties into two main parts: that dealing with planning, budgets and special studies and the other, a more conventional role of responsibility for the computer, operations research, internal auditing and systems reporting.

Two interesting variations were reported by Companies E and G. The former, which has a separate treasurer, reported that in addition to the more routine accounting functions attendant to a controller's duties, they also made the controller responsible for sales statistics through a separate reporting organization, and for credit and collections. Company G's controller was responsible for outside warehousing and transportation in addition to the more common functions.

Company J. which has a serious interest in computer output for marketing information, requires its controller to be highly EDP oriented:

> The financial function includes elements of finance and statistics. One part of the financial function, the treasurer, is "self-sufficient." The primary responsibility is the maintenance of proper cash balances and employee benefits. The area is independent of other departments.
>
> The other portion of the financial function is supportive and consists of a controller, primarily EDP oriented, and a deputy controller. The key function of the supportive groups is maintenance of an EDP logistics control system, a marketing information system, and a centralized accounting system.

Just as in the prior section about marketing, there is apparent disagreement as to the nature of finance. Data processing's role in the responses has been referred to but it should also be noted that ten companies considered credit to be a financial function, and one considered distribution and warehousing as a financial function. These replies are in stark contrast with Company K, which earlier positioned these definitely in marketing.

What may be emerging from these answers is the thought that:

> The hypothesis that branches of a corporation work together as a team is far more realistic than are the traditional approaches to corporate organization, which view the dynamism of a corporation as a series of unrelated functions. Thus, organizational philosophy may now return to the true "gestalt" idea that the form follows the function.[14]

There is little excuse, in a modern organization, to view the controller's function narrowly. Marketing, as perceived by Eldridge, is the essence of the firm. All else is ancillary and support-

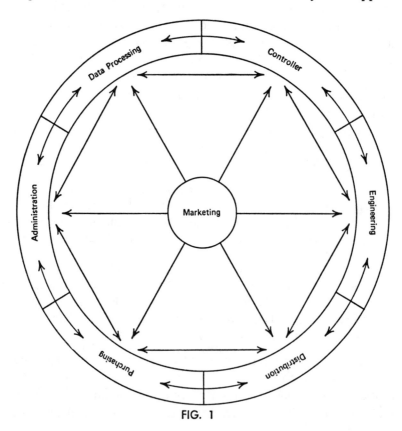

FIG. 1

ive. The concept is suggestive of the following diagram in which the arrows indicate lines of service and communication: (See opposite page.)

In terms of the evolution of the financial function, there has emerged from this study a confirmation of the old and the new. It is apparent that the Controllership Foundation study needs updating in its reporting of financial duties, although its main findings in the area are still valid. It should be noted that the study was based on a selective sampling of only seven companies.

Since 1954, the year of that study, the use of data processing equipment and the quantitative emphasis on decision-making have made the controller a likely vehicle for directing data processing and systems and procedures as ancillary duties. During discussions with the companies, a number of them implied that the rapid maturity of the total systems approach to business had resulted in plans to ultimately transfer data processing and systems and procedures to an information specialist. This implies the possible return of the controllership function to relative sterility unless dynamism and enlightment are introduced.

# Chapter IV

# Patterns of Organization of Marketing and Finance

The need for a "marketing controller" is strongly influenced by types of corporate organization and levels of decision authority. This chapter will probe the effect on that need of decentralized companies as contrasted with those which are centralized. In addition, decision-making prerogatives of managers in decentralized operations will be examined with regard to the extent of their license. The chapter will also explore the potential difficulties involved in division of formal authority over an individual.

The 1963 Schiff and Mellman study for the Financial Executives Institute Research Foundation, in its consideration of marketing organizational trends, concluded:

> Within the marketing organization, the traditional activities of research, advertising, promotion, and sales persist; but the organization needed to do an effective job has changed. The introduction of product managers and specialized sales managers results from the extension of product lines and the shift away from the purely geographic organization of the field force selling the entire line. These changes have been noted in many companies and are coming in others. It is safe to say that this trend in the marketing organization will continue in the future.
>
> There are implications here for marketing management as well as for the controller. Marketing management must constantly study the adequacy of its organization to meet the marketing

47

problems it faces. The controller, to provide an information flow system and assist in analysis and decision-making, must become familiar with the marketing organization, the specific functions delegated to personnel within that department, the individual areas of control—and decision-making, and the direction of changes. The controller must take the initiative in this. This additional effort is worth it, considering the dollars involved and the challenge for constructive work.[1]

There is strong evidence that both marketing and finance are beginning to appreciate the shortcomings of conventional organization patterns. In his 1966 article, Harold Jasper chided accounting for its ostrich approach to organizational change. "The accountant has always been involved in the process of gathering, measuring, processing, and disseminating information; it would be logical for him to extend his sphere of activity and influence to include this in broader information role total management information systems now needed in business and the economy."[2]

## Centralization versus Decentralization in Marketing

Of the twenty interviews, four respondents considered that their marketing efforts were highly centralized. The remaining sixteen respondents were decentralized companies, operating on a divisional basis.

Company D, a *centralized* company, grouped its marketing function under a marketing manager who was responsible for five product groups. The directors in charge of advertising and marketing development cut across all product lines in their advisory relationships and shared the basic responsibilities for multiproduct functions, such as corporate advertising. The officials of the company placed great emphasis on the point that they were highly conscious of the marketing concept and considered themselves a model of an aggressive, marketing-oriented company operating under that concept. Their view of themselves, though, is difficult to reconcile with their physical organization (Figure 1). The director of marketing, on the same level as the sales manager, shares the marketing function. Under the marketing

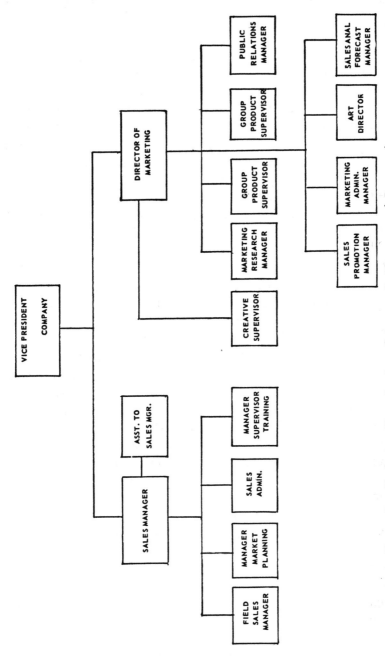

Figure 1. Marketing Organization, Company D (Canner and Processor)

49

concept, selling is but one ingredient of the marketing mix and should be under the control of the director of marketing. In the organization chart, some signs of this ambivalence are apparent: it can be seen that sales promotion and sales forecasting fall under the marketing director, but that the sales manager does not. In addition, as will be highlighted in other parts of this study, selling prices are determined by the controller, product managers do not have access to product operating data, and salesmen know little else about the product other than their assigned volume quotas. This is hardly the modern marketing concept in action.

Company F indicated that they preferred highly centralized marketing. A unique variation in this organization is that the sales force is *decentralized* because of the nature of the product lines and customers served. One segment of that sales force, the key account group, cuts across functional product lines. The arrangement is the antithesis of the organization structure as reported by many *decentralized* companies who indicated that their sales forces were centralized and cut across divisional lines.

Among the *decentralized* companies, two contrasting variations were found to be significant. Company P employed the marketing concept by having both the director of marketing and the director of sales report to the vice president-consumer products (Figure 2). The distinction between this format and Company D is that in Company P the two functions report to a marketing head, whereas in Company D they report to an administrative head. Company D thus suffers a lack of overall marketing guidance.

Company G also displays an awareness of the marketing mix by having each specialist report to the head of the marketing function (Figure 3). The equivalent of product managers report to the head of sales.

A further variation was exhibited by Company T. Under the decentralized, divisional organization, the sales force and advertising functions are essentially a staff operation and therefore the decision-making dynamics are carried on within each division. This divisional organization is shown in Figure 4.

A further question to those respondents who indicated that their marketing was decentralized asked if division managers have

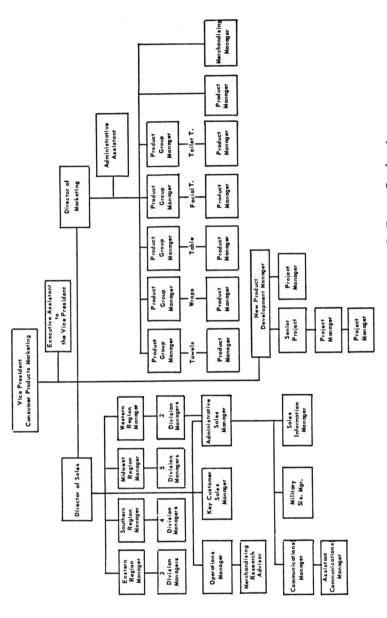

Figure 2. Marketing Organization, Company P (Paper Products)

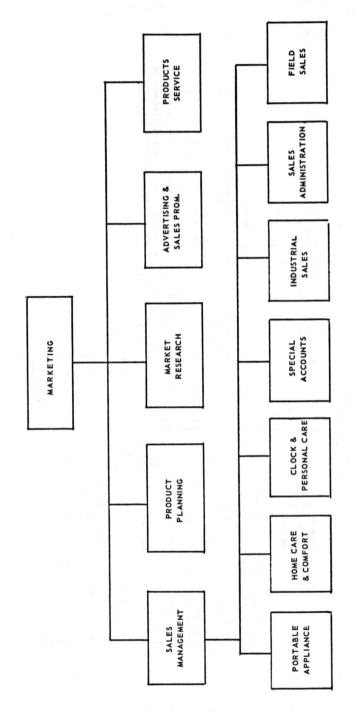

Figure 3. Marketing Organization, Company G (Consumer Appliances)

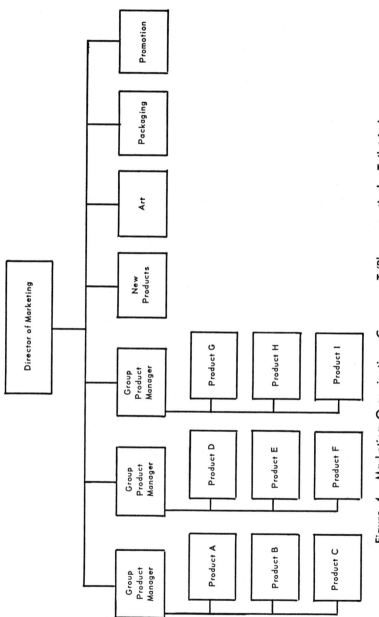

Figure 4. Marketing Organization, Company T (Pharmaceuticals, Toiletries)

53

ultimate authority in decision-making. There was a great deal of hedging in this area and no generalizations are really meaningful other than that a decision, if made within the framework of an approved plan, can be implemented by the division manager. Almost one-third of the division managers lacked a clear cut mandate to make decisions. Most, however, could do so *if it were within the context of an approved plan.*

A majority of the companies interviewed did not choose to elaborate on their replies. Some, however, provided meaningful commentary on modern corporate dynamics. Company H stated that, realistically, no one in a company truly has ultimate authority. In any event, they replied, even though division managers enjoy a great deal of freedom, sensitive pricing decisions must be cleared with superiors. On the other hand, minor changes for relatively minor products "generally may not require clearance."

Company J is governed by committee action. The ultimate authority rests with a management committee consisting of the president, vice-presidents for customer relations and administration, and the executive vice-president for operations. The committee meets weekly to review plans.

Something of a philosophical contradiction was evident in the reply from Company P. Typically, they agreed that division managers have the ultimate authority in most cases as long as the decision-making falls within the planned marketing efforts. The contradiction became evident when they further stated that even though an action falls within the scope of the marketing plan, it may nevertheless require approval from the executive committee if the decision affected profits in a manner *other than had been planned.*

One company referred to the distinction between existing products and new products. Company T said their division managers can make ultimate decisions on *existing* products if they are within the framework of the plan. *New products* decisions require higher corporate approval if the total cost in the first year exceeds $50,000.

Company M was one of the companies which replied that division managers *could not* make most high level decisions, even

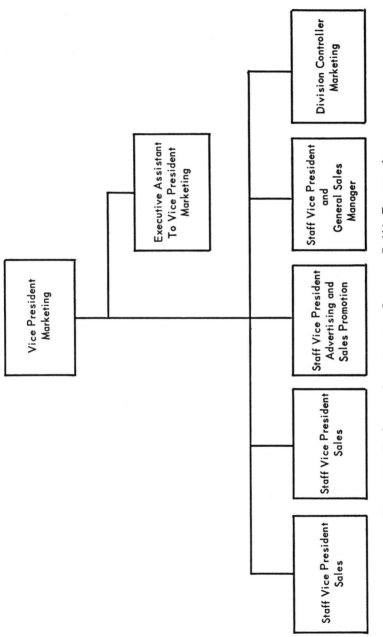

Figure 5. Marketing Organization, Company R (Air Transport)

though they exercise a great deal of authority from a day-to-day
point of view. All major decisions must pass before the chief
operating officer, who exercises ultimate authority. The author

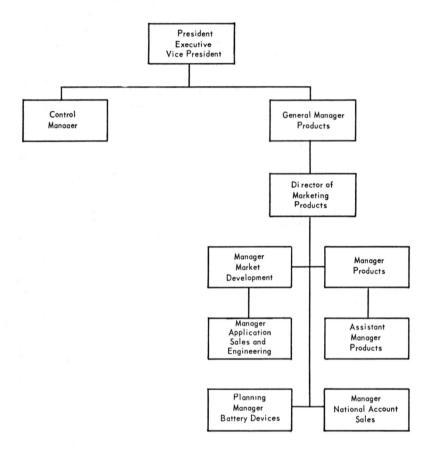

Figure 6.   Marketing Organization, Company S
(Chemicals, Plastics, Synthetics)

formed the distinct impression that this tight rein was an out-
growth of ego on the part of the chief operating officer, and of
a desire to keep his "fingers in the pie."

### The Product Manager Dilemma

Of the twenty companies interviewed, fifteen replied that they
employed a product manager system. Much has been written
about the product manager but few individuals have presented an
overview as effectively as Clarence Eldridge in his essay series.[3]
Conflicts had inevitably arisen from a responsibility point of view
and more and more young people were assigned this position.
Eldridge disagreed and placed the product manager in a status
akin to a marketing director, thus implying that the man was not
a youthful trainee but a mature marketing man with considerable
experience. Eldridge felt that the man's primary responsibility
should be advertising (he unconsciously contradicted himself in
essay number 15 by calling for an all-powerful advertising manager) and that because of a failure to maintain standards for
the position, the marketing director has not been able to dele-
gate tasks: ". . . as a result, the marketing director has had to
continue to perform functions which should be delegated to a
product manager. In this respect, the product manager system
has failed in its purpose."[4]

In another vein, the author wrote:

> Marketing personnel are becoming increasingly responsible
> for results expressed in quantitative profit terms and yet there is
> very reasonable doubt as to their ability to control their profit
> fate. There is little doubt that they can influence profits and prof-
> itability, but control implies a divine right of decision making
> and omniscient abilities to plan for seasonal, cyclical and com-
> petitive aberrations.
>
> As it is practiced by most companies today, the implementa-
> tion of the product manager concept leaves much to be desired.
> As understanding of the dynamics of the firm increase, the au-
> thor has little doubt that objectives and responsibilities of the
> position will be defined more clearly. Nevertheless, the profit
> onus hits the product manager. Yet it is not fair to ascribe profit
> responsibility to the man. He cannot purchase raw materials,

control plant efficiency, and, in some cases, does not choose his own media programs. If his product is a winner, a major one, it is doubtful if he can truly affect pricing, on a unilateral basis. The bigger truth is, as it is practiced today, any product has many managers—the product manager himself, the division manager, the manufacturing manager, the purchasing manager and the head of the company.

Shorn of his academic trappings, the product manager emerges as a man who can influence volume and promotional activity and, indirectly, working capital. The challenge to the marketing controller is to create a reporting system which will lend pragmatic truth to the exidence of the man's efforts. His likely target will be the one which will incorporate a measure of return on funds influenced.[5]

## Profit Responsibility through the Product Manager System

In the latter half of the 1950's and the early 1960's, the phrase *profitability accounting* became popular. As defined by Beyer, the philosophy states:

> A single unified accounting structure should satisfy simultaneously the objectives of financial (or custodial) accounting and those of managerial accounting. The system is complex, involving the integration of all the modern, profit-oriented, accounting techniques into a single, *decision-impelling,* management information system.[6]

Marketing has need for information which will enable it to make intelligent decisions. Most conventional accounting measures are simply not adequate for the task of implementing the "profitability accounting" concept.

> Current views of profit are deficient for decision-making purposes. Profits are reported to owners, to the government, to taxing authorities, to security analysts, and to owner/investors (including banks). Unfortunately, the reported profit may differ in amount depending upon to whom we are reporting and at what profit level we are submitting information. . . . The problems of distinguishing between profit and profitability are compounded by different uses of profit in corporate operations.[7]

Responsibility accounting, on the other hand, is the "concept of fitting the accounting structure to the organization structure so that performance measures can be compiled and reported in groupings which reflect individual responsibilities." The end-product use of "profitability and responsibility accounting" is its introduction into the marketing concept.[8]

One of the moving forces contained within the marketing concept is the evolution of the product manager. This evolution has had a profound effect upon managerial accounting systems, and its strengths and weaknesses have given rise to many of the questions probed in this book. Its weaknesses have been commented on as follows:

> It is rather because of a failure by top marketing management to define the respective roles of the advertising manager and the product manager, to provide operational guidelines within which each is expected to work, and thereby to establish a constructive and compatible relationship which can contribute greatly to an effective marketing program.
>
> In one division of a nationally prominent marketing organization there are five layers of marketing management, starting with the product manager and ending with the marketing director.[9]

This splintering of authority renders more important the efforts of the controller to ascribe meaning to his measurements of reporting responsibility. The development of measures to evaluate those with less than complete authority are the challenge before the controller. "The fact is that the product manager, at least in our system, has a great deal of responsibility, but very little explicitly stated authority. How then can he function efficiently? The answer lies mainly in implied authority."[10] The answer may lie in measuring such implied authority against a return on working capital *influenced*. This measure may incorporate, in the base, items such as receivables and inventories (finished goods). In his article, Michael Schiff states that, ". . . restriction of investment to accounts receivable and inventory minimize allocation problems and deals with assets *controllable* [italics supplied] by field sales management."[11] The base would then be measured against a return which incorporates a system of standard manufacturing costs that compensates for the lack of influence on the part of the product manager over manufacturing efficiency.

The same conceptual difficulties referred to by Eldridge and this writer were found in replies to a question which asked whether product managers are held responsible for product profits.

Fifteen of the companies employed a product manager system and in that group, ten stated that product managers *are* responsible for profits.

Among those ten companies, most took a realistic view of the limitations of that responsibility for profit. The reply from Company A called attention to the fact that they may also be responsible for "nonprofit." They conceded that ultimately the product manager is responsible for profits but that, in the short run, this responsibility may be tempered, since quite often the man may be riding herd on a new product that involves heavy investment spending in a period that precludes profitable operation. Their view is that it is more accurate to state that the man is responsible for adherence to the profit plan.

Company L rationalized that the product manager is held responsible for profits only in a staff capacity. They felt that division managers have the real responsibility because the "job of moving the merchandise" truly lies with the head of the division.

Company P conceded the weakness of its position. They stated that product managers are often held responsible for profits because "the things that they do affect profits." They added, however, that "in terms of the decision-making ability to affect profit, the answer must ultimately be no." The company did not care to comment further about the ambivalence of their statement and the fact that their product men were being judged on the basis of something they could not control.

Company T stated that although the product manager was being held to account for product profits, the activities were really a team effort and profits the responsibility of the entire division. They conceded that the man has limited influence in manufacturing and that he is not responsible for the sales force. He can initiate packaging changes and influence advertising and promotion policy. In a gross understatement they added that "even if it isn't the fairest system, it's the most efficient." In an effort to clarify this position they spoke further of their philosophy of responsibility and added that the man's performance rating does not rise or fall completely on profit attainment but is also influenced by the quality of his efforts in other areas of the marketing mix. Toward the close they confessed that he was *not* "literally responsible for profits," but *is* responsible within the framework of the world in which he lives.

Company M was equally frank but less confused and spoke about the relative ineffectiveness of the product manager. They recognized that the man cannot control the elements of profit; they felt it was reasonable simply to say that he affects profits through his actions.

Company B, in their reply, took pains to point out that their product men are responsible for maintaining the profit plan and that, in the strict sense, they are not held accountable for profit variations. They pointed out that their product men's responsibilities are set forth in writing. These are reproduced below:

| *Marketing Function* | *Responsibility* |
|---|---|
| Development | Responsible for collecting, evaluating and *circulating* all product information generated by the department and by services outside the department for inclusion in the Brand Book. This includes Field Sales, Advertising, Market Research, Management Assignments, Competitive Information, etc. |
| Sales Forecasts | Evaluates and recommends product product goals and develops sales forecasts according to established procedures. |
| Development of Objectives | Develops and proposes broad brand objectives and, consulting with appropriate departments, specific objectives for sales, promotion, price, publicity and packaging. |

| | |
|---|---|
| Advertising and Sales Promotion Budgeting | Serves and assists. |
| Advertising Strategy | The development of the broad advertising approach including the creative and media strategy is the function of a Strategy Committee, consisting of the Vice President—Marketing, the Marketing Manager, the Product Manager and the agency. |
| Media Strategy Framework | Collaborates. |
| Scheduling of Media by Area and Timing Within Strategy Framework | Initiates and collaborates. |
| Promotion Planning | Develops and proposes. |

Company D was one of the companies that claimed to have a product manager system but whose product men were not responsible for profit. Their reply makes the reason plain:

> Profit objectives are established in the controller's area. Prices are also established in the controller's area on the basis of a stipulated profit goal on a full cost basis. The goal is approximately 7% net after taxes.

The conclusion is inescapable that this question posed a great deal of difficulty for the respondents because it forced most of them to support untenable positions. These companies might benefit from a consideration of the following three points:

1. Those who wish to continue to hold the product manager responsible for profits of his product should charge to the product a standard cost which would not vary because of price or manufacturing efficiency variances.
2. An operating statement carrying only the operating costs for direct controllable marketing expenses, interest cost on inventories (if incremental) and cost of accounts receivable

should be introduced. If the product man controls distribution and elements of warehousing, a variant of these should be included.

3. Specifically delineated responsibilities such as those put forth by Company B could relieve some of the uncertainties in measuring job performance.

The product manager, in his current role, has been asked to assume responsibility without authority. He is required to do far more than glance at the bottom line of a profit and loss statement and report to management. Rather, he is expected to play an active part in improving the profitability of his product. In a sense the man is a "watchdog" over profits. As a staff man, however, he has very little line authority on matters directly affecting the costs and profits of his product. Yet, it is understandable why the various levels of marketing management are inclined to make each product manager feel responsible for the profitability of his product. A spokesman for Reynolds Metals once stated that the product manager should be accountable for sales and profitability targets as well as for product line results.[12]

In discussions of the implied responsibility of the product manager, the reluctance on the part of large companies to define the scope of the product manager's responsibility for losses has been rarely mentioned. Companies have apparently had difficulty in evaluating the degree of responsibility for loss on the part of the marketing manager in instances where he has failed to support the product manager adequately. However, *he* is the individual who has the greater access to the head of the non-marketing functions and who has authority over most of the factors that govern profit. In this sense, it is reasonable to charge the marketing manager with an even greater degree of profit responsibility than can be assigned to the product manager. In the final analysis, it is certain that if the authority for final decisions concerning pricing policy is wielded by the product manager, he can exercise a profound effect on profits. This is not to imply that pricing plays *the* major role in establishing profit levels; it is merely to state that pricing policy, among marketing tools, has the potential of being the more fluid variable.

The accurate measurement of the efficiency of the product

manager requires the design of a program that removes from consideration most of the variables affecting profitability for which the product manager has no responsibility. Among the likely areas are the costs of purchasing raw materials, plant manufacturing efficiencies, and, in those instances where a staff director of marketing is present, the direct advertising policy.

### Centralization versus Decentralization in Finance

Another question, similar to the question raised about marketing organization, probed the type of financial organization of the respondent companies. Over two-thirds of the companies considered themselves decentralized.

Centralization, according to the Controllership Foundation study, is a word of many meanings.[13] With reference to management problems, an administrative organization is centralized to the extent that decisions are made at relatively high levels in the organization. Conversely, decentralization implies lower level discretionary and decision-making authority.

The maturity of data processing systems and equipment is bringing about a change in the traditional financial interpretation of centralization and decentralization. Computer economics often preclude the maintenance of separate financial facilities by individual divisions. What is emerging in corporate decentralized organization is the assignment to divisions of quasi-financial personnel who assist in planning and control for decision-making and who have access to a central computer via on-line terminals.

Company J replied that they considered their financial function to be highly centralized; however, quasi-financial personnel are assigned to three marketing divisions and are called marketing services analysts. These groups are headed by a marketing services manager who reports to the divisional vice-president of marketing. The groups are primarily concerned with budgetary controls. The individuals are, according to the company, really "marketing economists" and have no corporate reporting responsibilities. The awareness of a need for servicing the marketing area with specialized, financially trained personnel comes very close to the spirit of the position contained in this study. The centralized portion of their organization is shown in Figure 7.

Somewhat similarly, Company I indicated that although the general accounting function of the financial area is centralized, all other financial functions are decentralized in the same manner as is marketing. One such decentralized organization for that company is shown in Figure 8.

The problem of reporting lines was raised in the reply given by Company C, which noted that financial functions such as cash and taxes are centralized but that most other functions are under the aegis of a division controller who reports directly to the division manager. Many of the decentralized marketing companies stated that their division controllers reported directly to the divisions heads but retained a "dotted line" relationship to the corporate controller. All indicated that this has proved to be a viable relationship, thus confirming the findings of the earlier Controllership Foundation study, which concluded that the evidence "indicates that a division of formal authority over the factory accountant is entirely workable."[14] This study further concluded than a man *can* serve two masters provided that the two masters are not working at cross purposes.

Company S indicated that although there is a conventional accounting function, most divisions maintain their own production and sales accounting groups and establish their own product costing systems. Data from those systems are fed into a centralized unit for purposes of consolidation.

An example of a completely centralized financial unit is illustrated by the structure of Company M, which is decentralized in marketing but centralized for all other functions. No division has any financial personnel except for an individual who acts as an "internal management consultant" and floats between the marketing division head and the corporate controller. Presently, the men report to the controller although in a new organizational plan, they report directly to the division head.

An organizational pattern has emerged in recent years which gives emphasis to informational assistance and techniques and which is consonant with the conclusions reached by Buchin. He spoke of the growing relationship between an understanding of quantitative reports and prudent management control. "Management planning and control appeared to be an inseparable process assisted by an intelligent use of quantitative information."[15]

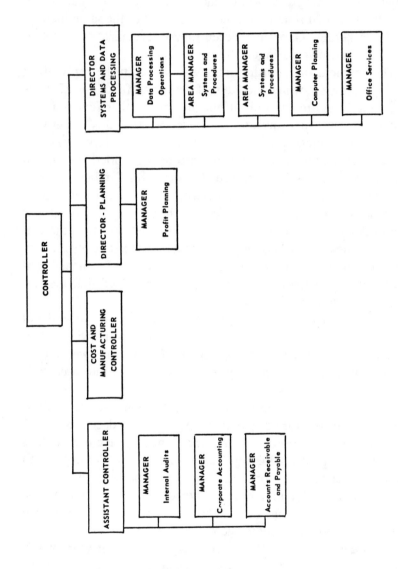

Figure 7. Financial Organization, Company J (Pharmaceuticals, Toiletries)

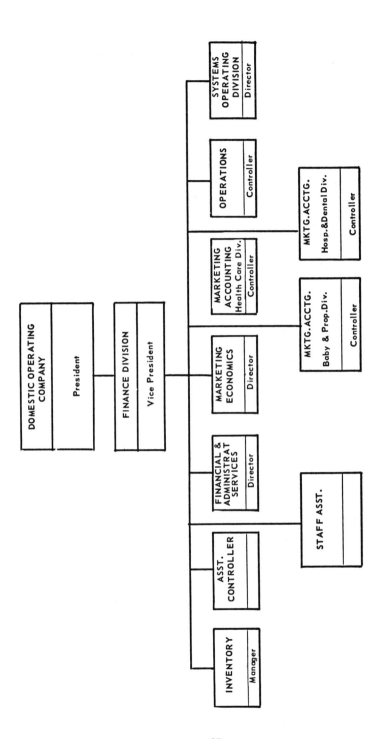

Figure 8. Financial Organization, Company I (Hospital, Health Aids)

67

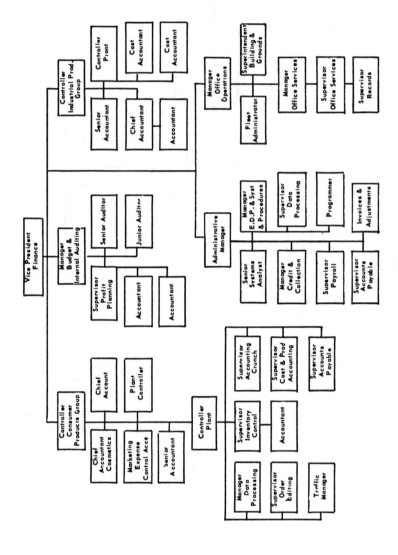

Figure 9. Financial Organization, Company K (Cosmetics, Toiletries)

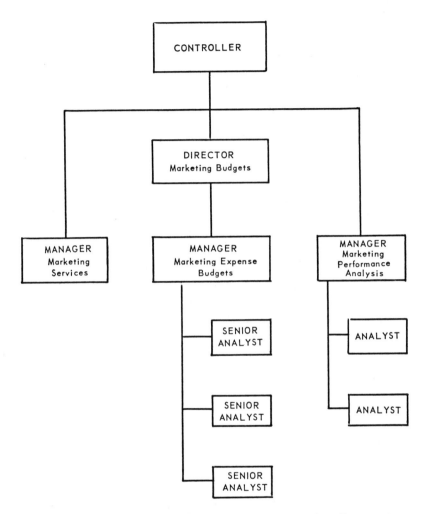

Figure 10. Financial Organization, Company R (Air Transport)

## Marketing Organization Specifically for Planning and Control

Marketing personnel were asked, "What type of organization exists within the marketing function specifically for planning and control?" For the most part (16 companies), marketing control was maintained by *financial* people.

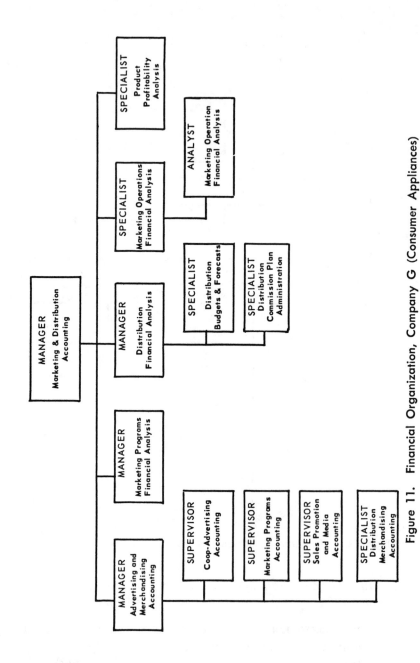

Figure 11. Financial Organization, Company G (Consumer Appliances)

70

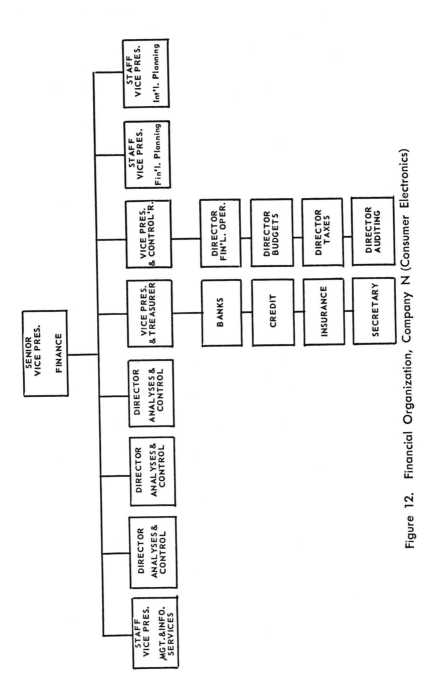

Figure 12. Financial Organization, Company N (Consumer Electronics)

71

Company A hired a media controller to track adherence to the plan. This was an innovative move that recognized marketing's role in planning. The most noteworthy response to the question came from Company H which stated that marketing planning and control "is not basically a marketing function." This may be self-rationalization. From a financial view, the company is superbly organized but the controller traditionally has wielded insignificant influence in the marketing area; consequently the marketing function has tended to use him and his assistants as a crutch, somewhat absolving themselves of the responsibility for control. The result, over the years, has been continuous friction between the financial analyst and the product man over the manner in which the "accountant's bookkeeping has fouled up marketing statistics," especially in instances when the product manager has overspent specific promotional funds. Recognition that control *is* a marketing function might go a long way toward ameliorating the friction.

Company T sketched its organization for their products division:

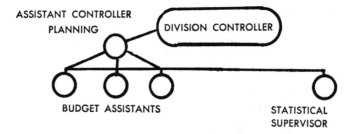

The division controller has three budget assistants whose main duties concern planning and control analyses, and report activities. In addition, there is a statistical supervisor, who is EDP oriented and concerned with current statistical information. The assistant controller for planning reports directly to the division controller.

Drucker succinctly analyzed the problem when he stated that ". . . most, if not all executives, including most controllers themselves, would consider it gross misuse and abuse of controllership were this 'controller' to use his 'controls' to exercise 'control' in the business."[16]

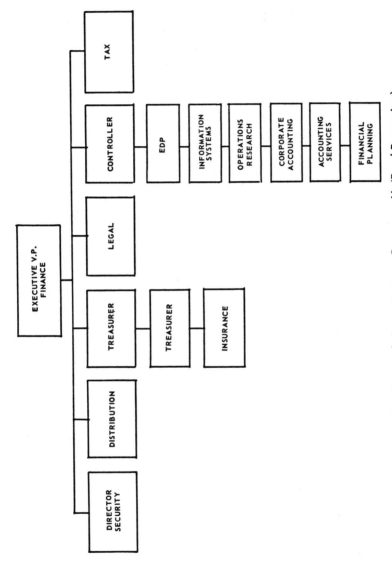

Figure 13. Financial Organization, Company H (Food Processing)

73

*Finance's Role in Services for Marketing*

Companies were asked, "Does any part of the financial function exist primarily to service the marketing area?" Only one company, Company Q, replied in the negative. This suggests that finance, as a function in the remaining companies, is aware of an implied responsibility to service marketing.

Company B indicated that there was a close working relationship between the staff controller and the division controllers. There are four analysts in the Food and Confectionery Divisions who are in a constant process of analysis and control.

Company D, which is highly centralized and sales oriented, replied that the real link for planning and control was the computer area which is working on a media coverage program called "MCA" that is designed to correlate information on physical sales in a media area. It seems that the systems people could be of additional assistance to the information-starved marketing group (see p. 50) by creating reports indicating the correlation of promotion policy to media area for each product. Regression analysis and exponential smoothing could aid in determining the degrees of influence on sales of media and promotion policies.

Within Company E, a division of a larger company, a budget group services the marketing area. Their individuals are assigned responsibility for the financial implications of product group activity. They prepare control data as well as financial data and "keep an eye on marketing funds."

Company J, which is highly committed to data processing, said that both the controller and the deputy controller, each of whom is EDP oriented, maintain an organization designed to equip the marketing services group within each marketing division with information adequate to assess the maintenance of gross margin. This emphasis on gross margin stems from their view that the product man's main job is to obtain volume and ensure stable selling prices. Package design, selling and distribution, and staff functions are relatively uncontrollable by individual product managers.

Company P, highly conscious of the marketing concept, said:

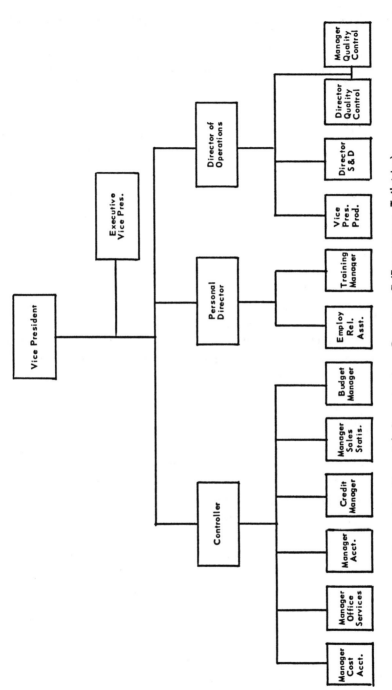

Figure 14.  Financial Organization, Company E (Fragrances, Toiletries)

Yes; one of the components of the controller's area is called marketing cost accounting. Its function is to provide measurement and control of a plan for consumers and industrial marketing. "All of their work is with the marketing organization." Another component of the controller's area is called sales and distribution accounting. This area provides historical accounting information on all sales and marketing activities except advertising and promotion. "Historically it has played a passive role which provides a service." Both of these components report directly to the assistant controller who works closely with marketing.

Company M employs what they call a "marketing services concept." Within their financial analysis and planning area, a select group of analysts who are highly marketing oriented, service marketing by accepting roving assignments from marketing managers, and also act as advisors. The range of assignments runs the gamut from computing the profitability of alternative strategies to preparing a complete marketing plan for a new product. In an effort to disassociate their image from traditional accounting, the men attend advertising agency strategy sessions, Nielsen review meetings, etc. They frequently have desks in the marketing area but a supervisory eye is kept on them by the manager of financial analysis and planning. This servicing approach completely recognizes the implied obligation on the part of the controller to provide marketing with quantitative assistance, and it has thus far been highly successful. It has also proved to be a springboard for promotion of the analysts to pure marketing product jobs.

An extension of this question asked, "If so, what specific training in marketing equips these personnel for their service function?"

With the exception of the negative response cited above, all respondents implied that the basic education derived from either exposure to marketing or simply experience over time. Company M saw fit to expand its answer:

They are equipped for their assignments as a result of a strong indoctrination in profitability concepts, a basic accounting edu-

cation and intense exposure to the marketing job through the use
of active participation in marketing sessions, attendance and
travels relative to sales meetings and, at times, maintenance of
their base of operations in the marketing area itself.

## The Role of the Controller in Decision Making

Respondents were asked to describe the role of the controller
in the decision-making process, specifically in the following
areas:

Purchasing policy
Pricing
New product ventures
Acquisitions
Sales incentive planning

Somewhat surprisingly, the responses indicated that the controller's role is generally limited to an ex-post responsibility.
Each of the above areas has within its parameters a potential
marketing decision; the table below indicates the degree to which
the controller is involved:

| Type of Role | Purchasing | Pricing | New Products | Acquisitions | Incentives |
|---|---|---|---|---|---|
| Major | 6 | 7 | 14 | 12 | 15 |
| Minor | 14 | 13 | 6 | 8 | 5 |
| Total | 20 | 20 | 20 | 20 | 20 |

It is apparent that the controller's role, save for new product
and acquisition evaluation, is limited in most companies. The
classification "major" and "minor" in the above tabulation is a
compendium based upon relies received giving the degree of
*decision-making* responsibility for the controller in each area. If
in incentive planning the role of the controller is merely to record
and compute, that role would be categorized as "minor." If, on
the other hand, he assists in creating and evaluating the plan, his
role would be classified as "major."

In the *purchasing* area, those companies indicating a strong role for the controller have in common the characteristic of sensitive raw material requirements and strong financial discipline. As an example, Company E indicated that it currently has a drive on to cut costs and in order to implement that drive, the general manager of the division and the controller make decisions on the long term impact of costs and inform the purchasing agent of specific prices which he should attempt to obtain.

Company I indicated that the controller has an active role in determining the purchasing policy and is responsible for informing the purchasing agent of "to buy" decisions made in order to meet profit plan requirements.

Similarly, Company M's controller keeps the purchasing agent completely informed of his current position for basic raw materials. He also informs the purchasing agent of his "to buy" position.

Company P feels that the controller should, in part, make certain that the purchasing department understands the proper value of volume discounts and the "consequent tying up of working capital." He is responsible for integrating the requirements of the profit plan into the purchasing function as it concerns material prices and inventory turnover. This definition of the controller's role stems from a change in the nature of the business from a small number of high volume brands to a multiplicity of low volume brands characterized by high raw material requirements.

The remaining fourteen companies expressed a diversity of reasons for the passive role of the controller in this process. One controller, in Company C, said that "the controller has little voice other than that of internal control. He exists in a service capacity only and has virtually no voice in decisions." It would not be too hard to conclude that the denial of a vigorous role in purchasing decision-making is but a reflection of that rather weak reply to the question.

Company H, quite financially sophisticated, sees the controller's role as a processor of information, feeding the profit plan data into the computer; it, in turn, formulates policy for the purchasing agent. In this role the controller merely supplies information and is bereft of any decision responsibilities.

Company Q "lives with any costs they can get"; consequently, all that their man has to do is to establish a standard material cost, and any purchasing differentials "will be thrown out in the form of variances."

The balance of replies indicated that they were either satisfied with the status quo or felt confident of their purchasing agents.

No single conclusion is possible about the above findings. Apparently the type of company, the reliance on volatile raw materials, the financial discipline extant, and the personality of the controller are all major influences on the dynamics of the controller's responsibilities in purchasing.

The *pricing* area is a particularly sensitive one because pricing divisions have traditionally been the prerogative of the marketing function. Contained within all profit plans are assumptions regarding pricing structures. Violations or deviations from that plan could have serious implications on operating results and, in addition, pricing policy frequently lives in the habitat of the highest executive levels. Given these considerations, it would seem at first blush that the natural administrator would be the man most familar with the requirements of the profit plan. That man is the controller.

This attitude, however, is not widespread. Seven companies, less than half the respondents, indicated that their controller plays a major decision role in pricing policy. Among those companies, Company D indicated that their controller establishes the selling prices for products based upon a full cost margin. This is the same company that claimed to be highly marketing-oriented and yet issued no financial data to marketing personnel.

Company I reported that their man plays an active role in pricing decisions; as a member of the division head's staff, he sits in on all meetings pertaining to pricing decisions. He does not, though, exercise a veto power unless there are truly significant possibilities of mispricing.

Company P replied that the controller is a party to all pricing decisions. The staff attests to the accuracy of pricing data and, in some instances, the controller takes the initiative in evaluating the adequacy of current pricing structures.

Company M indicated that the controller plays a dual role in pricing. The marketing services analysts participate fully in the decision process leading to a price change. Once a decision is made, the controller indicates his concurrence by signing the price change authorization. Actually many companies reported that the controller signs authorization documents, but this appears to be more of a notification to *him* rather than the expression of his decision authority. It is interesting to note that all the seven companies promulgate extremely aggressive marketing policies and are subjected to intense price competition.

Most of the companies in which the controller plays a "minor" role, indicated that pricing is basically a marketing function and out of the purview of finance. The most reasoned reply was given by Company H:

> The corporate controller does not have veto power in pricing decisions, although he is a party to it. A closer party to price change action is the division controller. Philosophically, a price change is not a purely financial or marketing decision. If a marketing manager cannot unilaterally make the decision himself, then in fairness, neither the corporate or division controller should have the power to veto such a decison. The basic role of the controller is to assess its financial logic. In these reviews, judgmental factors are opposed to functional reviews. In the final analysis, most of the onus for being a "watchdog," rests with the division controller.

Pricing is just one of the creative elements of the marketing mix. Judging from the lack of creativity thus far displayed by the financial function, it is not surprising that the area has, in most instances, not been invited to participate in the pricing process.

*New product ventures* proved to be the area in marketing subject to the greatest financial impact. Company B said it well when they responded that it was highly desirable for financial people to be involved in new product ventures, as early as in the conceptual stage. Review meetings are held one to two times each quarter to consider new product possibilities. At that time, an assessment is made of the product's potential contribution. A committee, called the New Products Committee, exists to perform that function. "There should be a happy point between the need to move and the desirability to move."

Company E involves its controller deeply, not in the conceptual stage, but rather in the formative stage. His responsibility is to evaluate cost implications and do a "complete marketing analysis."

Interesting replies came from Companies I, P, and H:

> In the area of new product ventures, the controller plays a role in the costing of a product. There is a great deal of room for improvement in this particular area, because not enough is being done in utilizing the available financial talent. The controller should be brought in, in this area, in the conceptual stage so that he may express a reasoned perspective on whether a product should be developed any further than its idea development. We have some projects now in motion which I am certain should never have reached that stage.
>
> From one point of view, the controller attests to the validity of financial assumptions and accounting data. From another view as an individual, the controller gets his "day in court." The controller must identify areas of crucial assumptions and also factors in learning curves.
>
> The controller is involved as soon as someone creates a budget. This beginning of involvement occurs when the investigator takes the result of an experimentation and decides to take a quantum leap into the product. After all, the decison to venture into the new product area infers market testing, pilot plants, high marketing rates, etc.

In Company M the marketing service analysts work closely with both the corporate and the division product development areas. They prepare cost estimates, calculate the impact upon profitability, and make extensive return on investment studies for individual products and for product concepts.

Not surprisingly, the area of *acquisition analysis* is heavily controller-influenced. All replies, save one, were perfunctory and emphasized the financial nature of acquisitions. This, of course, absolves any company of asking itself the basic reasoning behind *why* the acquisition is desired. As most later confessed, the core of the desire is most heavily weighted with marketing considerations. Even the reply by Company M could have been anticipated:

The primary responsibility for corporate action concerning acquisitions is within the controller's area. The Funds Analysis section of Financial and Planning exists mainly for that purpose. Frequently, in order to evaluate acquisition prospects, the controller will travel with the appropriate marketing division head who is likely to be affected by the acquisition, to the acquisition candidate and an on the spot marketing and preliminary financial evaluation is completed. It is then brought into headquarters for more detailed study.

*Sales incentive plans and planning* is graded most poorly in terms of controller participation. Actually, the area is a fine candidate for active participation in decision-making on the part of the controller. In his article in *Business Management,* the author wrote:

> An excellent example of constructive intrusion by the controller is in the area of *sales incentive planning,* a traditional marketing fortress whose drawbridge is raised or lowered by the sales manager. Most incentive plans revolve about volume (turnover) reward: This breeds a consciousness of sales into the selling force. What is not inbred, though, is an appreciation of *product mix,* the proportion in which products should be sold. Absence of this appreciation encourages the salesman to sell what is easiest for him to accomplish even though it may be one of the least profitable items for the company. Based on profitability concepts it would be a relatively simple task for the controller to *take the initiative* and demonstrate to the sales manager the optimum sales mix. Horrors, he may even suggest the playing down of an item easy to sell in favor of a more profitable but more challenging item to sell.

Nevertheless, most replies said that the controller assists the sales area in the "computation and evaluation" of incentive plans. For the most part, he is considered a monitor—he estimates the cost of a particular plan and then tracks the results against the estimate. In only one company did the controller have the temerity to propose a different type of plan, not based upon pure volume attainment. It was rejected for being too radical.

Thus, in an uncomfortably large number of instances, the controller has found that he is an "attestor." He has minimal roles in purchasing, pricing and sales incentive decisions, somewhat stronger roles in new product and acquistion evaluations. The former three areas are fertile ground for aggressive educational penetration by the controller.

### The Existence of Marketing Strategy and Decision Committees

Respondents were asked, "Are there standing committees which meet regularly and possess authority to evaluate marketing strategies and longer term decision implications? Are both marketing and finance represented on such committees?"

Among those with formal committees, Company B indicated that it has a marketing committee which meets at least once weekly, and monthly has both finance and marketing represented. Company C calls its group the Product Committee while Company J calls its the Management Committee. The latter consists of the administrative vice president, the consumer relations vice president and the executive vice president-operations. They meet at least once in each of twelve promotional periods.

Company P has lower level staff meetings weekly to consider and evaluate strategies. The assistant controller is present at all these meetings. Company S has an executive committee, consisting of the president of the division, the general manager of the business area and the control manager. They meet on the first and third Friday of each month to assess marketing strategy. On a daily basis, however, the general manager of the business area meets frequently with the control manager (finance.)

Company E has three basic marketing committee meetings: a weekly marketing group meeting at which the controller is present; a promotional planning committee consisting of the controller, marketing manager and managers of manufacturing and sales meets weekly; and a new products committee meets weekly.

# Chapter V

# Marketing
# Decision-Making Data
# and Techniques—
# Part I

## Criticism of Accounting

One of the contemporary mod things to do is to criticize the profession of accounting. Not only is it under attack by the Securities & Exchange Commission but also the Director of Internal Revenue. The profession has been chided in the courts in the Westec and Atlantic Research cases. Within its own community there is little agreement on the proper method to handle investment tax credits.

It should therefore not be surprising to see individual professionals disagree in print on the use of one of the many analytical techniques available. In his article dealing with "The Use of ROI in Sales Management,"[1] Michael Schiff contended that the most important measure that marketing men should employ for evaluating and decision-making is the return on investment. He is disputed by Bruce Henderson and John Dearden who wrote afterward that, "ROI fails in these ways (. . . . . evaluation and analysis) because it uses profit centers which really cannot be profit centers, transfers prices which are not really prices and investment bases which are not, in fact, relevant."[2]

Philip Scheuble earlier had written:

> However, the full potential of ROI analysis has not really been understood as a guide for day-to-day decisions throughout various levels of the organization. Perhaps its prime emphasis as a financial tool has limited its dissemination, but a more practical reason has been the lack of simple methods for calculating ROI and the limitations of classical accounting concepts in providing information in useable form.
>
> The fact remains that ROI guidelines, properly formulated, provide an insight for operating personnel that is usually obscured by profit and loss accounting."[3]

Robert Beyer, in discussing both direct costing and return on investment summarized the conflict:

> Since World War II, there have been only two significant developments in the technique of internal profit measurement, i.e., the substantial interest displayed in (1) direct costing and (2) return on investment. Neither of these concepts was new in the postwar period. Each had been discussed in textbooks for many years. The significant point is, however, that in neither case have we exploited the advantages for good internal accounting and control which are inherent in both of the concepts. Thus:
>
> Direct costing has frustrated many managers because of its clash with the principles of custodial accounting and its lack of acceptability by the Securities & Exchange Commission and the Internal Revenue Service.
>
> Return on investment as a tool has not made the headway it should because of the inability of most accountants and managers to integrate it with internal accounting procedures.
>
> The result has been that internal accounting limps along, to a great extent mimicking custodial accounting by making one pattern of figure recording do for two end products which, by their nature, have widely varying purposes.[4]

### The Adequacy of Accounting Data Supplied to Marketing

In his 1965 article, Feder recognized that accounting data for marketing is inadequate.

> To be sure, attempts have been made by many companies to identify by area the responsiveness of profits to marketing efforts.

Typically, however, they use a breakdown of accounting figures, and the value of traditional financial data for this purpose is severely limited. For one thing, the conventions which underlie the accounting system were originally designed for auditing. Accordingly, "generally accepted accounting practices" dictate that marketing expenditures be written off when they are incurred—not when they produce sales. Within this framework certain advertising and promotional activities which create retail movement of goods are expensed against unrelated segments of wholesale movement.

In many companies market area reports are further distorted by the allocation of unidentified costs and bookkeeping adjustments which are irrelevant from the standpoint of profit responsiveness. Under full costing assumptions, many products in many markets normally show losses. In fact, some of these products are profitable from an incremental standpoint, but the profitable areas are not usually identifiable. Differences in product mix and complicated accounting practices produce a situation in which the amount of allocated fixed costs is not uniform or recognizable by market area. In an effort to avoid taking incorrect action in a profitable area, marketing management is normally reluctant to enact spending changes on the basis of these reports.

To these two complicating factors we must add still another. Traditional accounting periods do not necessarily correspond to the time span during which an advertising campaign produces its full increment of sales. An analysis performed on the basis of the results achieved in any one month would probably exclude a substantial portion of the sales generated by the marketing effort expensed in that period. On the other hand, considerably longer periods (say, a year) probably combine the results of many spending decisions, concealing both overspending and underspending. Here again traditional accounting conventions preclude the measurement of profit responsiveness.[5]

Only three of the twenty companies in the study replied in the negative to a question which asked, "How adequate are accounting measures of profit to assess marketing profit responsibility? What criteria are used (ROI, volume, profitability)?"

Most of the companies interviewed said that their accounting measures for profit were "quite adequate." All claimed to use both volume attainment and "profitability" as criteria. Only 10 companies, however, used Return on Investment as a measure.

Revealingly, the responses of those companies which felt that the data was quite adequate clearly showed degrees of dissatisfaction.

Among the companies considering their data to be sufficient was Company A. Although they did not care to elaborate on their assessment, they did speak of the lack of criteria for judging the success of new products; volume is apparently the only measure of success. For established products, profit margin maintenance is the criteria for measurement of success. They do admit that there is no real minimum acceptable margin for established products, because much of the "story depends on the life cycle of the product which may vary from time to time." This reply indicates a lack of planning discipline. Margins are established as the criteria, but each criteria should have a goal against which to be measured. To place the blame at the doorstep of life cycle configuration is to release oneself from planning and influencing the degree and direction of life cycle movements. Life cycles are but a reflection of volume influences and these can be made to dance to a tune of period regeneration through marketing investment spending and product innovation.

Company C contended that their measures are "very good." They employ a net profit margin to sales concept for control purposes. They felt strongly that the technique of return on investment measure for division or product control cannot be used with facility in the company, for an interesting reason. The nature of the business is such that the basic investment and product costs are relatively minor compared to packaging and marketing costs. As a consequence, profits are higher relative to invested capital and it would be difficult to motivate a man by telling him to exceed the, say, 36% ROI he made last year: he is likely to reply that it is a very high ROI to begin with. Instead, motivation is achieved by reducing plans to an earnings per share basis and challenging the division manager to equal or better his planned contribution. The goal is controlled to the nearest tenth of a cent in per share earnings. The computation of earnings per share, however, includes corporate allocations of overhead which, admittedly, are beyond the control of an individual division manager. Divisions are allocated 1% of sales as corporate overhead, and are charged 6% on the corporate investment in the division.

Although a control and measurement system is in force here, the preoccupation with assigning period corporate charges to required profit quotas engenders something of a paradox. "The boundaries of a management control system . . . . . must not be drawn to conform with organizational structure merely because of that structure."[6] This assignment of uncontrollable period costs is in contradiction to elementary principles of responsibility accounting. The establishment of goals in terms of earnings per share is a unique device but it need not necessarily replace ROI as a measure. Any single ROI goal is relatively useless; when compared to a base it can be meaningful but there is no indication that this has been done.

Company F, which was satisfied with their data, commented that product profit and loss statements are continually published as an aid in evaluating alternatives; significantly, post audits comparing actual performance to plan are made. Plan, in this sense, also denoted an alternative strategy. Their reply was unique only in the sense that they were the only company to make a practice of post audit evaluations.

Company M likes their system and criteria very much. All three criteria of volume, profitability and ROI measures were being used with moderate success. The most interesting observation from the marketing side, however, was a statement saying that "the accounting boys could help us a great deal more by giving us data which would aid us in the simulation of results from alternatives. We also need more data, even better data in order to determine customer and geographic profitability."

Company K, smaller in comparison to other concerns, proved to be by far the most sophisticated in terms of utilization of financial techniques for marketing. They like their system but complained that there was not sufficient analysis of data. The job was being done by the product managers. The effectiveness of their performance is measured by adherence to the plan plus the maintenance of a minimum ROI performance. The base for the ROI calculations usually consists of types of working capital by accounts and inventories. They made an attempt to minimize allocations depending upon the level of profit being examined. The company stated that they "do not believe in allocations in instances where the recipient of the report can't exercise control over period costs." (See figure 15).

| MONTH OF | | | | | | | ITEM | CUMULATIVE YEAR TO DATE | | | | | | |
|---|---|---|---|---|---|---|---|---|---|---|---|---|---|---|
| THIS YEAR | % | LAST YEAR | % | PROFIT | % | Better or (Worse) than P.P | | THIS YEAR | % | LAST YEAR | % | PROFIT | % | Better or (Worse) than P.P |
| 1 | | | | | | | NET SALES | | | | | | | |
| 2 | | | | | | | Consumer Products Group | | | | | | | |
| 3 | | | | | | | Industrial Products Group | | | | | | | |
| 4 | | | | | | | | | | | | | | |
| 5 | | | | | | | | | | | | | | |
| 6 | | | | | | | TOTAL | | | | | | | |
| 7 | | | | | | | DELIVERED COST OF GOODS SOLD | | | | | | | |
| 8 | | | | | | | Consumer Products Group | | | | | | | |
| 9 | | | | | | | Industrial Products Group | | | | | | | |
| 10 | | | | | | | | | | | | | | |
| 11 | | | | | | | | | | | | | | |
| 12 | | | | | | | | | | | | | | |
| 13 | | | | | | | TOTAL | | | | | | | |
| 14 | | | | | | | MARKETING EXPENSES | | | | | | | |
| 15 | | | | | | | Consumer Products Group | | | | | | | |
| 16 | | | | | | | Industrial Products Group | | | | | | | |
| 17 | | | | | | | | | | | | | | |
| 18 | | | | | | | | | | | | | | |
| 19 | | | | | | | | | | | | | | |
| 20 | | | | | | | TOTAL | | | | | | | |
| 21 | | | | | | | GROUP EXPENSES | | | | | | | |
| 22 | | | | | | | Consumer Products Group | | | | | | | |
| 23 | | | | | | | Industrial Products Group | | | | | | | |
| 24 | | | | | | | | | | | | | | |
| 25 | | | | | | | | | | | | | | |
| 26 | | | | | | | | | | | | | | |
| 27 | | | | | | | TOTAL | | | | | | | |
| 28 | | | | | | | GROUP PROFIT CONTRIBUTION | | | | | | | |
| 29 | | | | | | | Consumer Products Group | | | | | | | |
| 30 | | | | | | | Industrial Products Group | | | | | | | |
| 31 | | | | | | | | | | | | | | |
| 32 | | | | | | | | | | | | | | |
| 33 | | | | | | | | | | | | | | |
| 34 | | | | | | | TOTAL | | | | | | | |
| 35 | | | | | | | GENERAL. ADMIN, RESEARCH, ETC. | | | | | | | |
| 36 | | | | | | | Non-Recurring Expenses | | | | | | | |
| 37 | | | | | | | Group Profit Reserves | | | | | | | |
| 38 | | | | | | | | | | | | | | |
| 39 | | | | | | | | | | | | | | |
| 40 | | | | | | | | | | | | | | |
| 41 | | | | | | | TOTAL | | | | | | | |
| 42 | | | | | | | | | | | | | | |
| 43 | | | | | | | Profit before Taxes | | | | | | | |
| 44 | | | | | | | | | | | | | | |
| 45 | | | | | | | Provision for Income Taxes | | | | | | | |
| 46 | | | | | | | | | | | | | | |
| 47 | | | | | | | | | | | | | | |
| 48 | | | | | | | | | | | | | | |
| 49 | | | | | | | NET PROFITS | | | | | | | |
| 50 | | | | | | | | | | | | | | |
| 51 | | | | | | | | | | | | | | |
| | | | | | | | PRODUCTS DIVISION - EARNINGS | | | | | Page | | 1-200 |

Figure 15.   Division Operating Statement, Company K
(Cosmetics, Toiletries)

Company S, a huge consumer products company, presents another contradiction. This is a company which considers its accounting measures of profit acceptable (as opposed to "quite adequate"). They produce an operating and revenue statement monthly for each major product. They feel that the statement is definitely product oriented because it details expense components for the product and, moreover, profit before taxes is measured against a base of *allocated* working capital. Their rule of thumb objective is to have sales increase at least twice the rate of period cost increases. It should not be too difficult for a company of that size and degree of data processing sophistication to compute the basic elements of working capital for the product rather than allocate them. Allocations by percentages are a great time-saver but product mixes, inventory positions, trade terms, etc., change frequently and allocation can result in a significant tradeoff in accuracy and control motivation. In another context the company mentioned that they did have access to receivables, payables and inventory data for specific products so the raw materials are there for the programming.

Although Company T considered their data to be acceptable, they were quite critical in their remarks about their own information system. It was felt that ROI measures were poorly utilized and that they relied too heavily on measures of profit and volume attainment. Little effort has been expended to measure working capital tied up in the business. There is difficulty from a decision point of view, because division statements conform to corporate reporting practices. One glaring example they cited was an instance where marketing personnel within the divisions requested that off-invoice deals to customers be reported as a marketing expense rather than as a deduction from sales. The controller's staff did not comply with the request because it was contrary to the corporate reporting format, which, in turn, was based on requirements set forth by the Securities and Exchange Commission. Most of the company's own commentary requires no elaboration, save for the observation that the responsibility for *reporting* is clearly being confused with that of special purpose *analysis*. Even though off-invoice allowances are a de facto decline over the short term, the fact remains that they are also a controllable marketing expense.

Among the companies considering the accounting measures of profit inadequate, Company P was one of the most outspoken. They felt that although they had come a long way toward rectifying inadequacies, the marketing area did not know how much profit was generated because too many fixed charges and overheads were "assigned on a rule of thumb basis." The Company uses three major profit criteria: return on investment, profit before taxes and gross margin reports. Results are compared to plan, and to the previous year. The company did not comment on the ability of their marketing personnel to appreciate the nuances of gross margin reports. This is a case of double jeopardy, because period factory charges are assigned to cost of goods sold but the marketing and distribution costs, that take up so great a part of the revenue dollar, are not even taken into account on the gross margin statement.

Company B was also outspoken in its criticism of accounting measures for profit responsibility. The vice-president of marketing indicated that the basic problem arose because operations were evaluated on a gross trading profit basis and that, therefore, marketing gross profit was disassociated from sales. That system took into account advertising, promotion, market research and packaging design costs, but no distribution costs. In addition, product statements were prepared annually for the mainline product but contained no provisions for elementary pack size profitability data. It is difficult to ascribe a cause to this gross lack of basic sophistication in the information-decision cycle. The most probable cause was the history of the company's preoccupation with volume growth without regard to the quality of the volume.

Earlier in the study reference was made to Company D and the role played by the sales force and the controller. In reply to the question at hand, the marketing respondent said, "I would personally like to know, with any individual product, what the profit structure is, under varying volume conditions." He felt that a marginal approach would be a decided improvement. It is extremely difficult to comprehend how marketing can make meaningful decisions under these circumstances. The implication is strongly implanted here, and confirmed by their organization chart (Figure 1), that the key is the measurement by volume attainment, a dubious criterion for profitability.

Company E complained of full cost absorption costing and the consequent inability to isolate incremental effects of marketing decisions. Volume and profit were the only accounting criteria used for assessing marketing profit responsibility.

In perspective, it does not appear that accounting, in the last six years, has made much progress in satisfying the needs of the marketing area. The critical areas of failure, as noted in the replies, are:

a. Nonuse of sufficient return on investment criteria
b. Insistence on traditional full costing for decision analyses
c. Inability to separate the reporting obligation from the service function
d. Imperfect understanding of the marketing concept
e. Lack of minimum acceptable goal-criteria
f. Disregard of working capital implications

Later sections will explore these points more fully.

### Finance's Appraisal of Its Own Information

Finance was asked, "Is financial data supplied to the marketing function adequate to assess profit responsibility? Assist in marketing decision making?" One company, Company D, bluntly replied that "no financial data is supplied to the marketing function." Of the remaining nineteen respondents, four expressed negatives and the remainder expressed degrees of satisfaction.

Dissatisfaction resulted from:

Lack of decision-making merits
No profit guidelines
Use of full costing
No expression of controllable variable expenses
No geographic data

One of the companies, B, was not satisfied with their data program and was restructuring it in a form that leads away from the "gross trading profit" concept.

Another company, E, replied in a firm, vocal manner:

> Definitely not. The financial data, at present, is lacking any decision making merits because of the number of factors. We have an acute shortage of manpower and in addition, there are no definite guidelines as to profit criteria. Unfortunately, the senior management in the company insists upon full cost allocation accounting and, because of this, it prevents marketing from making the proper decision. The configuration of the profit and loss statement considers that the following are direct product attributes:

> Gross Sales
> Full Cost, Cost of Sales
> Returns
> Freight
> Allowances
> Advertising and Promotions

> All other items are allocated to products on the basis of sales volume with one exception. The period factory costs included in cost of sales are allocated to products on the basis of direct labor dollars. In addition to the above, management insists upon seeing profit results for products expressed in terms of profit after taxes. They simply will not acknowledge the more sophisticated uses of marginal costs. (See figure 16.)

Company P was not satisfied and reasoned that they should construct measures designed to facilitate the evaluation of alternatives in terms of various controllable expenses. They (finance) felt that there was no basis in historical data to guide marketing in assessing volume changes resulting from different levels of advertising and promotion. They also intend to use geographic control areas for advertising and promotion levels.

The other company replying negatively was Company R. They felt that much more work should be done in "revenue" (sales) accounting so that geographical and functional performance could be measured. "We really don't know who sells what to whom."

There is a fine line of dissatisfaction relative to the data-output status quo; some of the companies were generally satisfied despite the fact that they, too, were not happy over the specifics mentioned above. What is most disturbing to the author is the passive attitude of the accounting functions, and their failure to

| | | | | | | PERCENT | | | | BUDGET | | Percent Growth From Prior Yr. Latest Estimate |
|---|---|---|---|---|---|---|---|---|---|---|---|---|
| **Division** | | | | | | | | Page No. | | | | |
| **Product Line** | | | | | | | | Responsibility Of | | | | |
| **Revises Schedule Dated** | | | | | | | | Date | | | | |
| *(All Dollars are Expended in Thousands)* | | | | | | | | | | | | |
| ACTUAL | | BUDGET | | LATEST ESTIMATE | | Of Budget | Latest Growth Prior Year | | | | | |
| $ | % | $ | % | $ | % | | | | | $ | % | |
| | | | | | | | | GROSS SALES | | | | |
| | | | | | | | | Returns | | | | |
| | | | | | | | | Freight | | | | |
| | | | | | | | | Allowances | | | | |
| | | | | | | | | NET SALES | | | | |
| | | | | | | | | COST OF SALES | | | | |
| | | | | | | | | PRODUCTION MARGIN | | | | |
| | | | | | | | | MARKETING & DISTRIBUTION EXPENSES: | | | | |
| | | | | | | | | Advertising - Print | | | | |
| | | | | | | | | Radio & Television | | | | |
| | | | | | | | | Promotions & Merchandise | | | | |
| | | | | | | | | Advertising & Promotions | | | | |
| | | | | | | | | Field Force | | | | |
| | | | | | | | | Demonstration Supv. Costs | | | | |
| | | | | | | | | Dept. Store Payments & Commiss. | | | | |
| | | | | | | | | Drug Store Payments | | | | |
| | | | | | | | | Market Research | | | | |
| | | | | | | | | Public Relations | | | | |
| | | | | | | | | Marketing Administration | | | | |
| | | | | | | | | Salvage - Net | | | | |
| | | | | | | | | Branch Expenses | | | | |
| | | | | | | | | Total | | | | |
| | | | | | | | | MARKETING MARGIN | | | | |
| | | | | | | | | OTHER DIVISIONAL EXPENSES: | | | | |
| | | | | | | | | Research & Development | | | | |
| | | | | | | | | General Administration | | | | |
| | | | | | | | | Other (Income) Deductions - Net | | | | |
| | | | | | | | | Total | | | | |
| | | | | | | | | INCOME BEFORE CORP. EXPS. | | | | |
| | | | | | | | | CORPORATE EXPENSES: | | | | |
| | | | | | | | | State & Local Taxes | | | | |
| | | | | | | | | Other Direct | | | | |
| | | | | | | | | Allocated | | | | |
| | | | | | | | | INCOME BEFORE FED. TAXES | | | | |
| | | | | | | | | FEDERAL INCOME TAXES | | | | |
| | | | | | | | | NET INCOME | | | | |
| | | | | | | | | EFFECTIVE TAX RATE | | | | |

Figure 16. Product Operating Statement, Company E
(Fragrances, Toiletries)

educate and convince their managements of the desirability of the information. Certainly in Company E, above, the role of the financial function has been reduced to one of bookkeeping despite the many examples of sophistication extant in their own industry. Company P is making headway and has a real campaign issue in its quest to achieve responsibility accounting. Finally, it is difficult to find one reason or justification for the policies of

| | | | | | | | | Division | | | Page No. | |
|---|---|---|---|---|---|---|---|---|---|---|---|---|
| | | | | | | | | Responsibility Of | | | | |
| *(All Dollars are Expended in Thousands)* | | | | | | | | Revises Schedule Dated | Date | | | |
| ACTUAL | | BUDGET | | LATEST ESTIMATE | | PERCENT | | | BUDGET | | Percent Growth From Prior Yr. Latest Estimate |
| $ | % | $ | % | $ | % | Of Budget | Latest Growth Prior Year | | $ | % | |
| | | | | | | | | GROSS SALES | | | |
| | | | | | | | | Returns | | | |
| | | | | | | | | Freight | | | |
| | | | | | | | | NET SALES | | | |
| | | | | | | | | COST OF SALES | | | |
| | | | | | | | | PRODUCTION MARGIN | | | |
| | | | | | | | | MARKETING & DISTRIBUTION EXPENSES: | | | |
| | | | | | | | | Advertising-Print | | | |
| | | | | | | | | Radio & Television | | | |
| | | | | | | | | Promotions & Merchandise | | | |
| | | | | | | | | Advertising & Promotions | | | |
| | | | | | | | | Field Force | | | |
| | | | | | | | | Demonstration Supv. Costs | | | |
| | | | | | | | | Dept. Store Payments & Commiss. | | | |
| | | | | | | | | Drug Store Payments | | | |
| | | | | | | | | Market Research | | | |
| | | | | | | | | Public Relations | | | |
| | | | | | | | | Marketing Administration | | | |
| | | | | | | | | Salvage-Net | | | |
| | | | | | | | | Branch Expenses | | | |
| | | | | | | | | Total | | | |
| | | | | | | | | MARKETING MARGIN | | | |
| | | | | | | | | Less: Dev. Brands Exp. | | | |
| | | | | | | | | ADJUSTED MKTG. MARGIN | | | |
| | | | | | | | | OTHER DIVISIONAL EXPENSES | | | |
| | | | | | | | | Research & Development | | | |
| | | | | | | | | General Administration | | | |
| | | | | | | | | Other (Income) Deductions-Net | | | |
| | | | | | | | | Total | | | |
| | | | | | | | | INCOME BEFORE CORP. EXPS. | | | |
| | | | | | | | | CORPORATE EXPENSES: | | | |
| | | | | | | | | State & Local Taxes | | | |
| | | | | | | | | Other Direct | | | |
| | | | | | | | | Allocated | | | |
| | | | | | | | | INCOME BEFORE FED. TAXES | | | |
| | | | | | | | | FEDERAL INCOME TAXES | | | |
| | | | | | | | | NET INCOME | | | |
| | | | | | | | | EFFECTIVE TAX RATE | | | |

Figure 16a. Division Operating Statement, Company E

Company D, whose financial area may not release any data to marketing. A modern company, especially one which claims to have adopted the marketing concept and the product manager system, can hardly expect those policies to be condoned.

Among the companies that expressed satisfaction with their data was Company G which prepares handy pocket digests of financial information called "brain books" for their marketing

| | | | | | | | | | Division | | | Page No. | | | |
|---|---|---|---|---|---|---|---|---|---|---|---|---|---|---|---|
| | | | | | | | | | Responsibility Of | | | | | | |
| | | | | | | | | | Revises Schedule Dated | | | Date | | | |
| | | *(All Dollars are Expended in Thousands)* | | | | | | | | | | | | | |
| ACTUAL | | BUDGET | | LATEST ESTIMATE | | | | | MAJOR PRODUCT LINE | | | BUDGET | | | |
| | | | | Dollars | | Percent | | | | | | Dollars | | Percent | |
| Sales Dollars | % of Total | Sales Dollars | % of Total | Sales | Of Budget | Growth From Prior Year | Of Total | | | | | Sales | Growth From Prior Year | Of Total | |
| | | | | | | | | | | | | | | | |
| Notes: | | | | | | | | | | | | | | | |

Figure 16b.  Division Sales Summary, Company E

executives. These books contain all decision-costs. A similar program is conducted by Company H, which updates the data in its quarterly "pocket data sheets."

Company J supplies current data to their marketing area. In addition to operating statements, data on direct account warehouse shipments is distributed—this can be then related to trade deal effectiveness. The increasing use of this data, which formerly

| | | | | | | | Division | Page No. |
|---|---|---|---|---|---|---|---|---|
| | | | | | | | Responsibility Of | |
| | | | | | | | Revises Schedule Dated | Date |
| *(All Dollars are Expended in Thousands)* | | | | | | | | |

| ACTUAL | | BUDGET | | LATEST ESTIMATE | | | | MAJOR PRODUCT LINE | BUDGET | | |
|---|---|---|---|---|---|---|---|---|---|---|---|
| | | | | Dollars | | Percent | | | Dollars | Percent | |
| Net Income | % of Total | Net Income | % of Total | Net Income | Of Budget | Growth From Prior Year | Of Total | | Net Income | Growth From Prior Year | Of Total |
| | | | | | | | | | | | |

Notes:

Figure 16c.  Division Income Summary, Company E

was available only to very large customers, stems from the recognition that most marketing research services (Nielsen, MRCA, etc.) measure *consumer* movement. Trade deals, however, are inducements for the trade to perform a function, and the measure of that success is the movement of merchandise *to* the shelf, something that Nielsen does not measure. Company M, for example, is initiating a financial program that will relate short term volume

| | | | | | | | | | |
|---|---|---|---|---|---|---|---|---|---|
| | | | | | Division | | Page No. | | |
| | | | | | Product Description | | Responsibility Of | | |
| | | | | | Revises Schedule Dated | | Date | | |
| *(All Dollars are Expended in thousands)* | | | | | | | | | |

| | BUDGET | | LATEST ESTIMATE | | Percent of Budget | | BUDGET | | Percent Growth From Prior Yr. Latest Estimate |
|---|---|---|---|---|---|---|---|---|---|
| | $ | % | $ | % | | | $ | % | |
| | | | | | | GROSS SALES | | | |
| | | | | | | Returns | | | |
| | | | | | | Freight | | | |
| | | | | | | Allowances | | | |
| | | | | | | NET SALES | | | |
| | | | | | | COST OF SALES | | | |
| | | | | | | PRODUCTION MARGIN | | | |
| Any Product In-ro-duced by a Divis-ion After January 1, of the Current Year Should be Considered a New Product. | | | | | | MARKETING & DISTRIBUTION EXPENSES: | | | |
| | | | | | | Advertising - Print | | | |
| | | | | | | Radio & Television | | | |
| | | | | | | Promotions & Merchandise | | | |
| Allocations of Overheads on this Statement Should be Made of the Same Basis as for Existing Product Lines. | | | | | | Advertising & Promotion | | | |
| | | | | | | Field Force | | | |
| | | | | | | Demonstration Supv. Costs | | | |
| | | | | | | Dept. Store Payments Commiss. | | | |
| | | | | | | Drug Store Payments | | | |
| | | | | | | Market Research | | | |
| | | | | | | Public Relation | | | |
| | | | | | | Marketing Administration | | | |
| | | | | | | Salvage - Net | | | |
| | | | | | | Branch Expenses | | | |
| | | | | | | Total | | | |
| | | | | | | MARKETING MARGIN | | | |
| | | | | | | OTHER DIVISIONAL EXPENSES | | | |
| | | | | | | Research & Development | | | |
| | | | | | | General Administration | | | |
| Over 100% Growth | | | | | | Other (Income) Deductions - Net | | | |
| | | | | | | Total | | | |
| | | | | | | INCOME BEFORE CORP. EXPS. | | | |
| | | | | | | CORPORATE EXPENSES: | | | |
| | | | | | | State & Local Taxes | | | |
| | | | | | | Other Direct | | | |
| | | | | | | Allocated | | | |
| | | | | | | INCOME BEFORE FED. TAXES | | | |
| | | | | | | FEDERAL INCOME TAXES | | | |
| | | | | | | NET INCOME | | | |
| | | | | | | EFFECTIVE TAX RATE | | | |

Figure 16d.  New Product Operating Statement, Company E

fluctuations in warehouse movement to trade promotion expense, a type of return on investment analysis.

Company J chooses to advise headquarters people rather than sales personnel of profitability by brand or district. Although marketing operations at headquarters do not specifically receive operating results of other marketing divisions, the information is available to them.

| | Division & or/Plant | | Page No. |
|---|---|---|---|
| | Product Line | Responsibility of | |
| (All Dollars are Expressed in Thousands) | Revises Schedule Dated | Date | |

| | $ | % | $ | % | $ | % | $ | % | $ | % |
|---|---|---|---|---|---|---|---|---|---|---|
| NET SALES | | | | | | | | | | |
| COST OF SALES | | | | | | | | | | |
| PRODUCTION MARGIN | | | | | | | | | | |
| MARKETING & DISTRIBUTION EXPENSE | | | | | | | | | | |
| MARKETING MARGIN | | | | | | | | | | |
| OTHER EXPENSES & ALLOCATIONS | | | | | | | | | | |
| INCOME BEFORE TAXES | | | | | | | | | | |
| INCOME TAXES | | | | | | | | | | |
| NET INCOME | | | | | | | | | | |
| TOTAL MARKET | | | | | | | | | | |
| PRODUCT SHARE OF MARKET | | | | | | | | | | |
|   DOLLARS | | | | | | | | | | |
|   PERCENT | | | | | | | | | | |

Figure 16e.   New Product Five Year Plan, Company E

Company Q is seeking to clarify their contribution statements and the assignment of "overhead at various levels of responsibility."

Company M spoke of marketing's unwillingness to think in terms of probabilities in judging its own data. They expressed a desire to do more work in assessing the probabilities of future occurrences. They felt that marketing people have a "natural reluctance" to quantify their certainties even though they will readily participate in baseball and football pools based upon odds. It was a strange reply because it was an admission both of hope and of misunderstanding of the marketing function.

The hope lies in the promising area of the application of Bayesian reasoning to financial analysis: the misunderstanding exists in the lack of appreciation of the fact that every time marketing issues a volume forecast, *an intuitive probability is already built in*. Whether Company M's controller recognizes it or not, the use of probabilities in his analysis is one of the greatest potentials of the application of creative accounting. The controller, once wedded to the past, will be equipped to explore the occurrences of tomorrow.

### Marketing's View of the Data It Needs

In the last section, marketing was asked its assessment of currently supplied accounting criteria for measuring marketing responsibility. This section devotes itself to a probe of marketing's "druthers" relative to decision-inputs from the accounting area. They were asked "what types of financial data are required for marketing decision-making?" In general, the replies asked for less accounting-oriented data and more data arrayed to provide:

> Operating statements by product line
> Contribution margin detail
> Simulation input
> Customer, geographic profitability report

Company B strongly felt the need for more product line statements. They had once considered various alternative flavors for a new product concept. A cost differential of 10¢ existed for the different packages, depending on the flavor. They felt that had they known the implications of their decision at the time, they could have saved the company $5 million by simply developing the flavor which had the lower packaging cost.

Company P wanted to see data that would permit them to evaluate the profit effect of alternative marketing strategies. They also were dissatisfied with their product criteria of Return on Funds Employed. They felt that the allocation of plant period cost to a product manager had little significance at his level, although they conceded its validity at higher management levels. Company's P's problem could be solved by using a different assest base such as controllable working capital, for the product manager, essentially the concept advanced by the Schiffs.[7]

### *Return on Investment as a Technique*[8]

The abstraction of measuring what one receives in return for what one has given—return on investment—has been used professionally for almost three quarters of a century. Like its brother, the present value concept, ROI has gone through periods of fads and times when the idea was so pregnant with possibilities that it became popular to improvise on its uses and assign to it glamorous terminology.

That an abstraction almost three quarters of a century old can still have a popular mystique is truly remarkable. After all, it is only a refinement of intuitive logic. It is analogous in some respects to the process of creating detailed step-by-step procedures and timetables to accomplish an objective and calling it the Critical Path Method (CPM); the aura renders a familiar concept somewhat less recognizable.

Because there are innumerable variations of profit levels, a proper question, initially, is *what return* is being used for the measure? Examples of profit levels are profit before royalties (including or excluding interest payments), profit before taxes, profit after taxes, cash flow, division profit contribution, factory contribution, or sales region or district contribution.

Any of the above are useful, depending upon the investment base being used.

Again, one could ask, "Return on *what investment?*" It may be total parent company investment, total investment of subsidiary, total assets, manipulative assets (excluding intangibles), funds employed (tangible working capital), or selected bases (receivables, inventories, cash, etc.).

The remaining question is, *whose investment?* The investment of the stockholder differs in concept with the operating investment of the firm. Use of each may give startlingly different results, especially in the case where tangible funds employed in a firm are contrasted with the stockholder's investment if large amounts of good will have been capitalized.

## Advantages of Approach

The above are problems of definition. Once these have been solved, the evident truths about the usefulness of the ROI measure revolve around the following advantages:

> . . .It eliminates, in part, distortions caused by changes in price levels.
> . . .Current efficiency can be measured against historical, planned, or standard measures.
> . . .Decision makers can determine optimum investment avenues.
> . . .It is especially useful for the evaluation of new products and capital investments.
> . . .It is most useful when measured against a predetermined objective.

Profit does not exist in a vacuum; it must be supported by resources. When we speak of return on investment, we are really speaking of return on funds, and funds have economic value. Moreover, we are talking about the efficient use of funds. Like "profitability," itself an elusive concept, ROI is a flexible tool which can be adapted and shaped to fill specific needs.

Many of our great corporations have grown by the seat of their managers' pants. The expectations were that a reasonable return should be earned on the money placed in the business. Those managers who survived proved to be the skilled entrepreneurs. Their intuition was such that their sixth, seventh, and probably eighth senses led them in the right direction. We are all aware that today we are being given more tools to enable us to make decisions and, as a consequence, the seats of our pants are less shiny than those of our counterparts of forty or even thirty years ago.

## Difficulties of Approach

In an effort to compartmentalize and isolate the important factors of control and information in a business, managements have splintered the enterprise into subsidiaries, divisions, or, even further, into cost centers. Theoretically, if one can measure the return on an entire business, the return on its segments should also be measurable. Unfortunately, measurement of these segments is still difficult, and the effects of operations continue to be hard to determine. The basic cause of the difficulty is the attempt to assign assets to the segments of a business. Corporations often face the "Hamlet" conundrum: to allocate or not to allocate. When they do allocate, as some must, they may face further problems.

Some years ago, *Business Week* had a feature article about the American Telephone and Telegraph Company which dealt with the problem of how the FCC attempts to change, in effect, the ratemaking structure of the company. An AT&T is permitted under law to earn a stipulated return on corporate investment. A significant area of the inquiry dealt with the concern of the FCC with the mix of the various subsidiaries' returns.

A paragraph in that article says the FCC ordered an investigation into the revenue requirements of all Bell System companies, including the "reasonableness and propriety of procedures used in *allocating investment costs.*" (Italics mine.)

Another difficulty involves the treatment of the subject in the academic world. Although incremental working capital requirements are alluded to in some texts, their importance is largely played down in illustrating practical approaches to ROI. Frequently, the importance attached to time value of this item overshadows the original investment itself. In addition, academicians have not reached agreement concerning the elusive concept of future patterns of incremental cost of capital. The difficulty is not so much one to measure what the cost of capital has been as it is to project its configuration after a given decision has been effected. As used here, cost of capital will be considered as the minimum cutoff point for investments, or as a target rate of return.

Although it has come to be a vital and necessary part of business decisions, the cost of capital concept is excruciatingly difficult to grasp. There are two ways to approach the calculation of a firm's cost of capital. The first way is to look at the computation as being the cost of an alternative use for money. In other words, if a company is presented with a project which will earn a 6% rate of return, it can measure its satisfaction with a 6% return against a possible option to earn 9% with the same money by investing the money in municipal bonds. In this sense, the cost of capital is an opportunity cost; it is not a number which will be found written down on any piece of paper. Nevertheless, it is a very practical and very real tool.

The second view of the cost of capital uses a different computation. A weighted average of the debt and equity position of a company's capitalization is computed. The answer is expressed in terms of an interest rate. This then becomes the criteria for acceptability of a project. For example, assume a corporation's capital structure includes 50% common stocks and 50% bond debt. Further, assume that the common stock sells for a price earnings multiple of 10 and that the bonds have an interest rate of 6%. The computation in this instance would involve the following:

Calculate the capitalization rate of the common stock. This is the reciprocal of the price earnings ratio. In this example, it would compute to 10%. Since one-half the company's capitalization is in common stock, the impact of the capital return for common stock on the cost of capital is 5%. Further, the bond interest, which is tax deductible, effectively carries an after tax return of 3%. Since 50% of the capitalization is in debt form its impact on the cost of capital is 1.5%. Therefore, the composite cost of capital, for the firm is 6.5%. No project should be accepted which has a return on investment less than that number.

*Horizons for ROI*

Thus far, we have been concerned with the difficulties of the ROI concept. It is time now to elaborate on its positive characteristics and to develop workable techniques from which meaningful, practical results can be derived.

There will be no attempt here to restate all that has been written about ROI. Indeed, probably too much has been written, comparing time value with non-time value techniques. In the following illustrations, the technique known as "discounted cash flow" will be used, mainly because of the author's preference. This technique has the following relative advantages:

> . . .It disciplines planning, in that projects may be evaluated over a useful life span.
> . . .It recognizes the time value of money.
> . . .Reinvestments are not assumed to be made at the cost of capital rate.
> . . .It avoids the fiction of computing, in advance, an exact cost of capital rate by using input data to find a rate.

Most explanations of the use of ROI techniques deal with capital project analysis or possibly the creation of a new product. These are probably the most popular uses for the technique aside from aggregate corporate measurement. One large company interviewed chooses not to motivate its division managers by using ROI goals because, with relatively small divisional investments and consequent high divisional ROI, motivation becomes a meaningless numbers game of degrees. Instead, the company relies on the tool of profit margin goals.

There are many practical applications of ROI. The examples which I will cite will deal with the following situations:

> Capital project analysis for a new product
> Establishment of a price for a product
> Evaluation of a market area
> Evaluation of a marginal salesman

## Capital Project Analysis for a New Product

Of all of the applications of the ROI technique, capital project analysis is probably the most familiar. Exhibits A through D illustrate the application of ROI in a project analysis.

Assume that in 1970 a company planned to construct a small plant costing $200,000 to house a manufacturing and packaging line for a new product. In the next year, machinery and equipment costing $1,400,000 were to be installed. Projections indicated that at some future point an additional $400,000 of machinery and equipment would be required to support the volume. It is important to note that all amounts shown are incremental and may not add precisely because of rounding. The incremental approach says, in effect, that if the product was not marketed, there would be no numbers in Exhibit A.

## Establishing a Price for a Product

The pricing function is always difficult to conceptualize. Marketing specialists contend that, except for bid and cost-plus contracts, pricing should have nothing to do with cost. The essence of pricing is that it reflects the competitive situation and the uniqueness of a product. The approach here to the problem is not in conflict with the marketing specialists' point of view; rather, it assumes that, if the option is available, a product may be priced based upon an ROI goal.

Assuming that the desired ROI for the product is 20 per cent, (twice the cost of capital), the problem uses essentially the data shown in Exhibits A through C with the addition of the following volume input (millions of pounds):

| | |
|---|---|
| 1970 | 5.8 |
| 1971 | 8.0 |
| 1972 | 9.3 |
| 1973 | 10.9 |
| 1974 | 12.2 |

In this case, everything is known except sales dollars. We know, for example, that cash flow must total $1.9 million on a dis-

Exhibit A
## COMPANY ALPHA
Capital Project Analysis

---

*Assume:*

Product X, a new product is being considered for manufacture and distribution. With a new product of this risk class, policy requires a return on investment of at least twice the cost of capital. Data is shown as follows:

| | |
|---|---|
| Estimated cost of plant | $ .2 million 1970 |
| Estimated cost of machinery and equipment | 1.4 million 1971 |
| Estimated cost of machinery and equipment | .4 million 1974 |

Capitalization:

| | *Amount* | *Interest* | *Total* |
|---|---|---|---|
| Common Stock | $ 500,000 | 15% * | $ 75,000 |
| Debt (after tax) | 500,000 | 5% | 25,000 |
| | $1,000,000 | | $100,000 |

Cost of Capital                                        10%

*Reciprocal of price/earnings ratio

---

counted basis in order to result in a 20% ROI (see Exhibit D). The aim is to back into sales dollars by utilizing the known inputs of cash flow required, variable costs, marketing costs, and incremental period expenses. Division of the sales figure by the approximate number of units arrives at a trial selling price of $.55 per unit. If many years and numerous pack mixes are inherent in the problem, it may lend itself easily to computer simulation.

From a quantitative point of view, this is the correct solution. However, from a marketing view, it represents only a first step in the determination of whether this is a reasonable price. It does at least provide a starting point and a base. Another approach to the same problem was a formula developed by I. Wayne Keller in his book, *Management Accounting for Profit Control*. A good summary of this effective formula is contained in the NAA Research Report #35, "Return on Capital as a Guide to Managerial Decisions."

The formula states that

$$\text{selling price} = \frac{\dfrac{\text{cost} + (\%\ \text{return} \times \text{fixed capital})}{\text{volume}}}{1 - (\%\ \text{return} \times \%\ \text{current assets to sales}}$$

Exhibit B
PRODUCT X
Profit and Loss
(dollars in millions)

| Year | Sales $ | Variable Cost | Variable Profit | Adv. & Prom. | Direct Profit | New Plant Period Cost | *Deprec. | Before Taxes | Profit after Taxes | Add Deprec. | Cash Flow | Total |
|---|---|---|---|---|---|---|---|---|---|---|---|---|
| 1970 | $ 3.0 | $ 1.6 | $ 1.4 | $ 1.6 | $ (.2) | $ .2 | $ — | $ .4 | $ (.2) | $ | $ (.2) | $ (.3) |
| 1971 | 4.2 | 2.3 | 1.9 | 1.5 | .4 | .4 | .2 | (.2) | (.1) | .2 | .1 | (.2) |
| 1972 | 5.3 | 2.9 | 2.4 | 1.5 | .9 | .4 | .2 | .3 | .1 | .2 | .3 | (.1) |
| 1973 | 6.0 | 3.3 | 2.7 | 1.2 | 1.5 | .4 | .2 | .9 | .4 | .2 | .6 | .4 |
| 1974 | 6.5 | 3.6 | 2.9 | 1.3 | 1.6 | .4 | .2 | 1.0 | .5 | .2 | .7 | .6 |
| 1975 | 7.0 | 3.8 | 3.2 | 1.3 | 1.9 | .4 | .2 | 1.3 | .6 | .2 | .8 | .6 |
| 1976 | 7.4 | 4.1 | 3.3 | .9 | 2.4 | .4 | .2 | 1.8 | .9 | .2 | 1.1 | .8 |
| 1977 | 7.7 | 4.2 | 3.5 | .8 | 2.7 | .4 | .2 | 2.1 | 1.0 | .2 | 1.2 | .9 |
| 1978 | 8.0 | 4.4 | 3.6 | .8 | 2.8 | .4 | .2 | 2.2 | 1.1 | .2 | 1.3 | .9 |
| 1979 | 8.4 | 4.6 | 3.8 | .8 | 3.0 | .4 | .2 | 2.4 | 1.2 | .2 | 1.4 | .8 |
| 1980 | 8.7 | 4.8 | 3.9 | .8 | 3.1 | .4 | .1 | 2.6 | 1.3 | .1 | 1.4 | .9 |
| 1981 | 9.0 | 5.0 | 4.0 | .9 | 3.1 | .4 | .1 | 2.6 | 1.3 | .1 | 1.3 | .9 |
| 1982 | 9.3 | 5.1 | 4.2 | 1.0 | 3.2 | .4 | — | 2.8 | 1.4 | | 1.4 | 1.0 |
| 1983 | 9.6 | 5.3 | 4.3 | 1.0 | 3.3 | .4 | — | 2.9 | 1.4 | | 1.4 | 1.0 |
| 1984 | 9.9 | 5.4 | 4.5 | 1.1 | 3.4 | .4 | — | 3.0 | 1.5 | | 1.5 | 1.1 |
| 1985 | 10.2 | 5.6 | 4.6 | 1.1 | 3.5 | .4 | — | 3.1 | 1.6 | | 1.6 | 1.1 |

*Does not add because of rounding

The required input factors, using hypothetical data, are as follows:

|  |  |
|---|---|
| Total manufacturing costs | $ 50,000 |
| Administrative costs | 30,000 |
| Sales and other costs | 10,000 |
| | $ 90,000 |

|  |  |
|---|---|
| Required rate of return | 15% |
| Fixed capital investment (net) | $100,000 |
| Number of units to make | 15,000 |
| Ratio of current assets to sales | 25% |

Substituting these figures in the formula gives:

$$\text{selling price} = \frac{\dfrac{\$90,000 + (.15 \times 100,000)}{15,000}}{1 - (.15 \times .25)}$$

The unit selling price computes to $7.47.

Exhibit C
PRODUCT X
Computation of Working Capital
(dollars in millions)

| | | Accounts Receivable | | Total | |
|---|---|---|---|---|---|
| Year | Sales | ÷ 24 | Inventories | Working Capital | Increment |
| 1970 | $ 3.0 | $ .1 | $ .6 | $ .7 | $ .7 |
| 1971 | 4.2 | .2 | .8 | 1.0 | .3 |
| 1972 | 5.3 | .2 | 1.1 | 1.3 | .3 |
| 1973 | 6.0 | .2 | 1.2 | 1.4 | .1 |
| 1974 | 6.5 | .3 | 1.3 | 1.6 | .2 |
| 1975 | 7.0 | .3 | 1.4 | 1.7 | .1 |
| 1976 | 7.4 | .3 | 1.5 | 1.8 | .1 |
| 1977 | 7.7 | .3 | 1.5 | 1.8 | — |
| 1978 | 8.0 | .3 | 1.6 | 1.9 | .1 |
| 1979 | 8.4 | .4 | 1.7 | 2.1 | .2 |
| 1980 | 8.7 | .4 | 1.7 | 2.1 | — |
| 1981 | 9.0 | .4 | 1.8 | 2.2 | .1 |
| 1982 | 9.3 | .4 | 1.9 | 2.3 | .1 |
| 1983 | 9.6 | .4 | 1.9 | 2.3 | — |
| 1984 | 9.9 | .4 | 2.0 | 2.4 | .1 |
| 1985 | 10.2 | .4 | 2.0 | 2.4 | — |
| | | | | | $2.4 |

## Exhibit D
### Discounted Cash Flow
### (dollars in millions)

| Year | Investment Fixed Assets | Investment Incremental Working Capital | Investment Total | Trial 20% | | Trial 25% | |
|------|------|------|------|------|------|------|------|
| 1970 | $ .7 | $ .7 | $ .9 | .9063 | $ .9 | .8848 | $ .8 |
| 1971 | 1.4 | .3 | 1.7 | .7421 | 1.3 | .6891 | 1.2 |
| 1972 |  | .3 | .3 | .6075 | .2 | .5367 | .2 |
| 1973 |  | .1 | .1 | .4974 | — | .4167 | — |
| 1974 | .4 | .2 | .6 | .4072 | .2 | .3255 | .2 |
| 1975 |  | .1 | .1 | .3334 |  | .2535 |  |
| 1976 |  | .1 | .1 | .2730 |  | .1974 |  |
| 1977 |  | — | — | .2235 |  | .1538 |  |
| 1978 |  | .1 | .1 | .1830 |  | .1197 |  |
| 1979 |  | .2 | .2 | .1498 |  | .0933 |  |
| 1980 |  | — | — | .1227 |  | .0726 |  |
| 1981 |  | .1 | .1 | .1004 |  | .0566 |  |
| 1982 |  | .1· | .1 | .0822 |  | .0441 |  |
| 1983 |  | — | — | .0673 |  | .0343 |  |
| 1984 |  | .1 | .1 | .0551 |  | .0267 |  |
| 1985 |  | — | — | .0451 |  | .0208 |  |
|  | $ 2.0 | $ 2.4 | $ 4.4 |  | $ 2.6 |  | $ 2.4 |

### Discounted Cash Flow
### (dollars in millions)

| Year | Total Receipts | Trial 20% | | Trial 25% | |
|------|------|------|------|------|------|
| 1970 | $ (.2) | .9063 | $ (.2) | .8848 | $ (.2) |
| 1971 | .1 | .7421 | .1 | .6891 | .1 |
| 1972 | .3 | .6075 | .2 | .5367 | .2 |
| 1973 | .6 | .4974 | .3 | .4167 | .3 |
| 1974 | .7 | .4072 | .3 | .3255 | .2 |
| 1975 | .8 | .3334 | .3 | .2535 | .2 |
| 1976 | 1.1 | .2730 | .3 | .1974 | .2 |
| 1977 | 1.2 | .2235 | .3 | .1538 | .2 |
| 1978 | 1.3 | .1830 | .2 | .1197 | .2 |
| 1979 | 1.4 | .1498 | .2 | .0933 | .1 |
| 1980 | 1.4 | .1227 | .2 | .0726 | .1 |
| 1981 | 1.3 | .1004 | .1 | .0566 | .1 |
| 1982 | 1.4 | .0822 | .1 | .0441 | .1 |
| 1983 | 1.4 | .0673 | .1 | .0343 | — |
| 1984 | 1.5 | .0551 | .1 | .0267 | — |
| 1985 | 4.0* | .0451 | .2 | .0208 | .1 |
|  |  |  | $ 2.8 |  | $ 1.9 |

Difference + .2     — .5

$$\text{R.O.I.} = 20\% + \frac{5\% \times .2}{.2 \times .5} = 21.4\%$$

*Evaluation of a Market Area*

The evaluation of a market area is shown in Exhibit E. Two inputs are required: the amount of the incremental contribution and of the incremental investment.

Sales reports showing volume and product mix can provide the sales input in the configuration shown in Exhibit E. Cost records showing the factory production mix on a variable cost basis provide the input for cost of goods manufactured. It is assumed that

Exhibit  E
DISTRICT ALPHA
Return on Investment

*Given:*
Company Vega, aware that R.O.I. techniques are used to evaluate overall performance, asks the Controller to why such techniques could not be used for evaluating the profitability of geographic areas and customers.

The configuration of District Alpha shows:

| | |
|---|---:|
| Sales .......................................... | $3,500,000 |
| Cost of Goods Manufactured ....................... | 2,000,000 |
| Gross Margin ................................. | $1,500,000 |

Less:
Incremental District Expenses:

| | | |
|---|---:|---:|
| Salaries and Fringe Benefits ............. | $500,000 | |
| Travel and Entertainment ............... | 200,000 | |
| Sales Office & Warehouse Expense ......... | 40,000 | 740,000 |
| Incremental District Profit  (Before  Tax) ........... | | $  760,000 |
| Profit After Tax ............... | | $  380,000 |

Assets Employed:

| | |
|---|---:|
| Receivables ......................... | $  700,000 |
| Inventories (Finished Goods) ........... | 300,000 |
| Warehouse (Net Value) ............... | 300,000 |
| | $1,300,000 |

$$\text{Return on Investment} = \frac{\text{profits}}{\text{sales}} \times \frac{\text{sales}}{\text{investment}}$$

$$= \frac{\$\ 380,000}{\$3,500,000} \times \frac{\$3,500,000}{\$1,300,000}$$

$$= \quad 10.8\% \quad \times\ 2.7\%$$

$$= \quad 29.2\%$$

finished goods inventory policy is corporate and not incremental to the sales district.

Following next is a selection of incremental district expenses. These might include items such as spot media, point of sale material, and advertising and display contracts for the district. If desired, costs of national media, such as network television, could be reasonably approximated for the district, based upon "point of origin." The district cost can then be related to the national cost.

## Analysis of the Sales Force

Companies regularly receive data from a variety of sources giving sales information within geographic areas. The data, usually expressed in terms of units, cases, and dollars may be reported for geographic entities as small as counties, probably the lowest hierarchy of practical reporting units. If sales figures are known, then it would follow that the manufacturing costs are also known. From that point all incremental expenses attributable to the existence of the geographic area should be calculated. Total *direct* expenses are then compared to the asset investment *attributable to the existence of the geographic area.*

Assume the following correspondence:

"TO:        Sales Manager, Company Vega
FROM:       Marketing Controller
SUBJECT:    PROFITABILITY OF ADDITIONAL SALES-
            MEN

The cost of an additional salesman (based on a salary of $7,200) is approximately $16,500. Broken down into major expense category, it loks like this:

| | |
|---|---:|
| Salary | $ 7,200 |
| Bonus | 550 |
| Benefits | 1,050 |
| Car | 2,100 |
| Travel & Entertainment | 800 |
| Other Expenses | 700 |
| | $ 12,400 |
| Add ⅓ due to Turnover | 4,100 |
| | $ 16,500 |

A word of explanation is in order concerning the turnover figure. Of the 52 men hired in 1969, we now have 35 still on the payroll, an approximate turnover of 33%. Those men who leave in less than a year never really are self-sufficient; therefore, the cost of their expenses must be considered when considering taking on new men. Accordingly, we have considered the likelihood of losing a man before he' is on his own as being 33% and have added ⅓ to the cost per man.

If this new man can sell $55,000 worth of *incremental* volume, we are breaking even. This figure was calculated as follows:

| Cost of new salesman | $16,000 |
|---|---|
| Divided by average division rate of variable profit less promotion, | 30% |
| Equals breakeven figure. | $55,000 |

Taking this analysis one step further, we can calculate a return on the investment in this new salesman. Assuming he generates $100,000 worth of *incremental* sales, at a 30% variable profit less promotion rate, this would generate $30,000 incremental profit. Of the $30,000, $16,500 would be used to pay for the salesman, leaving $13,500 that the company would realize. This amount when divided by the investment in the salesman ($16,500) would yield an ROI of 82%, obviously acceptable by any measurement.

In conclusion, let us emphasize that all the data discussed in the previous paragraphs are based on incremental volume (the volume that we would not have enjoyed had we not hired a new salesman). Volume transferred from another salesman's accounts should not be considered."

### Contemporary Uses for Return on Investment

The question posed to the companies asked, "Are any of the following advanced techniques used for marketing decision-making?" The first named technique was return on investment. Seven of the twenty companies replied that they did not use ROI techniques at all. The remainder of the companies primarily used the technique to evaluate new products and capital projects.

Other secondary uses cited were for acquisition analysis, plant evaluation and divisional analysis. No company used the technique to evaluate the return in geographic areas, sales efficiency, or for pricing purposes.

An example of the misunderstanding of the theory of time value techniques is shown in the reply from Company I:

> Return on Investment is used occasionally for the evaluation of new products and only very rarely for the evaluation of capital projects. The basic technique used is a payback technique and the minimum acceptable criterion is payback within three years. If any project cannot pay back its investment in a three year time period, it is considered to be a marginal decision. Discounted cash flow has occasionally been used by the company to evaluate projects; however, we feel that it is somewhat meaningless in our particular case, *since the company does not do any outside borrowing and finances all projects from internal funds.* We have also used that technique to evaluate the purchase or sale of a new product.

The immediate criticism that comes to mind is that internal funds are not cost free. There is always the opportunity cost of alternative investments. The misconception is somewhat similar to that which holds that a firm's cost of capital is the cost of its borrowed funds. Always financing internally may not be a virtue either, as there is no opportunity to exercise leverage on behalf of the stockholders.

Company L indicated that in employing the return on investment concept, a cost of capital is considered to be the minimum acceptable return. When dealing with a new product, the incremental investment is considered. A standard investment for this product may be computed for eventual comparison to actual amounts invested.

Company N, a consumer company, employs elements of the ROI concept. For example, two-thirds of their product lines are gauged by three factors:

Turnover
Percent profit margin on sales
Return on allocated assets

Company P is in the process of segmenting the asset base to reflect the company's vertical integration. In effect, ROI is being applied to timberland, pulp, and other operations. Thus, transfer prices are being developed. The company did not choose to elaborate on the type of transfer price being considered. Period charges based upon throughput are being calculated. Papermaking, with its specialized machinery, is a direct operation and its assets can be segregated.

Other corporate charges are allocated on the basis of sales and/or cost of sales. They admit that it is arbitrary, but assert that the control point is the source of expenditure. The decision-making profit level, moreover, does not include corporate charges.

Company H employs the concept of return on funds employed to evaluate marketing divisions and product *groups*. A specimen of their format is shown in Figure 17. Their technique considers an average return on an average investment, ignoring time value considerations. A distinct plus in their analysis, however, is the use of cash flow as the base for the measurement of return.

Company H utilized the format shown in Figure 17 for various types of projects and recognized that, in assessing the criteria for payback and return on funds employed, differing products will have differing risk factors. One major group of projects is recognized for purposes of safety and convenience. For these types of projects, payback and ROFE data are not required. However, the request for funds must demonstrate the need for the project and the lack of acceptable alternatives. In addition, requests for nonproductive facilities should emphasize the effects of owning rather than leasing. The emphasis on owning, as an operating concept, stems from the fact that the company generally owns integrated facilities and thus the introduction of rented or leased properties might complicate the long range planning or development of the area.

Projects associated with quality justifications need not contain payback and ROFE calculations. However, justifications must be made for the fact that the improvement is identifiable and justifiable.

The most critical group of projects are those which are justified on the basis of increasing profit. Those projects which are justified primarily by cost reduction potentials must provide a payback for up to 10 years and a 10-year ROFE of at least 20% before taxes. Those projects meeting these criteria merit consideration.

Those projects designed primarily to increase production capacity for an existing product should return the initial investment within a 10-year period and generate a before-tax ROFE of at least 20%. In a similar vein, projects oriented toward the development of new products are required to return a much higher rate of return, commensurate with the increased risk involved. These projects are required to return the initial investment within a 10-year period but must generate a before-tax ROFE of at least 10%.

### FUNDS EMPLOYED AND PROFIT AND LOSS PROJECTIONS

| DIVISION | | LOCATION | | PROJECT TITLE | | | | PROJECT NO. | | SUPPLEMENT No. | |
|---|---|---|---|---|---|---|---|---|---|---|---|
| RETURN OF NEW FUNDS EMPLOYED | Pay Back Years from Date of Completion | | | RETURN ON NEW FUNDS EMPLOYED | | | | Five Year Avg. | | Ten Year Avg. | |
| | Number of Quarters to Pay | | Years | | A-Avg. Funds Employed Line 14 | | | • | | • | |
| | Part Year Calculation | | Years | | B-Profit Before Taxes-Line 32 | | | • | | • | |
| | Total Years to Pay Back | | Years | | C-Calculated Return B & A | | | | % | | % |
| FUNDS EMPLOYED | | | 1st Year | 2nd Year | 3rd Year | 4th Year | 5th Year | 5-Year Avg. | 6th Year | 7th Year | 8th Year | 9th Year | 10th Yr. | 10-Yr.Avg. |
| 1 Cash | | | | | | | | | | | | | |
| 2 Receivables | | | | | | | | | | | | | |
| 3 Inventories | | | | | | | | | | | | | |
| 4 Prepaid & Deferred Expenses | | | | | | | | | | | | | |
| 5 Current Liabilities | | | | | | | | | | | | | |
| 6 Total Working Funds 1 thru 4-5 | | | | | | | | | | | | | |
| Gross Cost | | | | | | | | | | | | | |
| 7 Land | | | | | | | | | | | | | |
| 8 Buildings | | | | | | | | | | | | | |
| 9 Mach. & Equipment | | | | | | | | | | | | | |
| 10 Engineering | | | | | | | | | | | | | |
| 11 Other (Explain) | | | | | | | | | | | | | |
| 12 Expense | | | | | | | | | | | | | |
| 13 Total Capital Funds 7 thru 12 | | | | | | | | | | | | | |
| 14 Total New Funds 6 & 13 | | | | | | | | | | | | | |
| 15 Cumulative Depreciation 8 thru 11 | | | | | | | | | | | | | |
| 16 Cum.Net Front & Deprec. Line 37 | | | | | | | | | | | | | |
| 17 New Funds to Repay 14 & 15-16 | | | | | | | | | | | | | |
| 18 Unit Value | | | | | | | | | | | | | |
| 19 Gross Sales | | | | | | | | | | | | | |
| 20 Deductions | | | | | | | | | | | | | |
| 21 Net Sales | | | | | | | | | | | | | |
| 22 Cost of Goods Sold | | | | | | | | | | | | | |
| 23 Gross Profit | | | | | | | | | | | | | |
| 24 G.P. % Net Sales | | | | | | | | | | | | | |
| 25 Advertising | | | | | | | | | | | | | |
| 26 Selling | | | | | | | | | | | | | |
| 27 General and Administrative | | | | | | | | | | | | | |
| 28 Research | | | | | | | | | | | | | |
| 29 Start-Up Costs | | | | | | | | | | | | | |
| 30 Other (Explain) | | | | | | | | | | | | | |
| 31 Adjustment (Explain) | | | | | | | | | | | | | |
| 32 Profit Before Taxes | | | | | | | | | | | | | |
| 33 Taxes-Fed. & State Income | | | | | | | | | | | | | |
| 34 Net Profit | | | | | | | | | | | | | |
| 35 Annual Depreciation | | | | | | | | | | | | | |
| 36 Annual Net Profit & Deprec. 34-35 | | | | | | | | | | | | | |
| 37 Cum. Net Profit & Depreciation | | | | | | | | | | | | | |

Figure 17. Financial Justification, Company H (Food Processing)

Company T uses ROI rarely except for selected large capital projects and all new products. Their format is shown in Figures 18, 19, 19a, and 19b. They, however, do not use the cash flow

To insure good Ozalid reproduction
please use a No. 2 pencil to fill out this
form, making the clearest mark as possible.

Plan Due . . .
Seasonalization Due . . .

(Dollars Stated in Thousands)

| LINE | ACTUAL Amount | % | LATEST ESTIMATE Amount | % | PLAN Amount | % | DIFFERENCE Amount | % | ( ) IN DIFFERENCE COLUMN - UNVAVORABLE | 1st Quarter Amount | % |
|---|---|---|---|---|---|---|---|---|---|---|---|
| 1 | | | | | | | | | GROSS SALES | | |
| 2 | | | | | | | | | Returns & Allowances | | |
| 3 | | | | | | | | | NET SALES | | |
| 4 | | | | | | | | | COST OF GOODS SOLD | | |
| 5 | | | | | | | | | At Standard of Direct | | |
| 6 | | | | | | | | | Raw Material | | |
| 7 | | | | | | | | | Finishing Supplies | | |
| 8 | | | | | | | | | Direct Labor | | |
| 9 | | | | | | | | | Overhead | | |
| 10 | | | | | | | | | Outside Processors | | |
| 11 | | | | | | | | | Period Overhead | | |
| 12 | | | | | | | | | Expenses | | |
| 13 | | | | | | | | | Deferred to Inventory | | |
| 14 | | | | | | | | | Variance from Standard | | |
| 15 | | | | | | | | | Purchase Price | | |
| 16 | | | | | | | | | Spending | | |
| 17 | | | | | | | | | Volume | | |
| 18 | | | | | | | | | Material Usage | | |
| 19 | | | | | | | | | Other Merchandise Expenses | | |
| 20 | | | | | | | | | Mailage | | |
| 21 | | | | | | | | | Rework & Redress | | |
| 22 | | | | | | | | | Prov. for Inventory Obsolescence | | |
| 23 | | | | | | | | | Prov. for Inventory Shrinkage | | |
| 24 | | | | | | | | | Manufacturing Royalties | | |
| 25 | | | | | | | | | Overhead on Supplies | | |
| 26 | | | | | | | | | Inventory Write-Off | | |
| 27 | | | | | | | | | Other | | |
| 28 | | | | | | | | | GROSS PROFIT | | |
| 29 | | | | | | | | | DIRECT COSTS | | |
| 30 | | | | | | | | | Total Promotion | | |
| 31 | | | | | | | | | Total Advertising | | |
| 32 | | | | | | | | | Media | | |
| 33 | | | | | | | | | Other Advertising | | |
| 34 | | | | | | | | | Miscellaneous | | |
| 35 | | | | | | | | | Outside Market Research | | |
| 36 | | | | | | | | | Packaging Design | | |
| 37 | | | | | | | | | Total Selling | | |
| 38 | | | | | | | | | Sales Promotion Plan | | |
| 39 | | | | | | | | | Field Sales Force | | |
| 40 | | | | | | | | | Total Operating Expense | | |
| 41 | | | | | | | | | Freight | | |
| 42 | | | | | | | | | Packing & Shipping | | |
| 43 | | | | | | | | | Cash Discount | | |
| 44 | | | | | | | | | PROFIT CONTRIBUTION | | |
| 45 | | | | | | | | | INDIRECT COSTS - SERVICE DEPTS. | | |
| 46 | | | | | | | | | Own Division | | |
| 47 | | | | | | | | | Other Division | | |
| 48 | | | | | | | | | OPERATING PROFIT | | |
| 49 | | | | | | | | | Other Income Deductions | | |
| 50 | | | | | | | | | NET PROFIT BEFORE INCOME TAXES | | |

Figure 18.   Division Operating Statement, Company T
(Pharmaceuticals, Toiletries)

concept even though depreciation charges are clearly included in the "fixed-overhead" portion of cost of goods sold. By including the fixed overhead in the cost of goods sold estimate for their product evaluation, they deprive themselves of making meaningful, marginal analysis. Another point of interest on Figure 19a is that in Section A, the "return on assets," they do not stress that capital expenditures, inventory, or working capital should be as-

|  | TEST MKT. | REGIONAL INTROD. | NATIONAL INTROD. |
|---|---|---|---|
|  | ☐ | ☐ | ☐ |

**Estimated Dates for Starting:**

Division _____

MD No. _____

Proposed Prod. Name _____

Date _____

Production _____

Selling _____

Shipping _____

Advertising _____

I. PRODUCT DESCRIPTION:

    A. Product Name or Reference on Official Specification Directions, if different from name above:

    _____

    B. Formula or Technical Specification _____

    C. New Product ☐ or Basic Formula Change ☐ or Packaging Change ☐ or Size Change ☐ or Discontinuance of Regular Product ☐

    D. General Description of Product or Change: _____

II. TECHNICAL INFORMATION:

    A. MANUFACTURE OF PRODUCT

        1. a) Our Manufacture ☐ b) Indicate Manufacturing Location(s) _____

            c) Outside Processors ☐ _____

        2. Is new equipment required? Yes ☐ No ☐
           If yes, give details, estimated costs, and state whether expenditure will be capitalized or charged to expense.

        3. Origin of Materials to be used. Comment only if problem is anticipated

        4. Special Manufacturing Problems.

    B. FINISHING SUPPLIES

        1. Type of container (state composition).

        2. Package design (attach sketch or photo if possible).

    C. PRODUCT STABILITY

        1. Shelf life.

        2. Container compatability

        3. Other stability problems.

Signature (Production Dept.) _____

Figure 19. Marketing Decision Guide, Company T

sessed on an incremental basis. In addition, the capital expenditure figure does not show the inclusion of the expense portion for capital projects that are not normally included in capital expen-

### III. FINANCIAL EVALUATION:

A. COST OF GOODS ESTIMATE FOR     UNITS

|  | (a) $ | (b) % |
|---|---|---|
| 1. Raw Materials | | |
| 2. Finishing Supplies | | |
| 3. Direct Labor | | |
| 4. Overhead - Fixed | | |
| 5. Overhead - Variable | | |
| 6. Outside Processors | | |
| 7. Royalties or other | | |
| Total | $ | ____% to Gross Sales |

Cost of Goods Sold Ratio - Similar Products:
a. _____ b. _____

B. RETURN OF ASSETS
1. Direct Cost Basis

|  | 19 | 19 | 19 | 19 |
|---|---|---|---|---|
| Capital Exp. | | | | |
| Inventory (Avg.) | | | | |
| A/B Cash etc. (Avg.) | | | | |
| Total Dir. Invest. | | | | |
| Ret. on Assets | | | | |

2. Allocated Cost Basis

|  | 19 | 19 | 19 | 19 |
|---|---|---|---|---|
| Total Dir. Invest. | | | | |
| Alloc. Capital Exp. | | | | |
| Total Adj. Invest. | | | | |
| Ret. on Assets | | | | |

### IV. PRICING:

A. PRINCIPAL COMPETITION

BASIC DISCOUNTS & PRICE DATA | SALES EST.

| PRODUCT NAME | MANUFACTURER | SIZE OR FORM | Price to Public | Price to Direct Retail | % Prof. | % Disc. | Price to Indir. Retail | % Prof. | % Disc. | Price to Whlsn. | % Prof. | % Disc. | Factory Sales Last Yr. (Dollars) |
|---|---|---|---|---|---|---|---|---|---|---|---|---|---|
| 1. | | | | | | | | | | | | | |
| 2. | | | | | | | | | | | | | |
| 3. | | | | | | | | | | | | | |
| 4. | | | | | | | | | | | | | |
| 5. All Others ///////////////////////////////////////////////////////////////////////////////// | | | | | | | | | | | | | |
| B. PRICING FOR THIS PRODUCT | | | | | | | | | | | | | |
| C. PRICING POLICY | | | | | | | | | | | | | /////// |

### V. FORECAST

| | 1st. YEAR ( Mos.) Net Value ____ Units ____ | | 2nd. YEAR Net Value ____ Units ____ | | 3rd. YEAR Net Value ____ Units ____ | | 4th. YEAR Net Value ____ Units ____ | |
|---|---|---|---|---|---|---|---|---|
| | $ | % | $ | % | $ | % | $ | % |
| A. Gross Sales | | | | | | | | |
| B. Returns & Allow. | | | | | | | | |
| C. Net Sales | | | | | | | | |
| D. Cost of Goods Sold | | | | | | | | |
| E. Advertising | | | | | | | | |
| F. Direct Promotion | | | | | | | | |
| G. Direct Selling | | | | | | | | |
| H. Direct Operating | | | | | | | | |
| I. Profit Contribution | | | | | | | | |
| J. Indirect Costs | | | | | | | | |
| K. Net Profit | | | | | | | | |
| L. Net Profit (after taxes) | | | | | | | | |
| M. Cum.after tax Profit | | | | | | | | |

Signature, (Controller's Department) Section III., IV. and V.

### VI. MARKETING: (Discuss following items on attachment)
A. MARKETING RATIONALE    B. SALES FORECAST    C. PROMOTION AND ADVERTISING

### VII. GENERAL:
A. TRADEMARK REGISTERED
B. F.D.A. APPROVAL OR MEDICAL CLEARANCE
C. ROYALTY PAYMENTS

RECOMMENDED    PRODUCT DIRECTOR _____ Date _____

APPROVED    DIVISION HEAD _____ Date _____

Figure 19a. Marketing Decision Guide (Finance), Company T

diture numbers. In the "forecast" portion of the form (part V), note that although profit contribution is isolated in the sense that all direct costs attributable to the existence of a product are properly shown, there is no attempt to segregate the direct costs into variable and non-variable elements. Again, this deprives the analyst of assessing the impact upon profits of changes in volume; many of the direct charges cited, such as advertising, are of a period nature. There is also an implication in line (L) of the "forecast" portion that there is a profit after taxes attributed to the product. This is something of an economic fallacy since there is no such thing as a net profit for a product: products do not pay taxes.

In attempting to evaluate the future potential of new products, the individual completing this form would really have no alternative but to include the aggregate tax rate, perhaps 50%, and apply it to the operating results of the product. Frequently, however, the tax rate paid by the *aggregate company* does not approx-

| V. FORECAST | A - TEST Market Net Value ___ Units ___ $  % | B - Regional Introduction Net Value ___ Units ___ $  % | C - National Introduction Net Value ___ Units ___ $  % | D - TOTAL Net Value ___ Units ___ $  % |
|---|---|---|---|---|
| A. Gross Sales | | | | |
| B. Returns & Allowances | | | | |
| C. Net Sales | | | | |
| D. Cost of Goods Sold | | | | |
| E. Direct Advertising | | | | |
| F. Direct Promotion | | | | |
| G. Direct Selling | | | | |
| H. Direct Operating | | | | |
| I. Profit Contribution | | | | |
| J. Indirect Costs | | | | |
| K. Net Profit | | | | |
| L. Net Profit (After Tax) | | | | |
| M. Cumulative After-tax Profit | | | | |

Figure 19b. Marketing Decision Guide (Finance), Company T

imate the nominal tax rate stipulated by the government. The investment credit, the method of company organization, including subsidiaries, and the effect of tax loss carried forward or carry-backs may have a significant effect on the tax rate.

Thus, it would appear that there is not enough effort devoted to evaluating divisional ROI. There are probably many valid reasons for not applying the concept to product evaluation since products may share common fixed asset investments. At the very least, however, product groupings should be considered. The use of payback as a new product criteria is a poor substitute for an incremental ROI analysis of such products. Despite the alleged sophistication of the companies in the study, they have demonstrated poor utilization of ROI, a technique which is close to a century old.

### Profit vs. Profitability

The word "profit" has become a euphemism. Its widespread, ill-advised use has led to many attempted reforms in the accounting profession, such as those prompted by feelings of the Securities and Exchange Commission and the Accounting Principles Board of the American Institute of Certified Public Accountants that the investing public has been deceived by generally accepted accounting principles which permit the creation of instant earnings through the concept of pooling of interests in acquisition accounting. Prior to this latest irritation, profit had undergone many attacks from various parties, notably in the areas of latitude permitted financial executives in reporting their companys' income. In the strictest sense, profit is not an accounting concept. It is more of an economic concept, related to the productivity of capital.

From a down to earth point of view, profit is a number which must be reported to the government on tax returns. In this sense, and in most reporting senses, profit is a residual; it is simply what is left over. The implication here is that all that lies before the residual comes into being must be scrutinized to ascertain its fairness, its correctness and its relevance to decision-making. After all, there are many kinds of profit. Which one is the best one for making a particular decision? gross profit?, operating profit?, gross trading profit?, profit before taxes?, profit after taxes?, marketing profit? Of course, any of these may be the correct answer to the question, but like the concept of cost, the proper usage of profit depends upon the particular problem being attacked. It must be remembered that as a profession, accounting is accustomed to looking backwards. Until very recently, accounting's major responsibility has been to report what happened yesterday. As such, the accounting calculation of profit has been geared to a reporting function much more than to decision-making.

The concept of profitability as espoused in this book is a much more dynamic way of approaching the problem. In reality, what we are trying to determine is a rate of change of profit as a result of changes in activity. If product A has a profitability rate of 2¢ per unit, the sale of two units should produce an incremental profitability of 4¢, the sale of three units 6¢ and so on. This progression should be unmarred by the considerations that go into the compilation of the traditional profit. For example, depreciation may have no bearing on changes in the volume of a product. Similarly, administrative overhead may not affect changes of volume. The concept of profitability owes its birth to the contribution margin techniques originally propounded by those who espoused the concept of direct costing. Unfortunately, the use of contribution margin techniques has been limited principally to the area of manufacturing profit. Since most of the revenue dollars are not consumed in production, but in the distribution function that includes advertising and promotion, it behooves us to advance to further stages of analysis. Progress should be directed toward a more meaningful type of technique which is called, appropriately, relevant cost determination. This will be discussed in the next section of our compilation of practical applications for marketing control of profitability.

Most of the current uses of profit are not well suited for purposes of making decisions. The conventional accountant in reporting profit must serve too many masters. He is responsible for reporting profit to the stockholder/owner of the company, to governmental agencies, and to owner/investors which may include banks and insurance companies but exclude the conventional smaller stockholder. He may also have to report profit to security analysts. Unfortunately, in this morass, that profit figure may differ, depending upon the individual or group to whom profit it being reported. The most blatant admission of this seeming contradiction is the simple fact that on federal tax returns for corporations, there is a separate Schedule M; its sole purpose is to adjust the income reported on the books of a company to the income which is reported to the government on the tax return.

The profit/ownership confrontation is compounded by the various uses of profit within the corporation itself. Internally, contemporary profit computations may be used for various purposes. Product managers are interested in the profits of their product; division managers are interested in the profit of the division. Individuals may wish to use the profit as a basis for establishing a selling price. Groups who are involved in government contract work may use the profit to establish cost/plus pricing guidelines. This conflict between end-receivers of information and the users of information, has inevitably led to the distribution of a set of statistical variables. For example, the profit reported to the government for cost/plus pricing purposes may be completely different than the profit which might be reported to a security analyst for purposes of writing a market letter.

In all of this, generally accepted accounting principles have been of little help, because the financial executive in the company has been left with too many options that can influence the magnitude and the direction of profits. Within reason, it is not a very difficult task for the financial executive in any company to customize the results that the chief executive officer wishes to report.

Various financial strategies can have a profound effect upon reported profits. There is a conflict for instance, between straight line vs. accelerated depreciation accounting. Accelerated depreciation has come about in the more recent years and was designed originally as an incentive for American business to accelerate its turnover of capital investment.

Depreciation on a profit and loss statement is an expense. As an expense, it is deductible for income tax purposes. Therefore, it behooves any company that wishes to reduce its income tax payment to the minimum, to report as high an amount for depreciation as is legally possible. Depreciation itself, is an odd kind of expense because no money is expended for this item: it is a *non-cash charge*. As a financial executive of a company, I can simply take my hand, place it on a piece of accounting paper and create the entry, debiting depreciation and crediting reserve for depreciation. By doing so, I have legitimized a proper expense which will be reported on the financial statement. It should be kept in mind, however, that in the creation of that account, I have not spent any money. It is an economic expense: a recognition of an apportionment of the original cost of an item.

The controversy over the expense arises in its apportionment. Shall we apportion the cost in equal installments over the expected life of an asset?, or shall we, if permitted by governmental authorities, lump or bunch the installments in earlier years so that we give recognition to the economic fact that the major portion of the expiration of the physical life of a machine takes place in its earlier years? The techniques for accomplishing either of these objectives may be either straight line apportionment of cost, or an accelerated apportionment of cost. On a straight line basis, if a machine costs $100 and is expected to have a useful life of 10 years with no scrap value at the end of that period, we can charge $10 to each of ten annual profit and loss statements as legitimate expenses. Under accelerated depreciation, we can choose either of a few devices to give recognition to a bunching of the cost expiration in the earlier years. One of these devices is called the *sum of the digits* method, in which the expected total life of a machine might be apportioned as follows:

*Machine A has an expected life of 10 years*

$$
\begin{array}{r}
1 \\
2 \\
3 \\
4 \\
5 \\
6 \\
7 \\
8 \\
9 \\
\underline{10} \\
\overline{\overline{55}}
\end{array}
$$

Using this device, the depreciation for the machine at the end of the first year would be 10/55 of $100 or $18. In the second year, the depreciation for the machine would amount to 9/55, in the third year 8/55, and so on. Another method of accelerated depreciation is called *double declining balance*. Still others are also available. Rather than going into the details of each of technique suffice it to say that there are options available. The point is that companies can switch from one technique to the other technique for essentially the same item, in order to influence their profit reports. Many companies which are very conscious of investor relations and maintenance of per share earnings have, in more recent years, switched from accelerated depreciation to straight line depreciation. This has had the effect of shrinking the amount of reported depreciation in any one year and thereby increasing the reported profit. They have done this despite the fact that they may be paying a penalty in the form of higher tax payments than they would under accelerated depreciation.

Another financial strategy which can be used to influence the magnitude and the direction of profits, is the choice which companies face when considering whether to capitalize or expense certain items. An expense, by definition, should relate to current year operations. It should be identified with a situation in the current year which has produced the expense. If, however, a company chooses to make expenditures for an item which is more properly related to events which will take place subsequent to the current operating period, it has the choice of recognizing the expense now or, in effect, postponing the expense to that future period when revenues from such an expenditure may take place. The postponement of expenditures to future periods is called *capitalization*.

Unfortunately, any attempt to apply meaningful guidelines to capitalization will probably go the way of the four winds. After all, a justification can be made for opposing the conventional accounting treatment of advertising. Any savvy marketing man knows that when, in September of a given year, he commits his advertising budget for the next year, the results in terms of sales and profits from that advertising campaign may not take place until the next year. They may, in fact, take place in the second subsequent year. Conventional accounting treatment holds that advertising is an expense in the current operating year. If we are talking about the year 1970, for example, when Company A spent $1 million for an advertising campaign which would take place in the year 1971, the expenditure of $1 million would be treated as an expense in 1970. Economically, and from a marketing point of view, accounting is engaging in a fiction. In fact, it is violating its basic precepts that expenditures should be matched to revenues received. In each operating period, there should be every attempt made to show a cause/effect relationship.

The expending of advertising in 1970, in this case, is completely at variance with the marketing knowledge that the revenues from the $1 million may not begin to be received until 1971 and perhaps even 1972. One of the most recent striking examples of the deferred impact of advertising took place recently when Bristol-Myers decided to drop its old line toothpaste brand called Ipana. Some enterprising entrepreneurs in the mid-west decided to create a product under that name and market it themselves. Their experience showed that people recalled the advertising messages from over twenty years ago for the product and that this had a significant effect on the sales power of the product. How should or how could the accountant of two decades ago, truly have accounted for the advertising in any one year for Ipana toothpaste?

The same type of rational argument can be made for the accounting treatment of research and development. The lead time which takes place between concept development prototype, and national marketing of a product may be as much as eight years in some industries. Accounting treatment of research and development varies. Many companies choose to expense it. Many of the younger, newer, more dynamic techniology-oriented companies have chosen to defer research and development spending on their operating statements. There is a perfect justification for this; however, the wary investor must also be aware that he is not looking at earnings per share in comparison with other companies. In fact, one computer company in its recent financial statement, deferred an amount of research and development for future years which, if expressed in terms of expenses per share, exceeds the earnings per share for the current operating period.

Another source of the accountant's hang-up is in the grey area of capital projects which can subjectively be evaluated as either an infusion of new capital which will introduce a new asset, or prolongation of the life of an existing asset. One alternative is to "patch" assets to make them look nicer or to make minor repairs or adjustments. We might consider, for example, two adjacent factory buildings owned by the same company. If a company chooses to install a common air-conditioning system for the two buildings, it is obvious that the adjoining wall separating the two buildings must be torn down. There is not much doubt that the air-conditioning system itself would be considered an infusion of new capital in the creation of a new asset. One of the reasonable questions to be asked, however, is whether the demolition of the wall between the building prolongs the life of the new asset, or is merely a type of refurbishing?

It is in this area that accountants must use judgment in making classifications. When an item is introduced as a new asset, it is shown on the balance sheet of the company. As such, it is entitled to be diminished only by the amount of annual depreciation for that asset. The opposite side of the coin, expensing of a capital item, can reap very quick tax benefits for a company. The amount is simply considered as another expense on the profit and loss statement similar to depreciation or advertising, and it will be given the prevailing tax rate.

The financial executive may also influence the profit number by his choice of inventory evaluation methods. Certain acronyms describing these techniques have grown up in the field of finance. FIFO is a technique which assumes that the earliest materials purchased will be consumed first in production. Literally, it denotes *first-in, first-out*. It should be easy for the reader to visualize the impact of this technique in times of rising or falling prices. In times of rising prices, this technique will produce higher profits. The lower cost materials, which were purchased initially, were consumed and sold. This means that the higher priced materials remained in the carryover inventory and were not consumed in production.

LIFO stands for *last-in, first-out*. This approach is often used by companies in times of rising raw material prices, when they wish to minimize their reported profits and thereby minimize their calculation for tax payments. It places the highest priced material into production and clears them through sales. In times of rising prices the highest priced materials are the last ones to be placed into production and the first ones to be credited to sales. The remaining inventory contains the lower cost materials, bought in the initial phase of the price rise cycle. This has the effect of reducing reported earnings. Other techniques are available, including one that will average the cost of inventory valuations over a period of time.

The above discussion is only a fragmentary list of the possibilities for manipulation by the financial executive of the reported profits of a company. The implication for the marketing executive is that the reported profits of a company are frequently traced back to individual divisions or individual products; when they are traced to these segments of the business, they invariably affect the profit performance of individuals. Why should a product manager ostensibly be held responsible for the profits of his product when, in reality, he may not control the elements which create profits, and certainly may not be able to anticipate the various alternative strategies which the financial executive in the company can employ to affect reported profit? The essential key to solving the dilemma of how to attain the objective of profitability reporting lies in the concept of relevant costing as defined in the next chapter.

## Use of the Profitability Concept

The phrase "profitability accounting" has come increasingly into vogue within recent years but still apparently causes confusion. In 1967, this author wrote:

> In discussing the distinction between profit and profitability, we are entering the debate between those who espouse traditional accounting reporting and those who are representative of modern corporate finance.
>
> To the former, profit is a residual. It is a static, historical term, more geared to a reporting function than to decision-making. Profitability, on the other hand, is somewhere in the background and is espoused by those individuals using contribution tech-

niques, such as direct costing, to view isolated marketing production problems.

The modern corporate finance man views the distinction between profit and profitability as a test of ownership. Profit is an
owner-oriented concept and is tied into the ownership shares of
national income and the provision of equity capital for business
enterprises. In substance, it is the measure of wealth maximization and the yardstick for distribution of potential wealth to enterprises. Profitability, on the other hand, is an internal measure
of new wealth generation.[9]

One question asked whether the "profitability concept" is used.
Even among those replying in the affirmative, the term had different meanings.

As an example, Company J indicated that elements of the
profitability concept are contained in the structure of product
and division operating statements. In the statements, Figures 20
and 20a, it can be seen that the firm operates on a gross trading
profit basis (already decried by Company B). The statements
are surprisingly unsophisticated considering the size and marketing expertise of the company. No effort is made on the product
statement to segregate variable from nonvariable expense elements, thereby precluding marginal analysis. In addition, there
is no provision for attributing direct freight and warehousing
expenses to the product. On the division statement (Figure 20a),
corporate period charges are allocated to the division, making
controllable division operating elements less obvious.

Despite the fact that Company I answered in the affirmative,
they stated that they differentiate between reporting and analysis
purposes. Their reporting statements for products include both
allocated divisional charges and corporate charges. A sample
division statement is shown in Figure 21. Valid marginal analysis
is precluded because on the product statements, period costs are
assigned to products before the gross profit level, although they
may not be incremental to the products. Under the category
"Programmed Costs," promotion is noted as having the characteristics of a period cost, at least to the extent that the cost will
vary more with respect to time than to unit volume. This may not
be true, especially over the short term. This statement, then, has

its maximum use for viewing the operating characteristics of a product over a long period of time.

The format of the statement *does* approach the concept of relevant costing and, if used properly and if understood by the marketing brand men, can be an extremely useful tool for gaining a perspective into the performance of their products. Reporting

Brand _____

| | | | | |
|---|---|---|---|---|
| VOLUME DATA (M Standard Cases)<br>Consumer Sales .....................................<br>Share of Market - % of | | | | |
| Trade Stocks ........................................ | | | | |
| Shipments to Trade ................................<br>Samples ...........................................<br>  Total Distributed (000 Omitted)<br>  Std. Cases ..................................<br>  Net Sales Revenue ....................... | | | | |
| GROSS MARGIN - Per Case ...........................<br>        - Pct. of Net Sales Revenue ....... | | | | |
| TRADING PROFIT: (000 Omitted)<br>Gross Profit ........................................<br><br>Advertising ..........................................<br>Promotion ...........................................<br>  Total ............................................<br>Continuous Cooperative Advertising ...........<br>  Combined Total.............................<br><br>Gross Trading Profit ............................... | | | | |
| PER STANDARD CASE<br>Advertising ..........................................<br>Promotion ...........................................<br>  Total ............................................<br>Continuous Cooperative Advertising ..........<br>  Combined Total ............................<br><br>Gross Trading Margin ............................. | | | | |
| PERCENT OF NET SALES REVENUE<br>Advertising ..........................................<br>Promotion ...........................................<br>  Total ............................................<br>Continuous Cooperative Advertising ..........<br>  Combined Total ............................<br><br>Gross Trading Margin ............................. | | | | |

Figure 20. Product Operating Statement, Company J (Foods, Soaps)

and analysis under this format are carried on by the division controllers within the domestic operating company. They are being increasingly oriented toward free form and creativity in their reporting to management. This company is making great strides toward the marketing controller concept.

Similarly, Company G claimed to use the profitability concept

| AMOUNT | %<br>OF SALES | | AMOUNT | %<br>OF SALES |
|---|---|---|---|---|
| | | Total Distributed - Std. Cases ........................................ | | |
| | | NET SALES REVENUE .................................................. | | |
| | | Cost of Goods Sold ..................................................... | | |
| | | GROSS PROFIT .......................................................... | | |
| | | Advertising and Promotion ............................................ | | |
| | | Continuous Cooperative Advertising ................................ | | |
| | | GROSS TRADING PROFIT - Before Adj .......................... | | |
| | | Prior Year Adjustment - Adv. & Prom. .......................... | | |
| | | Provision for New Products ......................................... | | |
| | | GROSS TRADING PROFIT - Adjusted ............................ | | |
| | | Operating Expenses:<br>  Direct:<br>    Mktg. Div. - Headquarters ..................................... | | |
| | | - MRD Projects ..................................... | | |
| | | Total Direct Expenses ..................................... | | |
| | | Allocated:<br>  Selling ................................................................ | | |
| | | Consumer Relations ............................................ | | |
| | | Plant Overhead .................................................. | | |
| | | Research and Development ................................... | | |
| | | Other Operating ................................................. | | |
| | | Total Allocated Expenses ............................... | | |
| | | TOTAL OPERATING EXPENSES ................................ | | |
| | | NET TRADING PROFIT ........................................... | | |

Figure 20a.   Operating Statement, Divisional Summary, Company J

for reporting and analysis. Their operating statement, Figure 22, clearly indicates corporate staff expenses applied to marketing. Note that their statement separates what they term decision costs from marketing costs. There is an interesting semantic implication

INCOME STATEMENT

DOMESTIC OPERATING COMPANY

| DESCRIPTION | $ | % | $ | % |
|---|---|---|---|---|
| UNIT VOLUME    BEFORE PRICE CHANGES | | | | |
| PRICE CHANGES - | | | | |
| UNIT VOLUME    REFLECTING PRICE CHANGES | | | | |
| LESS: TEMPORARY PRICE CONCESSIONS | | | | |
| INTO STOCK & INCENTIVE ALLOWANCES | | | | |
| RETURNS | | | | |
| GROSS SALES | | | | |
| LESS: CASH DISCOUNTS & ALLOWANCES | | | | |
| NET SALES | | | | |
| PRODUCTION - DISTRIBUTION COSTS | | | | |
| VARIABLE PRODUCT COSTS | | | | |
| VARIABLE DISTRIBUTION COSTS | | | | |
| TOTAL VARIABLE COSTS | | | | |
| MARGINAL INCOME | | | | |
| FIXED PRODUCT COSTS | | | | |
| FIXED DISTRIBUTION COSTS | | | | |
| TOTAL FIXED COSTS | | | | |
| GROSS PROFIT | | | | |
| PROGRAMMED COSTS | | | | |
| ADVERTISING - PRODUCT ACTIVITY - MEDIA | | | | |
| - PROMOTION | | | | |
| MULTI - PRODUCT ACTIVITY | | | | |
| MARKET & CONSUMER RESEARCH | | | | |
| SPECIAL DIRECT CHARGES - MERCHANDISING | | | | |
| ENGINEERING | | | | |
| PRODUCT RESEARCH & DEVELOPMENT | | | | |
| OTHER MANUFACTURING & DISTRIBUTION COST | | | | |
| BRAND CONTRIBUTION | | | | |
| DIVISION MARKETING COSTS | | | | |
| DIVISION CONTRIBUTION | | | | |
| GENERAL ADMINISTRATIVE COSTS | | | | |
| PROFIT OR (LOSS) BEFORE TAXES | | | | |
| PROFIT OR (LOSS) AFTER TAXES | | | | |

Figure 21.   Operating Statement, Company I (Hospital, Health Aids)

in that format; it suggests that there are no decisions involved in the marketing program. Expenses allocated to marketing expenses, of course, have no bearing on the incremental performance of any one product nor, indeed, should they have any important effect upon the performance of a division's operations.

In a similar manner, the division contribution is masked under the category of "other operating costs;" costs associated with cor-

| | Current Month | | | | | | Year to Date | | | | | |
| | 197 | | | 197 | | | | 197 | | | 197 | | |
| | VE% | Amount | % of Sales | Amount | % of Sales | V% | VE% | Amount | % of Sales | Amount | % of Sales | V% |
|---|---|---|---|---|---|---|---|---|---|---|---|---|
| *(Dollar amounts in thousands)* | | | | | | | | | | | | |
| NET SALES BILLED | | | | | | | | | | | | |
| DECISION COSTS IN SALES: | | | | | | | | | | | | |
|   Material | | | | | | | | | | | | |
|   Conversion Costs | | | | | | | | | | | | |
|   Other | | | | | | | | | | | | |
|   Total | | | | | | | | | | | | |
| DECISION MARGIN | | | | | | | | | | | | |
| MARKETING COSTS: | | | | | | | | | | | | |
|   Adv.& Sales Pro. | | | | | | | | | | | | |
|   Sales Plans | | | | | | | | | | | | |
|   Direct | | | | | | | | | | | | |
|   Allocated | | | | | | | | | | | | |
|   Total | | | | | | | | | | | | |
| MARKETING MARGIN | | | | | | | | | | | | |
| OTHER OPERATING COST: | | | | | | | | | | | | |
|   Product Design & Prod. | | | | | | | | | | | | |
|   Liquidation Variance | | | | | | | | | | | | |
|   Complaint Liq. Var. | | | | | | | | | | | | |
|   Finance: | | | | | | | | | | | | |
|    Trans. Liq. Var. | | | | | | | | | | | | |
|    Warehousing | | | | | | | | | | | | |
|    D.F.O. Service Charge | | | | | | | | | | | | |
|    Other | | | | | | | | | | | | |
|   Overseas H'swares Dept. | | | | | | | | | | | | |
|   Relations & Facilities | | | | | | | | | | | | |
|   Advance Development | | | | | | | | | | | | |
|   Business Planning | | | | | | | | | | | | |
|   Legal & Patent | | | | | | | | | | | | |
|   Administration | | | | | | | | | | | | |
|   G.O. Assessment | | | | | | | | | | | | |
|   Total | | | | | | | | | | | | |
| INCOME FROM SALES | | | | | | | | | | | | |
|   Other Income | | | | | | | | | | | | |
| TOTAL INCOME | | | | | | | | | | | | |
|   Federal Income Taxes | | | | | | | | | | | | |
| NET INCOME | | | | | | | | | | | | |
|   Residual Income | | | | | | | | | | | | |
|   Res.Inc.to Contr'b.Vol. | | | | | | | | | | | | |
|   Earnings per Share | | | | | | | | | | | | |
|   Aver. Investment | | | | | | | | | | | | |
|   Return on Investment | | | | | | | | | | | | |
|   Cash Flow-gen./(used) | | | | | | | | | | | | |

Figure 22. Division Operating Statement, Company G
(Consumer Appliances)

porate service areas such as legal and patent services and administration and general office are assigned to the division on arbitrary bases. The bases for allocation may have stemmed from past studies or estimates of time spent and this does not detract from the argument that, even though the computations may be statistically valid, they may be pragmatically misapplied.

Company T recognized that the concept was only partially used. They consider their statement (Figure 18), to be constructed on a "modified direct cost basis." They can, however, through the construction of their accounts isolate variable manufacturing cost. The problem faced in Figure 18 is essentially the same problem that the previously cited companies faced. In effect, the information to be gained from marginal analysis techniques has been lost by the inclusion of period expenses in the wrong areas of the operating statements. Gross profit, in Figure 18, includes three specific references to period overhead. Thus, it would be difficult to analyze the effect of incremental changes in volume on profits. In addition, under the category of "direct costs," total promotions are considered in the same manner as total advertising, belying the fact that one is a true period cost, whereas one tends to vary with volume over certain time horizons.

Company M had the best product operating statement (Figure 23), and clearly demonstrated a knowledge of the profitability concept. Their statement creates three specific decision-making levels of profit. Variable profit is the level for making marginal evaluations since it isolates factors incremental to a product. Another level, not highlighted, but used for marketing decisions isolates the unit value of variable profit less promotions. This enables the analyst to deal with the effect of short-term volume fluctuations when promotional expense is variable. The last level of profit for decisions is direct profit, or that profit which is incremental to and attributable to the existence of a product.

Company S was one of the companies which answered the question in the negative:

> In general, pricing of our consumer products was determined more in the marketplace than by consideration of incremental sales volumes that might be attainable. I would agree that we do

Form No. 5685
7/70

PRODUCT PLAN – PROFIT AND LOSS ACCOUNT

Revision 1  19     Original  19     Product _____

| | PER LB. | AMOUNT | % | PER LB. | AMOUNT | % | PER LB. | AMOUNT | % | PER LB. | AMOUNT | % |
|---|---|---|---|---|---|---|---|---|---|---|---|---|

Plan Sales Units - Pounds . . . . . . . .
Bonus Goods - Pounds . . . . . . . .
TOTAL . . . . . . . .

Net Proceeds from Sales . . . . . . . .
Variable Cost of Goods Sold . . . . . . . .
V R A D U L E   P X R O D D U C T   Freight and Charges . . . . .
Warehouse Expenses . . . . . .
Spoiled Goods . . . . . . .
Cash Discount . . . . . . .
Distributors' Discount . . . . .
Commissions . . . . . . . .
TOTAL VAR. EXP. . . . .
VARIABLE PROFIT . . . . . . .

D I R E C T   P R O D U C T   C O S T   Advertising - Media . . . .
Promotions . . . . . .
Co-Promotion . . . . . .
SUB-TOTAL . . . . .
Extraordinary Promotion . . .
Prior Years Adv./Promotion . .
Market Research . . . . .
Other . . . . . . .
TOTAL DIRECT PRODUCT COST .

DIRECT PROFIT . . . . . . .
Less-Provision for Contingency . . . . . .
NET DIRECT PROFIT . . . . . .

Period Factory Expenses . . . . . .
Direct Divisional Expenses . . . . . .
Other Period Expenses . . . . . .
NET PROFIT (LOSS) . . . . . .

Sugar Cost per Lb. . . . . . .
Green Coffee Blend Cost per Lb. . . . .
Cocoa Bean Cost per Lb. . . . . . .
Cocoa Butter Cost per Lb. . . . . . .

Comments: _____

Financial Analysis and Planning - By _____  Date _____  Product _____
Yearly Class _____  Page No. _____

Figure 23.    Product Operating Statement, Company M

not use these techniques on a routine basis or as regularly as the return on investment measurement, but believe we do employ them in some form in special studies from time to time.

There is confusion evident in the above reply. It implies that the raison d'etre for the profitability concept is pricing evaluation. This could not be farther from the truth: profitability deals with all the elements of the marketing mix.

| PRODUCT | | YEAR | SUBJECT | PROVISIONAL PRODUCT BUDGET PROFIT & LOSS ACCOUNT |

| | ORIGINAL BUDGET PREVIOUS YR. | | ACTUAL ESTIMATED PREVIOUS YR. | | ORIGINAL BUDGET OCT 1 | | REVISION 1 JAN 1 | | REVISION II APR 1 | | REVISION III JULY 1 | | REVISION IV OCT 1 | |
|---|---|---|---|---|---|---|---|---|---|---|---|---|---|---|
| Sales ——— Units | | % | | % | | % | | % | | % | | % | | % |
| Gross Sales $ | | 100.0 | | 100.0 | | 100.0 | | 100.0 | | 100.0 | | 100.0 | | 100.0 |
| | | | | | | | | | | | | | | |
| Gross Profits $ | | | | | | | | | | | | | | |
| Advertising | | | | | | | | | | | | | | |
| Promotion | | | | | | | | | | | | | | |
| Market Research | | | | | | | | | | | | | | |
| Package Design | | | | | | | | | | | | | | |
| Total Mer. Exp. | | | | | | | | | | | | | | |
| | | | | | | | | | | | | | | |
| Gross Trading Profit | | | | | | | | | | | | | | |

| | 1st QUARTER | | 2nd QUARTER | | 1st HALF | | 3rd QUARTER | | 4th QUARTER | | 2nd HALF | | FULL YEAR | |
|---|---|---|---|---|---|---|---|---|---|---|---|---|---|---|
| Sales ——— Units | | | | | | | | | | | | | | |
| Gross Sales $ | | 100.0 | | 100.0 | | 100.0 | | 100.0 | | 100.0 | | 100.0 | | 100.0 |
| | | | | | | | | | | | | | | |
| Gross Profit $ | | | | | | | | | | | | | | |
| Advertising | | | | | | | | | | | | | | |
| Promotion | | | | | | | | | | | | | | |
| Market Research | | | | | | | | | | | | | | |
| Package Design | | | | | | | | | | | | | | |
| Total Mer. Exp. | | | | | | | | | | | | | | |
| | | | | | | | | | | | | | | |
| Gross Trading Profit | | | | | | | | | | | | | | |

Approvals Initial and Date

| BRAND MGR. | MARKETING MGR. | ADVERTISING DEPT. | V.P. MARKETING | EXEC. V.P. |
|---|---|---|---|---|
| | | | | |

Page No. _____

Figure 24.  Operating Statement, Company B

Company B was another company replying in the negative, but added that the concept will be instituted shortly. The reasons are evident in their operating statement (Figure 24). It is another variety of the gross trading profit type, and ignores the effect of incremental factors such as freight and distribution. Factory period costs are included in gross profit, inhibiting marginal analysis.

# Chapter VI

# Marketing Decision-Making Data and Techniques— Part II

*Relevant Costs*

Traditional accounting and marketing philosophies do not stand the test of time in today's marketing environment. Unfortunately, accounting philosophy, especially that concerned with period costs, has contributed to the demise of more profitable new products than many of the efforts more directly related to the marketing of those products. How many times have you run up against the situation in which a new product has been developed and, prior to the official decision to market the product or not, someone asked whether the product would be profitable on an "in-business" basis? The calculation was then handed over to the financial executive who produced a profit and loss statement for the product that included the allocation of corporate overhead. On that basis, many a decision has been made which said "this product will show a loss after overhead has been applied; therefore, we cannot go ahead and justify a decision to make this product."

The financial executive has failed to mention that by taking the overhead costs from elsewhere in the corporation and diverting them to this new product, he has, at the same time, made an existing product more profitable by removing its overhead charge. Overhead, by its very nature, is an expense that changes very slowly or, quite often, not at all. When was the last time your financial executive had the courage to tell you that overheads have no relevance whatsoever to decision making, unless it is a new overhead that is incremental to the decision in question? This is expressed in the economic axiom that a "sunk cost cannot affect a future outcome." Deprecating overhead allocation can be a dangerous game for any author, because these costs are real money and they do count. A more dangerous game, however, attempts to place too much importance on overhead in decision-making strategies. Companies try to recover overhead many times over in their pricing decisions. Service industries, in particular, are notorious for over-recovering. Consider, for example, a service industry that bids for jobs. If the financial executive reviews the pricing structure and inserts overhead factors into the pricing formula, he will probably feel secure that he met the accounting criteria. Yet, consider the argument that should the company have a very good year and win more bids for services than had been anticipated, its accountant will have more than recovered the amount of overhead currently in existence. Results of this type can warm the heart of any chief executive of a company. There is the possibility, on the other hand, that the company will experience a bad year. If the same rigid overhead formula is adhered to, overhead may not be recovered through the formula and in fact, in tight competitive situations, jobs which should have been gotten, may not be gotten at all.

Relevant costing is a rather new and innovative approach to the problem of isolating the important factors in a decision. It is innovative in the sense that it considers all factors in a business situation. To date, accounting systems have been very much oriented toward solving production problems. Standard costing, absorption costing and even the newer technique of direct costing, are all production-oriented systems. We have seen, however, that the bulk of expenses which deplete revenues received are applicable to the distribution function. What techniques, then, are available for analyzing the expenses which lie beyond the factory door? It is here that traditional financing techniques have utterly failed to assist the marketing executive in making a proper decision.

Relevant costing is an evolutionary technique of analysis which succeeds the earlier, more cumbersome techniques of standard and direct costing. Standard costing is a production-oriented technique that seeks to devise optimum performance characteristics for direct material, direct labor and factors of overhead, without discriminating as to the type of overhead involved. The standard cost thus devised is then used as the base for multiplication by the actual and planned volume; comparison of the results yields variance amounts. The variances show actual performance versus the planned performance in manufacturing costs. Other types of income or expense, separate and apart from the standard cost of production, would be considered in addendum.

Direct costing was an attempt to apply contribution margin analysis, which is essentially an economic concept, to accounting. It was devised in the mid-1930's and sought to analyze manufacturing costs in terms of those expenses which were *variable* in contrast to those which were *non-variable*. The element of variability is measured in relationship to the physical volume of goods produced. Thus, if the variable cost per unit is 2¢ per pound for product A, the production of two pounds of product A should bring an aggregate cost of 4¢, but the unit rate will remain at 2¢ per pound. On the other hand, the non-variable costs, under direct costing, are called period costs because they vary more over a period of time than they do with physical output. In addition, their unit costs tend to change as changes in volume occur, but the aggregate dollars remain the same. For example, when a company contracts for an aggregate dollar level of advertising in a given period, the dollar level will not change whether the company sells one unit or sells five million units. If our company spends $1 million for advertising and expects to sell one hundred thousand units, we can say, at this point, that the advertising cost per unit is $10. If however, we sell two hundred thousand units, our $1 million expenditure would not change but the cost per unit would be reduced to $5 per unit.

Direct costing was an innovation in its day. Unfortunately, it has been primarily oriented toward the manufacturing function. It does not, for instance, describe variable and non-variable cost behavior patterns for advertising, sales promotion, salesmen's expenses, warehousing or for any other marketing or distribution cost. This is where each of the aforementioned systems has thus far failed to assist in marketing decision-making.

Relevant costing goes that one critical step further by taking all parts of a company and examining them in two steps. First, it isolates those cost elements which are direct to the entity being measured versus those which are indirect. By entity being measured, I am referring to a product profit and loss statement, a division operating statement or a group product operating statement. The word *direct* is really a synonym for "directly attributable to the existence of." Secondly, relevant costing takes the direct costs, once isolated, and separates them into variable and non-variable components. Again, the word variable refers to volume fluctuations. Under this concept, we might define labor, or direct materials, or even freight, warehousing and spoilage as direct costs attributable to the existence of the product. Advertising and sales promotion may also be direct costs attributable to the existence of a product. The distinction, though, is that whereas direct materials, direct labor, freight or warehousing costs may vary directly in proportion to the units of production, advertising and sales promotion may not.

We are essentially concerned with costs that change. Moreover, we are concerned with *future* costs. Relevant costing therefore, is *not* a replacement for custodial accounting systems; it is an adjunct to existing systems, and is designed specifically for analyses purposes.

A transition to the new technique can best be accomplished by adopting a form of operating statement similar to Exhibit B. On the product statement and the division statement, variable profit is shown as a highlighted profit level. That the profit level expedites the preparation of break-even analysis is clearly seen on Charts 1 through 6.

In order to clarify the uses and philosophy of relevant costing, four simple problems and their solutions are shown below. Additional uses and an expanded discussion of the subject are also contained in my earlier work, entitled *Techniques of Profitability Analysis.*

## Problem #1

Product Z has the following highlights:

> NOTE: Product Z is one of thirty products sold by its division and accounts for about 2% of annual divisional sales dollars.

> *Per Unit*
> Selling Price—$2.00
> Variable Manufacturing Cost—$1.00
> Distribution Cost—$.20
> Advertising (Share of Divisional Total)—$.10
> Sales Force Expense (Share of Sales Salaries)—$.25

> At present, it appears that Product Z will overrun planned volume by 5,000 units or 2% of its volume. How much will this increase profit?

Solution:

> Advertising and sales force expenses are allocated and will not change in total if budget is exceeded by a small sum. Hence, the calculation is as follows:

| | | |
|---|---|---|
| Selling Price | | $ 2.00 |
| Less: Manufacturing Cost | $1.00 | |
| Distribution Cost | .20 | 1.20 |
| Variable Profit Per Unit | | $ .80 |
| Volume Increase | | × 5,000 units |
| Profit Increase | | $ 4,000 |

## Problem #2

The XYZ Company paid $5,000,000 three years ago to purchase a company manufacturing magnetic tape drives. This company has been operated as a division of XYZ and has lost $500,000 each year since its acquisition.

The outlook for this division is as follows:

1. It should break even this year and next.
2. Two years from now, when a new product is fully developed, it should return a profit of approximately $500,000.

3. That profit should continue each year for the foresee-able future.

Recently the APEX Corporation offered to purchase this division from XYZ for $3 million. Should XYZ accept this offer?

Solution:

A return on investment study should evaluate the antici-pated profit against the worth of the investment in the divi-sion. Since the $5 million and the $500 thousand lost in each of the first three years cannot be recouped, they are regarded as "sunk" costs and should not be considered in this study. The worth of the investment is, in reality, the $3 million offered for the division by APEX. Hence, the evaluation by the XYZ Corporation must be made by bal-ancing an annual $500 thousand of profit against the $3 million offer for the division. Undoubtedly, the profit would be considered acceptable by most corporate standards.

Accordingly, the offer would probably be declined.

*Problem #3*

Determine true profitability of a product in multi-product plant and/or operation.

*Given: Product A*
  Sales Volume—1,000,000 Units
  Variable Profit Rate per Unit—$1.50
  Total Allocated Expenses—$1,300,000

| | | *Total Expenses* | |
| *Expense Classification* | *Total* | *Allocated* | *Incremental* |
| Period Factory | $  500,000 | $  50,000 | $450,000 |
| Sales Force | 300,000 | 150,000 | 150,000 |
| Head Office | 500,000 | 400,000 | 100,000 |
| | $1,300,000 | $600,000 | $700,000 |

Incremental Expenses included in allocated expenses—$700,000

*Solution:*

  1,000,000 units × $1.50 variable profit rate—$1,500,000
  Less: Incremental Expenses . . . . . . . . . . . .     700,000
  True Profitability . . . . . . . . . . . . . . . . . . . .   $  800,000

## Problem #4

Determine effect on profit of increasing volume of Product B by 100%

*Given*:

       Current Volume—500,000 Units

       Variable Profit Rate per Unit—$1.00

       Current Allocated Expenses—$300,000

       Additional Expenses Incremental to volume increase (supervision for second shift, shift premium, additional sales force and administrative expenses, etc.)—$100,000

*Solution*:

    500,000 units × $1.00 variable profit rate—$500,000

| | |
|---|---:|
| Less: Expenses that are incremental to additional volume | 100,000 |
| Profit Effect | $400,000 |

## The Use of Relevant Costing

The survey pointed out that the term "Relevant Costing" is not well known in industry. Horngren, one of the proponents, states that " . . . to be relevant, a cost must be an expected future cost. But *all* future costs are not necessarily relevant to a given decision; only those costs that will be *different* under alternatives are relevant. Thus, relevant costs may be defined as those *future* costs that will be *different* under available alternatives."[1]

In addition, the author has written:

> Direct costing is a misnomer and a euphemism in the sense that it has become a crutch to management accountants and the end of all of their creativity. Certainly the costs may not all be direct, and moreover, the system only accounts for manufacturing costs. Once a product leaves the factory, it still must be marketed. A better name for the system is variable manufacturing costing.
>
> Charles Horngren, in his fine text *Cost Accounting: A Managerial Emphasis*, recognizes this and devotes pages to this newer and better technique which permits evaluation of alternatives

which have not yet occurred. Future costs are not begat from sunk costs. This is the most compatible accounting technique to economics thus far developed. In a recently published article, the author explored the ramifications of relevant costs, particularly with reference to the marketing function.[2]

Earlier the author in his article dealing with marketing analysis said:

> Relevant costing is much more of a solution than direct costing because it attempts to infer precision and relevancy to the economic existence of the item being measured. Any cost is relevant if it generates a negative answer to a question such as: "If we did not do this (make the product, build the factory, add a flavor, a size, etc.) would we still have the cost?" Plainly, we are dealing here with an economic concept of incremental costs."[3]

Respondents were asked if they used the technique of relevant costing. Only two claimed to use it completely; seven used it partially.

Company M, one of the two companies that replied that they used the concept, said they recognized that many costs are attributable to the existence of a product although they may not be completely variable (such as media costs). This was the reason they have extended the concept of direct costing further to include principles of relevant costing. Their experience thus far has shown that the concept is far more easily understood by marketing personnel who identify closely with the delineation of marketing cost behavior and with the implication that they are the cause of the costs. Previously, their exposure under direct costing was limited to the behavior of manufacturing costs.

Company F also uses relevant costing concepts. However, in formal operating statements, cost of goods sold includes factory period costs. They feel period costs are such a minor factor that it would not destroy the utility of the reports for analytical purposes. They compute profits at a variable and direct level.

Company J partially uses relevant cost concepts. They stated that they really considered it to be an adjunct of direct costing. Yet, there is no attempt to segregate marketing and distribution costs into variable components. In addition, they deviate from direct costing by including maintenance, insurance and depreciation costs in cost of goods sold. Their philosophy holds that products must absorb these fixed charges other than "plant period costs" which they consider to be a corporate burden. Their key measure is gross trading profit which they define as gross margin less advertising, promotion and cooperative advertising. Their objective for profitability holds that products should yield a gross trading profit of at least 25%. This is sufficient to cover average period cost factors of about 12%, and to show a profit before tax of about 13%.

Other companies partially using the concept claimed that they could isolate needed costs through the construction of the chart of accounts. Those not using the concept either professed ignorance of its implications or indicated that it was too new to employ.

Marketing involves evaluating alternatives. The concept of relevant costing was developed to aid in the understanding of that which will occur tomorrow. It is clear from the pattern of the above replies that the majority of companies interviewed either do not use it or do not understand it. There can be no question that thinking professionals—businessmen as well as academicians—have a long overdue date with the Marketing function. The same degree of effort that gave direct costing to manufacturing must now be applied to providing marketing with its set of analytical tools.

### The Origins of Mathematical Models

The development of mathematical models began as an operations research attempt to investigate all of the variables that are attendant to the new product process. The use of these models has created a split in the marketing world, pitting the traditionally oriented individuals against those who like to consider themselves innovative. It is not enough to say that models in the new product process are merely concepts devoid of practical value. As with all innovations, they contain many useful elements.

The balance of this chapter will deal with four major questions:

1. How did the process of applying mathematics to new product decision models begin?

2. What are these models: are they useful, have they been tested?
3. Why are they not more widely used?
4. How do they effect new product development?


1. Operations research, as a functional area, has a mixed heritage. It was used sucessfully in Great Britain during the waning days of the war in connection with radar installations. Commercially, it was first used successfully to relate inventory and production data. As a technique, it has been in the business realm for approximately 20 years. Its place in marketing is still rather negligible.

The first published marketing decision models appeared in the mid-1950's and admittedly were somewhat primitive. The majority dealt with problems of optimization, mainly in the areas of advertising, the allocation of sales resources and pricing of products. Each of the mathematical models faced the criticism of its existence. More and more complex models were developed and these in turn, regenerated the cycle so that the more complex models became, in effect, constantly the first generation of models to be criticized. By the early 1960's, a few, highly original, marketing models were developed. One of the first companies to invest funds for research into marketing model building was Du-Pont. Their initial avenues of inquiry dealt with the definition of how advertising works, problem solving in the new product development and introduction areas, and in product pricing.

The Scott Paper Company and Monsanto Chemical each conducted field advertising experiments and attempted to develop a total systems approach that would assist marketing management in analyzing a variety of marketing problems. Following on the heels of these basic investigations, other companies began to develop further the use of marketing models, all seeking the ultimate goal of simulation of marketing environmental conditions. General Electric and Ford have been working now for many years on developing simulation processes for marketing. In addition, other large companies have now joined the list of marketing model users, including Pillsbury, Union Carbide, Anheuser-Busch, Lever Brothers and Westinghouse.

An interesting sidelight has been the entrance of service agencies into the field. In addition to specialized marketing research agencies, advertising agencies such as Batton-Barton-Durstine and Osborne and Young & Rubicam have developed sophisticated models which delve into the area of media selection and new product development. In 1966, a rather exhaustive study by the Diebold group concluded that the areas of greatest application for mathematical models in marketing were internal profit analysis, market analysis, competitive strategy, sales effort effectiveness and pricing. Among the techniques which appeared to be the most promising ones were simulation, linear programming and critical path analyses.

In his fine book dealing with the use of mathematical models in marketing, Robert Buzzell[4] makes the point that in the early sixties, marketing management made sparse use of mathematical models. Many companies claimed to be exploring potentials of such devices, but actual success stories were few and far between. It seemed that model building achieved success, not so much as a tool for decision making, but as a catalyst for discussion of the many considerations involved in analysis of the consumer marketplace.

Of company types which have utilized model building for marketing, two in particular stand out. The technically oriented company which has a core of engineers, statisticians, mathematicians and other quantitatively trained individuals has been highly receptive to the quantitative techniques involved in model building. Another group which has been quite prominent is the industry type that deals heavily with the consumer market, particularly those companies in the cosmetics and food industries. The intense competition among the companies in this group requires that each continuously seek to gain an edge. Model building was seized upon as one of the devices which might provide the clue to gaining such an edge.

2. Mathematical model building can be viewed as a four-stage process:

    a. *Formulation.* This stage consists of a study of the marketing situation, listing all of the factors which might influence the outcome and the interrelationships between the variables involved. A flow chart is usually created that mirrors the situation. A generalized model is created based upon the qualitative representation shown in the flow chart.

b. *Data collection.* The basic data required to derive numerical estimates of the various parameters indicated in the generalized model are collected.

c. *Computation.* Once the parameters have been evaluated, they are converted from the generalized model into a specific planning and control model.

d. *Verification and adjustment.* The model is subjected to objective proof by comparing the estimates generated by the model with the actual figures. On the basis of this comparison, variances are noted and adjustments made in the model in order to eliminate any deviations.

## DEMON, SPRINTER, AND NSPM

Three major mathematical models are now or have been in use for new product development. These models have been given the acronyms of:

### DEMON, SPRINTER, and NSPM.

In order to understand how these models evolved, it is necessary for us to very briefly review their forerunners. There are two well known models which were widely used in the area of new product development, prior to the evolution of the above, more sophisticated, techniques. They are the Baysian Decision Model and the Monte Carlo Simulation Model.

I discussed the Baysian Decision Theorem in an article in the May, 1969 issue of *Innovation* magazine. I would refer the reader to that article for a more detailed explanation of Baysian logic. The Baysian approach to decision-making under uncertainty uses a decision rule which considers expected values. Various possible outcomes for a given decision are assigned probability weightings that reflect the decision maker's willingness to act. The Baysian Model, therefore, calls for executives to define the company's objectives, possible alternative strategies and, indeed, any of the major events which may affect the outcome of each strategy. In addition, the probability of these events occurring and the profit values resulting from different outcomes are considered. This technique permits the calculation of the unexpected profit of each strategy, including the strategy of simply gathering more information *before* acting. When the nitty gritty of semantics is stripped away from explanations of this and other techniques, the truth is that we are really speaking of the creation of intuitive odds in the mind of the decision maker. Baysian logic is no different from the estimate of success which the individual makes each time he crosses the street in the face of oncoming traffic. The individual must deal in probabilities: certainty is expressed as a unit of one. We will often reason to ourselves that we have 80 per cent chance of obtaining success in something. This type of logic is the essence of the Baysian Decision Theorem. It is no more than a quantification in dollar terms of our intuitive probability.

In the statistical sense, the Baysian model, although it did introduce the probabilistic nature of rates of return, did not compare the probability distribution of the different strategies but, instead, calculated the arithmetic means of these distributions. The means are the expected values of the Baysian analysis and the decision which is generated results from the choice of a strategy with the largest expected present value. For example, in the instance where strategy (a) may have a greater mean rate of return than strategy (b), a conservative management may very properly choose strategy (b), because of the lesser risk of incurring a substantial loss.

Monte Carlo Simulation overcomes many of the problems inherent in the Baysian Mode. It has the advantage of allowing a market strategy to be spelled out, and takes into consideration assumptions about the marketing environment. It almost mandates executives to quantity their uncertainties regarding estimates of sales, costs, prices and marketing investments. The uncertainties lead to probability distributions, and by drawing simulated observations representing prices, sales, costs and investments, it is possible to derive the earnings and investment cash flows. These cash flows are then discounted to reflect the time value of money in order to arrive at a rate of return for each simulation. Each of the simulations are in turn, repeated several times so that a probability distribution for the various rates of return may be derived.

There are special computer programs to handle simulations such as the Monte Carlo method, notably IBM's General Purpose Simulation system. The GPSS is programmed to repeat prescribed simulations as many times as it is instructed to do. It takes only seconds for the computer to run through the repeated calculations hundreds of times; it is only on this basis that simulations can be economically run.

Despite its advantages over the Baysian Model, the Monte Carlo Simulation also has its own weaknesses. For instance, it treats price, unit cost and investments as an independent variables, but each can really only be seen in a relative context. After all, a higher price should lead to a lower sales level, a higher unit cost and possibly lower annual investment than expected. Another weakness is that in many of the sets required to complete a Monte Carlo simulation, a great deal of computation is required to determine the value of *additional* information. This very brief and somewhat superficial introduction to the three main models under discussion has necessarily skirted the main issue of step-by-step programs.

### DEMON

One of the fallacies of evaluating new product development is that the last phase of the marketing plan, which normally is the testing of a new product, is the great contributing factor in the decision as to whether to market the product. Actually the decision is a continuous process which has its inception in the birth of the idea for the product. DEMON, an acronym for *decision mapping via optimum GO, NO networks,* considers that every aspect of the product's developmental sequence is considered in relation to the total marketing environment. Each factor in the total marketing plan is related in terms of its contribution to achieving the goal of maximum profitability on the investment. It recognizes that test marketing is an important factor in the total process but only *one* of the factors.

As a new product moves through development and testing, information is continuously needed to determine the desirability of introducing the product and the best manner in which introduction should take place. DEMON is structured so that optimum decisions regarding purchasing information will be reflected on criteria appropriate to decisions about the introduction or dropping of a product. DEMON is structured to achieve two other advantages. Quite often marketing research is considered in the light only of the latest information available. Thus, marketing decisions may not be made on the basis of accumulated information. DEMON incorporates a method for integrating all that is known about a product at the time just prior to the next marketing planning decision, so that an optimal decision related to an optimal objective will result. DEMON deals with outputs of all past studies and uses these bases for selecting further study possibilities in order ultimately to reach a best possible decision.

One of the critical management problems in new product marketing is to *evaluate* all of the information that has been collected about the product. DEMON attempts to solve the problem of disorganization information describing the new product market. No matter how complex the sorted data, the decision maker can really have only three options. He can say that consumer acceptance is sufficient to can go national. On the other hand, if acceptance is poor and profit is low or nil, he may drop the product. A third alternative which is neither GO, as in the first instance, or NO, as in the second instance, derives from that area where consumer acceptance appears uncertain. This decision might be designated as ON and calls for more data to improve the marketing mix of information. An ON decision simply means that we will make another evaluation of the alternatives.

DEMON explores, in a cumulative fashion, all of the facts at hand about a product. Information about price, copy, consumer distribution and other marketing facts are weighed and balanced to provide great flexibility in planning. Once, however, that decision has been made, the system is entered at each evaluation mode and, at each mode, one of the three choices must be made: GO, NO, or ON. When a product is evaluated and an ON decision results, it becomes necessary to collect additional information in order to get a better fix on product acceptance. The DEMON system will, in addition to specifying the ON decision, help choose that factor of the marketing mix which should be altered or tested. The new data is than added to the original data for a second evaluation. Another decision based upon the *cumulative* information is made. This sequence of new data, evaluation and decision is repeated until a GO or NO decision is reached.

Because the objective becomes one of plotting an optimal path through a quantitative model, it is necessary for the path to be subjected to guidelines in the form of quantitative constraints. The constraints that characterize the DEMON model are:

1. Payback period
2. Horizon planning period
3. Minimum acceptable profits for a GO decision
4. Minimum acceptable profits for an ON decision
5. Total marketing research budget
6. Minimum degree of confidence needed for a GO decision
7. Minimum degree of confidence needed for an ON decision

The above are used in conjunction with those input factors which are critical to the development of sound marketing plans. In the course of assembling a sound marketing plan, DEMON established goals for each of the factors in the marketing mix. These goals are advertising, budget, promotional expenditure, advertising awareness, virtual reach, distribution levels, price, product trial, product usage and usage rate. Each combination of these marketing factors produces consumer acceptance, and one of the combinations will give greater acceptance than the others. Thus, it is possible at each step in the development of a new product, to evaluate components of the mix in terms of maximum product acceptance. The input for a model of this complexity is not as vast as it might first appear. Dave Learner, the creator of the model, cites the following as required inputs:

1. The length of the planning period, usually the payoff period plus two or three going years.
2. The minimum acceptable profit over the planning period.

3. The level of expected profit at which the company would immediately go natiqnal.
4. The cost of going national. This should include filling the pipe line, production expense, sales training, sales promotion and expenses other than consumer advertising and promotion required to get the product from the factory to the retail outlet.
5. The amount of the initial study budget. This should include an estimate for all consumer research, advertising research, test markets, use tests, product placement tests, etc.
6. The profit per unit.
7. The length of the payout period.

An important facet of the DEMON model is that it has the capability of balancing risks and profits. Evaluating the tradeoff between these two variables is in direct contrast to much of current planning, which looks at either payout or profit with no possible way of explicitly balancing changes in profits against changes in risks. It should be emphasized that with this latter capability, DEMON provides is a very significant advantage from a management point of view. Another distinct advantage is that the system will maximize profit over the planning period. The design of the model permits one to plan cumulatively, taking advantage of all information on hand and it chooses the next best factor of the marketing plan to alter so that a consistent move is made towards profit maximization. Every change in the marketing plan which is recommended by the model, is a change for the better. It points out that critical nature of collating retail distribution with advertising expenditures so that advertising, for example, would not be scheduled in areas where the product is unavailable.

Why is DEMON not used in more widespread fashion? In the course of my own research, I interviewed one company which claimed to have used the DEMON model and achieved unsuccessful results. They attributed the basic fault to a degree of inflexibility in the model. As dynamic as it was, the model itself was not sufficiently flexible to compete with the even more rapid and vibrant dynamics of the marketplace. Corporations are extremely

sensitive to broadening the overhead base within companies and
it should be obvious from the description of the model that a
brand new breed of "cat" is required to simply interpret the findings for the conventional brand manager or sales manager. It is
axiomatic that the use of DEMON or any other mathematical
model will create a new form of overhead in the corporation.

The one problem to which DEMON neglects to give full treatment arises when a new product is related on the demand and
cost side to some other current company products. DEMON can
not economically evaluate single products within an entire product line.

### SPRINTER

SPRINTER has been developed fairly recently by Glen Urban.
Like DEMON, SPRINTER is also oriented towards yielding
a GO, ON or NO decision. The major distinction between
SPRINTER and DEMON is that the former does give very ex-
plicit consideration to the interactions of new and existing products in the line. Considerations of the product life cycle are inherent in the SPRINTER model in that variations in competitive
response are considered in the calculation. Estimates of demand
and costs are derived functionally from various sources, including
marketing plans, competitive actions and statistical measures.
SPRINTER is essentially a trial and error simulation that evaluates discreet points in a range of marketing programs. It identifies
the optimum price, and advertising and distribution levels for the
new product in each year of the planning period. In addition,
SPRINTER calculates a maximum differential profit as a result
of decisions made regarding the new product. The concept of the
differential profit is similar to the economic concept of out-of-
pocket increments to profit as a result of taking a certain action.
In essence, DEMON compares the profitability results of the existing product line before introduction of the new product, to the
profitability results of the product line with the new product. The
decision areas of GO, ON, or NO are plotted on a "profit uncertainty graph." This graph is somewhat similar to a graph employed in the decision grid for DEMON.

Profit uncertainty is the difference between total uncertainty (as measured by the variance of profit) with and without the new product. After the calculation of the differential profit is made for each year under the program involving the new product, the value of the maximum total differential profit is then compared to the differential uncertainty to see if the point when plotted on the profit uncertainty graph falls in the GO, ON, or NO area of the quadrant.

The SPRINTER model was run for a large chemical company that had developed a new nylon compound which carried both cost and performance advantages in several significant markets. The product would experience demand interactions with two other products currently being marketed by the firm. The starting point for the data gathering was a description of a specific marketing program that the particular firm and its executives could visualize for the product over the planning period of ten years. This program included the price, advertising and distribution plans for the new and old product and the competitive strategies for these products over the ten year period. It was assumed that execution of the marketing program would result in sales of the new product in each year. The firm's marketing executives supplied estimates for each year and based upon this input, the reference life cycle estimate for the model was drawn. This life cycle estimate was considered the reference point for the determination of the response function of the various parameters contained within the model. All response functions measured the deviations from the reference life cycle estimates produced by changing the variables of price, advertising or distribution.

The simulation technique for SPRINTER began by evaluating the company's proposed marketing plan. Initially, the pricing policy stipulated in the plan was $350.00 per carton for each of the first three years, and $200.00 per carton for the remaining seven years. It was assumed that the sales force allocation for the product would amount to approximately 1 per cent of the cost of the total sales force and, in addition, an incremental $10,000 per year of advertising would be purchased. If evaluated independently, the product, on an economic basis, could generate an incremental profit of approximately $8.5 million. However, the truth was that the product depended significantly upon the inter-action of other products already in the line. Therefore, on a differ-ential basis, the total discounted incremental profits were $6.0 million. The model is telling us that the differential of $2.5 million is, in actuality, a loss of products in the existing line. At this point, the decision would have been to reject the product since the total investment itself for the new product was $8 million. The SPRINTER then went into a trial and error search routine in order to establish a better marketing mix over the life cycle of the product.

In the course of an hour and one-half, SPRINTER evaluated a range of two million marketing programs. In the optimization program, the model recommended a price of $250.00 per carton for the first three years and prices near the $200.00 per carton level for the remaining seven years. On the basis of that mix, the total discounted differential profits accumulated to $10.8 million, an increment of $2.8 million over the total estimated investment. Even then there was not a clear-cut case for accepting the product because the probability of achieving the minimum rate of return was less than the standard of 90 per cent. The final decision made by the model was to add the new product to the line. That deci-sion was made after the variables within the marketing mix were juggled to produce a differential profit of $6 million more than the profit level originally recommended by the company.

The value in this type of demonstration lies not in the fact that SPRINTER was able to render a non-human decision, but in the saving of a vast amount of time which would be required to hand-simulate and calculate the financial implications of the various marketing alternatives.

*NSPM*

NSPM is another planning model which is now used very fre-quently by the clients of Young & Rubicam. The initials stand for a Natural Sales Projection Model. In 1959, Young & Rubi-cam became convinced that major fluctuations in the sales curve of a new product result from a curious combination of predictable activities of consumers in the marketplace. The major emphasis in their logic is based upon the rate at which new purchasers enter the marketplace, the rate of repeat purchasers and the time lag between individual purchases and purchases of comparable quantities. The model has been used somewhat successfully since its creation.

The major advantage of the model in the eyes of its developers is that it permits marketers to plan and to time marketing and promotional activities in order to compensate for disruptive fluctuations on the new products sales chart. Because of the structure of the model, a successful application would result in giving the marketeer the ability to (a) estimate market size and evaluate test market situations for the product (b) assess package design and package sizes (c) calculate payouts from sampling and couponing (d) determine advertising expenditures and frequency and predict long-term effects of change in advertising allocations.

This model, as opposed to DEMON and SPRINTER, comes much closer to the economic intuition of practicing marketing executives. Estimates of market potential for varying time periods contained in marketing plans are frequently calculated as the basis of repeat purchase patterns with factors allowing for the introduction of new users. In this sense, it is compatible with the qualitative logic used in the real world. The basic input to the model includes the answers to such questions as:

a. How many people will try the product?
b. How many of the people will try the product within the first season?
c. How will the acquisitions of these additional layers of purchasers be spaced?
d. What is the average time span between the purchases of products in the product class?
e. When will new layers which are constantly added on actually repeat their original purchase?
f. How much of the product is bought per buying occasion?

There is somewhat of a bias in favor of a media policy in the model. However, its bias is unimportant when considered in the context of the entire marketing mix. For example, media exposure, as a technique, will have a great influence on the rate of acquiring new layers of purchasers. Therefore, changes in media or promotion policy may show up as changes in the rate of entry of new layers of purchasers. The model is designed to aid the new product manager in determining in advance the amount of expenditures which will affect the number of new purchasers that he will get. The model is also somewhat biased in favor of the product brand loyalty theory. The repeat buyer curve is based upon the surprisingly stable return to a product by the consumer. Young & Rubicam found a step-wise decline in the number of those who repurchase a product in each cycle following that in which they first bought.

3. Even though DEMON and SPRINTER are the most complex and have some proven abilities beyond the scope of the simpler models, they do have limitations. The greatest limitation is the scope inherent in the models. They assume that new product ideas are proposed and analyzed one at a time. This may not always be true. In addition, unforeseen difficulties may arise in the timing of new product introductions, simply because one among the new products may become so successful in test marketing that it seems desirable to employ the larger portion of marketing investment funds in that product. This type of situation has recently occurred in the marketing program of one of the major divisions of the General Foods Corporation. The overwhelming success of one of its products which has been on the market for almost two years and the increasing success of a brand new product which has been on the market for approximately six months, has caused a delay in the introductory timetable for a third, very promising, product.

Although SPRINTER can supply differential profit and uncertainty information about each product, the model in its present form cannot select from a group of alternatives unless they are all in the same stage in the information network. The basic limitation of SPRINTER is that although the model specifies the GO, ON, or NO decision, it does not specify what studies to undertake if the ON decision is reached. SPRINTER indicates which relationships are most uncertain but it does not explicitly specify the optimal sequence of marketing research studies.

## Some Observations on Models

It should go without saying that all models are subject to limitations of the input data and the largest single flaw in input data can be found in all human beings: our bias towards optimism and our apparent unwillingness to reason in terms of probabilities. I do not mean to imply by this statement that all of us should suddenly become marketing undertakers. I *am* saying that in evaluating given decision situations we will increasingly be forced to accept a different posture from that of the pure marketing man holed up in his little world of marketing variables. We will, in the future, assume the position of an overall administrative executive concerned with the total impact of a decision upon the company. In addition, we will have to stop giving one-number-answers: this is at the heart of my stated concern about our apparent reluctance to deal in probabilities. As vocalizers we are much too prone to blurt out an intuitive, impulsive, one-number response to quantitative questions. It would be much more logical if we were to begin to think of providing a range of numbers and a *probable* answer within that range.

Another major limitation in the use of the model is their high cost potential. Model building is very expensive; the people who structure the models are highly salaried, and the time to run a machine sophisticated enough to accommodate the programs is still more expensive. The very real and unanswerable question has to be, "Is it all worth it?" Do the large, expensive models actually produce gains significantly higher than simple breakeven analysis?

I think that the answer to that type of question is rooted in two considerations. The first is the caliber of the people within the company and the number of new product introductions being undertaken by the company. In the business world we are currently witnessing a rather dramatic change in the type of business executive who is inhabiting the cloistered office. More frequently now he is the type an individual who has had a basic exposure to quantitative reasoning. If this type of executive is becoming predominate in your firm, I think he stands a good chance of wisely using the new product mathematical model building route.

The entire success of the model program depends upon the willingness of people to accept the concept of models. I believe further that high technology companies can benefit most from the new product simulations, if for no other reason than that the basic training of the better part of their personnel makes them uniquely suited to utilize the decision model.

That company which is in the highly competitive consumer market and which is saddled with the burden of multiple new product introductions at various intervals, may also benefit from model usage, even though the cost may initially appear to be large. After all, the cost of building and using an advance model is typically very small in relationship to the possible cost of making a wrong decision.

The payout potential of investment in marketing operations research can be illustrated by specific instances such as DuPont's ability to predict the sales response to a new advertising campaign within a few percentage points of the actual figures, or General Electric's reported savings resulting from the adoption of a market strategy suggested by a physical distribution simulation.

The food industry, only one segment of the consumer industry, now has sales of about $100 billion. A tremendous amount of waste has taken place in this industry because a rather careless approach to new product strategy. The pursuit of an individual consumer who acts irrationally, at least in the eyes of the manufacturer, has become a type of fun game in which various producers compete to gain his attention. Not only is media selection directed increasingly towards television exposure, but vast amounts of promotional funds are being spent either in the form of virtual bribes to the trade to carry the product on the shelf or to provide direct remittances to the consumer in the form of ostensive price reductions of products. Literally billions of dollars have been spent in an almost blind manner to protect and enhance their franchises. The executive who makes decisions by the seat of his pants will soon wither away along with the last of the pioneers. In his place will be the man who has learned to change and adapt to his new environment, the executive who refuses to become a dinosaur.

## Contemporary Uses of Management Science Techniques in Marketing

One of the phrases currently in wide use is the term *management science*. Its wide use threatens that it will become a cliche at an early age.

It is frequently used interchangeably with the term *operations research*. As defined by Toan it is:

> . . . that discipline, or skill or body of knowledge and experience which believes that it is both possible and valuable to use the techniques and approaches of the scientific method in order to represent most business functions as mathematical models or formulae.
>
> It believes it is practical to obtain useful and realistic values for use in these formulae and to produce answers which will be helpful to managers in planning, controlling and above all, making decisions about their business.[5]

Management science relies heavily on probability, statistics, algebra and calculus. Its use has evolved a variety of techniques. Vatter, in his study, enumerated these as:

Linear or other mathematical programming
Critical path scheduling (pert)
Queuing (waiting-line) models
Economic order size or other inventory models
Simulations
Factor analysis
Regression analysis
Statistical sampling
Other[6]

The Vatter study investigated *where*, within companies, operations research work is done. Significantly, in Table 6 of that study of eighteen departments or combinations of departments, marketing or marketing decision-making is not mentioned, despite the fact that 44 companies (12 per cent of the respondents) were manufacturers of consumer products. This apparent omission of interest in operations research applications for marketing decision-making is entirely consistent with the results of this study.

In the context of asking respondents which techniques were used for *marketing decision-making,* a question was raised about the use status of "other management science techniques." Nine companies didn't use them at all; of those who did use them, the major applications were in new products, sales forecasting, and distribution.

Among the nonusers, the meaningful comments display a combination of poor experience to date, inadequate education of management, and frustration over the inability of individuals to quantify risk and intuition.

Company F said that they have a "sophisticated setup," generally, but not in the marketing area. They consider their role as conservative and noninnovative. "Essentially our role is to keep score and our reports are by-products of the billing and invoice and inventory control systems."

Company G said that they are "not sure how useful they (management science techniques) are. We're really not sophisticated in their use."

Although they don't use it now, Company L said:

> The amount of activity of this type of technique is increasing. CPM is used on construction projects and the planning of other various activities. In other areas, it is also used for production planning, inventory management and distribution methods. It is not yet a sophisticated technique and is in the development stage. Over a period of time, we are convinced that it will become part of the marketing decision making function. "From a personal point of view, I am still skeptical. It simply takes too long to find out whether these techniques will work."

Company Q does not use management science techniques to any great degree (they use exponential smoothing to forecast sales), because of a very poor experience with DEMON.

It was plain from the replies that only a few techniques have achieved a degree of popularity. The replies indicated that they fall into the following categories:

| *Use* | *Technique* |
|---|---|
| New product evaluation | PERT, CPM |
| Sales forecasting | Linear programming, exponential smoothing |
| Purchasing, distribution | Value analysis |
| Warehouse location | Queing |

However, it should not be inferred that the companies have necessarily achieved satisfactory results. For example, Company M said:

> Operations research is used very little within the company. Frankly we have been somewhat disappointed in its results. We have used exponential smoothing techniques to try and forecast sales volume and specific products but this has not been successful. It is also quite expensive to employ a staff of analysts solely to work on these products. My basic objection to the reliance which is placed on these techniques is that in order for operations research to be truly effective, quantitative restraints must be present in any mode. In the real world, qualitative considerations often outweigh the quantitative ones and no model can express that.

Company Q, which, as indicated earlier, uses exponential smoothing to forecast sales, indicated that the effort thus far had not been wholly successful. Competitive actions which are difficult to forecast have directly affected sales projections.

Company K has used PERT in all instances of new product development as a means of proper scheduling. In addition, they employ linear programming to coordinate sales estimates and programming requirements.

Company I uses CPM for new product planning, and exponential smoothing to forecast sales.

Company J, a large company, admitted that management science techniques are used only selectively; their chief use is PERT for new product ventures.

Company N was held up in its applications of management science techniques for marketing because of an inability on the part of its personnel to agree on quantitative constraints and minimum acceptable criteria.

Company P uses venture analysis in the new products and purchasing areas to analyze "all the elements of capital" to be tied up in specific projects.

The replies certainly indicate an awareness of the techniques involved but demonstrably show a serious need for the pre-education of marketing and financial management in the potentials of operations research applications to marketing. It may also be that we have overestimated the tool. In an overview, we have implied that problems are subject to logic and that the variables of the problem are logically subject. In our zeal we may be overlooking this statement by Drucker:

> . . . there are equally important events that cannot be measured. To this comes the fact that the measurable results are things that have happened, they are in the past. There are no "facts" about the future. To this comes secondly that the measurable events are primarily inside events rather than outside events. The important developments on the outside . . . are not measureable until it is to late to have control."[7]

Financial respondents were asked, "Are marketing personnel capable of understanding the implications resulting from answers derived from these techniques (operations research)?"

The consensus of replies was a hesitant affirmative. Some of the replies were particularly interesting because of their insights into management policies.

Company Q said, "Yes; the president of the company, who is an astute individual, embodies the marketing function. He is, in effect, the director of marketing."

Company M said that, by and large, marketing personnel respond to the wishes of general management and that, unfortunately, too many of the marketing men, mostly the older ones, worship the "golden calf of gross profit and volume attainment." They have attempted to overcome the inertia through tactful teaching and, on at least one occasion, held a controller's seminar for marketing personnel to teach them about the implications of financial data and operations research. The author had occasion to speak to a few of the younger marketing men; their comments indicated that they were well satisfied with the efforts of the controller's area to educate them.

Company **P** indicated that their marketing men were well equipped to understand these techniques. "They are anxious to learn. They know that the goal is to maximize profits and per share earnings." It is true that their marketing men are pressured to understand quantitative techniques and results. They are given a general goal of increasing earnings per share by 10% annually. This filters down to the product manager level rapidly and even here there is a minimum required rate of 10% for return on funds employed.

Company **J** indicated that their marketing people needed help, but with the aid of the "marketing services" area (a financial group) they were becoming much more familiar with quantitative data. The two groups are cooperating on a mutual project which will standardize quantitative information. A basic nucleus of five data books is being prepared:

a. Brand Data Book—one for each product manager
b. District Data Book—one for each district sales manager
c. Category Data Book—for merchandising managers and marketing vice presidents
d. Management Committee Data Book—for Management Committee Members
e. Marketing Handbook—all purposes

   (The Category Data Book covers information about general product classifications such as detergents. The Marketing Handbook contains essential market research, trade and demographic data covering company and competitive operations.)

The table of contents for the above five books, which are produced under an automated information system, costing $750 million to develop, are shown in Figures 25 through 25h (see next nine pages).

It should be remembered that these replies were from *financial* respondents. Conversations with younger, lower echelon *marketing* executives gave a distinct impression of impatience with the

## VOLUME 1

**SUMMARY**

B10-1   Summaries—Nielsen and NOP* Data
B10-2   Market Profile—Percent of Consumer Sales by Demographic Groups

**HISTORY**

B20-1   Chart—Consumer Sales and Share of Market Trends; Six-Year History
B20-2   Chart—Share of Market and Merchandising Expenses; Six-Year History
B20-3   Chart—Product Developments; Six-Year History
B20-4   Gross Trading Profit; Ten-Year History
B20-5   Sales Volume; Ten-Year History
B20-6   Chart—Advertising and Promotion Expenses; This and Competitive
              Brands; Three-Year History
B20-7   Sales, Promotions and Gross Trading Profit; Six-Year History

**NOP/NET SALES**

B30-1   NOP by District by Region (Weekly)
B30-2   NOP by Zone by District (Promotion Period)
B30-3   NOP by Size by Zone by District (Promotion Period)
B30-4   NOP per Household and at National Annualized Rates (Semi-Annually)
B30-5   Net Sales by Customer Type (Semi-Annually)

**NIELSEN DATA—MONTHLY—NATIONAL**

B40-1   Shares—and Competitive Brands—Total U.S.
B40-2   Average Weekly Consumer Sales—and Competitive Brands—Total U.S.
B40-3   Cumulative Consumer Sales—and Competitive Brands—Total U.S.
B40-4   Distribution and OOS*—and Competitive Brands—Total U.S.
B40-5   Inter-Relation Among Consumer Sales, Shipment Received by Trade,
              and Trade Inventories

**NIELSEN DATA—BI-MONTHLY—NATIONAL**

B50-1   Consumer Sales and Shares—and Competitive Brands—National
B50-2   Consumer Sales and Shares by District
B50-3   Consumer Shares & Sales by County Size, Store Types
B50-1   Distribution and OOS by District
B50-5   Distribution by County Sizes
B50-6   Distribution by Store Types

TENTATIVE TABLE OF CONTENTS BRAND DATA BOOK COMPANY J

The table of contents shown for a series of Data Books by one of the respondents in the survey is a comprehensive attempt to bring together in one area, the pertinent information of a marketing and financial character in an efforts assist decision makers to make prompt and accurate evaluation. These books were created of great expense to the Company and are part of a fully automated system in which the computer updates information as often as the input is changed.

**Figure 25**

## NIELSEN DATA—INDICES AND TRENDS

B55-1  District Sales Development Indices by District by Quartile
B55-2  District Sales Volume as Per cent of U.S.; District Shares—This Product
       Group
B55-3  Analysis of Current Trend by District by Quartile
B55-4  Chart—Brand Distribution Trends by Store Type and Size
B55-5  Chart—Sales of This Brand and Related Products
B55-6  Chart—Consumer Sales Trend
B55-7  Chart—Sales Trend—Regular vs. Price-Off Packs
B55-8  Chart—Sales by Package Size
B55-9  Chart—Sales and Share Trends by Store Type and Size
B55-10 Chart—District Brand Performance
B55-11 Chart—District Share Trend Summary
B55-12 Chart—Distribution Trends by District
B55-13 Chart—Brand Distribution Summary

## RETAIL INVENTORIES

B60-1  By District by Region
B60-2  By Store Types
B60-3  Chart—Inventory Trends in Retail Stores
B60-4  Chart—Retail Inventory Trends by Product Size and Store Type

## ADVERTISING

B70-1  Advertising Flow Chart
B70-2  Advertising—Annual Plan or MYE
B70-3  Advertising—Two Year Comparison
B70-4  Advertising Calendar (Advertising Activity by Month)
B70-5  Advertising Expenses, Reach and Frequency—Total U.S. (Quarterly)
B70-6  Advertising Expense by District by Region (Annually)
B70-7  Four-Week Reach and Frequency by District by Region (Annually)
B70-8  TV Commercial Test Ratings (Schwerin—OATS)
B70-9  Commercial/Ad Usage (Quarterly)

BRAND DATA BOOK COMPANY J

**Figure 25a**

PROMOTION

B75-1   Promotion Flow Chart
B75-2   Chart—Competitive Promotion Activities by Zone by District
B75-3   Chart—Expenditures for This and Competitive Brands
B75-4   Promotion Calendar
B75-5   Expense Indices by District by Region (Annually)
B75-6   Expense by Type by District by Region (Annually)
B75-7   Chart—Consumer Sales Trends—Regular vs. Price-Off Packs
B75-8   Chart—Effect on Sales of In-Store Offers

PRICES

B80-1   Direct Price List
B80-2     and Competitive Predominant Shelf Prices by District
B80-3     and Competitive Pack Sizes, Weights, Dimensions, and Number of
          Packages Per Case

FINANCIAL

B90-1   Elements of Gross Trading Profit—Total and Per Unit—Four-Year
          Comparison
B90-2   Elements of Gross Trading Profit—Total and Per Unit—Actual vs.
          Plant (Monthly)
B90-3   Gross Trading Profit by District (Annually)
B90-4   Elements of Gross Profit Margin (Semi-Annually)

VOLUME 2

NIELSEN DATA—BY DISTRICT (BI-MONTHLY)

EACH DISTRICT

B100-1 Consumer Sales and Shares—and Competitive Brands
B100-2  Distribution and OOS—and Competitive Brands and Sizes

BRAND DATA BOOK COMPANY J

Figure 25b

SUMMARY
C10-1   Nielsen Summary
C10-2   Share of Market and Consumer Sales—(Company Names)
C10-3   Financial Summary—(Company Names)
C10-4   Advertising and Promotion Expense Summary—(Company Names)

HISTORY
C20-1, 3, 5, 7 Charts—Net Sales and Gross Trading Profit by Sub-Category
C20-2, 4, 6, 8 Charts—Share of Market by Sub-Category for (Company
                    Names)
C20-9   Charts—Long Term Growth Comparison by Sub-Category
C20-10 Market Breakdown by Brand, Sub-Category, and Company

SHARES AND CONSUMER SALES
C30-1   Nielsen Share of Market by Brand and Sub-Category
C30-2   Nielsen Consumer Sales by Brand and Sub-Category (Weekly Averages)

SALES ANALYSES
C40-1   Chart—Sub-Category Sales Trends
C40-2   Chart—Average Weekly Sales Trends
C40-3,4 Chart—Actual vs. Forecast Sales Comparison
C40-5   Total (Company Name) Franchise Trend by District
C40-6   Sales Trends by Store Type and Size
C40-7   Sales Changes by Sub-Category by District

TENTATIVE TABLE OF CONTENTS CATEGORY DATA BOOK COMPANY J

**Figure 25c**

## ADVERTISING AND PROMOTION

C50-1   Chart—Estimated Merchandising Expenditure Level and Trends—
        Total of Major (Company Name) and Competitive Brands
C50-2   Chart—Corporate Merchandising Expenditures—(Company Names)
C50-3   Chart—Corporate Advertising Expenditures—(Company Names)
C50-4   Chart—Advertising Expense Trends—Total of Major (Company Name)
        and Competitive Brands
C50-5   Chart—Advertising Expense Trends by Sub-Category
C50-6   Chart—Merchandising Expense Trends by Sub-Category
C50-7   Merchandising Expense Trends by Major Brand

## IN-STORE OFFERS

C60-1   Chart—In-Store Consumer Offers
C60-2   Chart—In-Store Offer Importance by Sub-Category
C60-3   Chart—Corporate In-Store Consumer Offers—(Company Names)
C60-4   Chart—In-Store Offer Importance—(Company Names)

## NIELSEN PROJECTIONS

C70-1   History and Forecast of Consumer Sales by Sub-Category

## SEASONAL FACTORS

C80-1   Seasonal Indices by Month by Sub-Category
C80-2   Relative Monthly Importance—Month as Percent of Year by Sub-
        Category

## FINANCIAL

C90-1   Elements of Category Gross Trading Profit—Total and Per Unit—Four-
        Year Comparison .
C90-2   Gross Trading Profit Breakdown—(Company Name) Brands
C90-3   Gross Trading Profit Breakdown—(Company Name) Brands

BRAND DATA BOOK COMPANY J

**Figure 25d**

SUMMARY
D10-1   Weekly and Cumulative NOP by Major Product Group (Last Year and This Year)

NIELSEN DATA BY PRODUCT GROUPS
D30a   Nielsen Data—Laundry Detergents
      D30a-1 Consumer Sales and Shares—and Competitive Brands
      D30a-2 Distribution and OOS—and Competitive Brands and Sizes
      D30a-3 Retail Inventories—and Competitive Brands
D30b   Nielsen Data—Light-Duty Liquids
      D30b-1 Consumer Sales and Shares—and Competitive Brands
      D30b-2 Distribution and OOS—and Competitive Brands and Sizes
      D30b-3 Retail Inventories—and Competitive Brands
D30c, etc.   Nielsen Data—Other Product Groups

WEEKLY NOP
D40-1   District Report—Brand Totals
D40-2   Area Report—Brand Totals

PERIOD NOP—DISTRICTS
D50-1   District Report by Brand and Size

PERIOD NOP—ZONES
D60-1   Zone Report by Brand and Size

NET SALES
D80-1   District Report by Zone and Major Product Group

PRIMARY ACCOUNTS
D90-1   Packs Shipped and Not Shipped to Primary Accounts

PRICES
D100-1 Direct Price List
D100-2   and Competitive Chain Store Shelf Prices

SIZES
D110-1 Standard Case Factors, Packed Weights, and Palletization Data

PROMOTIONS
D120-1 Promotion Calendar—Promotion Activity by Brand and Period

ADVERTISING
D130-1 Local Advertising Schedule

LOCAL REPORTS

EXCERPTS FROM MARKETING HANDBOOK

TENTATIVE TABLE OF CONTENTS DISTRICT DATA BOOK COMPANY J

**Figure 25e**

**MAPS**
M10-1   Map of U.S.
M10-2   Zone-District Maps

**POPULATION, INCOME, ETC.**
M20-1   Analysis of Population
M20-2   Analysis of Buying Income
M20-3   Personal Income Trends
M20-4   Shifts in Population and Income
M20-5   Sales Trend—75 Packaged Grocery Commodities
M20-6   Degree of Water Hardness

**POPULATION BY COUNTY**
M30-1   Population by County/Zone

**FOOD STORES**
M40-1   Growth of Large Food Stores
M40-2   U.S. Food Store Trends
M40-3   Food Store "All Commodity" Trends by Store Type and Size
M40-4   Number of Food Stores by Size
M40-5   Food Store Retail Sales

**DRUG STORES**
M50-1   Drug Store "All Commodity" Trends by Store Type and Size
M50-2   Drug Store Retail Sales

**MARKET COVERAGE**
M60-1   National Coverage—Number of Accounts by Type—Total U.S.
M60-2   Regional Coverage—Number of Accounts by Type by Region
M60-3   Zone and District Coverage—Number of Accounts by Type, Zone and
        District

**DISTRIBUTION**
M70-1   Origin of Customer Shipments—Listing of Distribution Centers
        Showing Zones Serviced by Each by Major Product Group
M70-2   Origin of Customer Shipments—Listing of Districts Showing
        Distribution Centers Servicing Each by Major Product Group
M70-3   Customer Warehouse Spillover Indices by Zone

**NOP**
M90-1   Volume Ranking by District by Major Product Group
M90-2   NOP by District and Brand by Major Product Group
M90-3   Percent of Total Brand NOP by District by Major Product Group

**WASHING MACHINE USAGE**
M100-1  Estimated Number of Washing Machines in Use by Type

**INVENTORY ASSESSMENT DATES**
M120-1  Assessment Dates by States

**ZONE DATA**
M130-1  Zone Statistical Data (one page for each zone)

**ZONE CHARACTERISTICS**
M140-1  Zone Characteristics (one page for each zone)

**SOURCES OF MARKETING INFORMATION**

TENTATIVE TABLE OF CONTENTS MARKETING HANDBOOK COMPANY J

Figure 25f

| 010 | | Nielsen Shares |
|-----|-----|-----|
| | 010 | Shares by Category |
| 020 | | NOP |
| | 010 | Weekly NOP by Brand |
| | 020 | Weekly NOP by District |
| | | Separate report for each of Schedules A, B and C. |
| 030 | | Weekly Averages |
| | 010 | Consumer Sales and NOP by Brand |
| | | Separate report for each of Schedules A, B and C. |
| 110 | | Laundry Detergents |
| | 010 | Category Nielsen and NOP Trend |
| | 020 | Category Summary NOP |
| | 030 | Competitive Market Summary |
| | 040 | Financial Summary |
| | 050 | Advertising and Promotion Summary |
| | 060 | Nielsen Shares |
| | 070 | Nielsen Weekly Averages |
| | 080 | Category Summary—Consumer Sales by Brand |
| | | Brands Within Category |
| | 111 | Nielson Data by Brand |
| | 112 | NOP by Brand |
| | 113 | Brand Data—Trading Margins |
| 120 | | Fabric Softeners |
| | | (Some reports as Category 110 above) |
| 130 | | Dishwasher Compound |
| | | (Same reports as above) |
| 140 | | Light Duty Liquids |
| | | (Same reports as above) |
| 210 | | Toilet Bars |
| | | (Same reports as above) |
| 220 | | Dentifrices |
| | | (Same reports as above) |
| 230 | | Toothbrushes |
| | | (Same reports as above) |
| 310 | | Margarines |
| | | (Same reports as above) |
| 320 | | Prepared Shortenings |
| | | (Same reports as above) |
| 330 | | Whipped Toppings |
| | | (Same reports as above) |
| 340 | | Maple Syrup |
| | | (Same reports as above) |

TENTATIVE TABLE OF CONTENTS MANAGEMENT COMMITTEE DATA BOOK COMPANY J

**Figure 25g**

800      Other Brands
   110    NOP Data
   113    Brand Data—Trading Margins
        Note: "Other Brands" will normally not have Nielsen Data reports.
910      Promotion Grids
   010    Brand by Period Grid
        (Separate Report for each Marketing Division)
920      Testing
   010    Test Panel Chart by Brand
        (Separate Report for each Marketing Division)
930      Testing Expenses
   010    Product and Market Testing Expenses
940      Margins
   010    Brand Margins
950      Inventory Write-Offs
   010    Actual and Possible Future Write-Offs
960      Back Orders
   010    Cancellations and Delays Resulting from Shortages
970      Lay-Offs
   010    Plant Lay-Offs of Hourly Paid Employees

MANAGEMENT COMMITTEE DATA BOOK COMPANY J

Figure 25h

older marketing teams in terms of sophisticated financial understanding.

## Decision Making and Mathematical Models

In the pragmatic sense, we are all models. Our heritage and learned responses together with our inherited genetic makeup, almost mandate that we behave in a predictable manner. It is not enough, therefore, for the individual merely to *express* resentment at being identified as a participant in behavioral patterns. Traffic jams develop because too many people are in the same place at the same time. The proper question of each of the individuals caught in the jam should be "Why am I here?" It is probable that each Monday morning and Friday afternoon sees monumental traffic jams either entering or leaving urban complexes. That many cars are involved results from limited accesses or limited exits. However, this is not the explanation for the mass behavioral pattern. What is really important is that after knowing that this event was likely to take place, each of the individuals still participated in the same movement. This type of phenomenon is the essence of the construction of a model of consumer behavior.

A model should be a representation of real alternatives. All mathematical models contain variables, and human behavior is the most important of these. The success or failure of the attempt to make meaningful mathematical models for marketing decisions, will rest upon the ability of the model builder to identify the variables involved in a marketing transaction and further, to apply the relevant correlations to human behavior.

Mathematical models are anathema to the humanist. Ego forces the individual to disclaim a model's ability to simulate the human environment. Because models are quantitative by definition, there is an implicit defensive posture taken, because so much of our business environment is involved in qualitative matters. The challange before mathematical model makers is to separate the qualitative from the quantitative facets and, if possible, to extract even from the qualitative facets, all of its quantitative juice. After all, how can one possibly quantify the virtue of integrity or moral character, two aspects of the business environment which play a major role in many decisions?

If the survival of the human race has been dependent upon the individual's adaptability to changing environmental conditions, then it follows that the profitable survival of corporate organizations lies in their ability to successfully innovate. Few, if any, of the vexing problems which businesses face each day are as intriguing or as complex as those of developing, introducing and profitably marketing new products. The maturing life cycles of many of our well established products require a continual infusion of new and exciting product ideas into the marketplace. Billions of dollars are devoted to the research, development, and marketing of these future products. Despite all the corporate capital, management skill, and sophisticated techniques, many of these products fail at one stage or another between the genesis of a new product idea and the period of national distribution.

It has been recently estimated that by the year 1975, the number of consumer products carried by the average supermarket will increase from the current 7500 items to approximately ten thousand. Of this amount, it is probable that new products will comprise of about one-third. This means that 3300 items on supermarket shelves in 1975 will be new products. The past history of new product attrition has suggested that of approximately 60 new product ideas submitted and worked upon, only one survives. Thus, the 3300 new product items on the supermarket shelves in 1975, represent the end product of approximately 200,000 new product ideas.

Because of the extremely high mortality rate for product ideas, and the difficulty in assessing in advance the technical feasibility of development costs or the realistic market potentials for a product, a new and exciting area of marketing inquiry has emerged. This new area recognizes that failures beyond concept and screening stages could probably be avoided if a more objective analysis and systematic handling of information were accomplished through the use of a mathematical model, a tool which is derived from a framework for organizing arrays of data.

## The Uses of Data Processing in Market Decisions

One of the more interesting revelations in the Dean summation of the Booz, Allen & Hamilton study of the computer[8] is a pie chart illustrating probable future uses of the computer. Finance and administration usage declines sharply from the current estimate of 44% of time usage to a projected 29% three to five years hence. Marketing's usage is expected to increase marginally from 13% to 15%. The above hardly suggests vigorous, dynamic, growth in decision-making methods.

A few years ago, the rash of computer-oriented marketing articles that appeared augured well for marketing. Joseph N. Froomkin, marketing administrator of IBM's Data Processing Division, said, "The only way you're going to be able to do better next year is by analyzing what's happening this year. Eventually, a firm should run a balance sheet by sales territory, calculating profitability of that territory on a weekly, monthly, semi-annual and annual basis. If properly utilized, this can give you profitability, share of market and growth of market, so you can estimate marketing and marketing expense on a viable basis."[9]

The promise of the statement has not yet been realized, perhaps because of deficiencies in the mathematical tools which are the input for the computer. Merle Crawford said it well:

> To date, the marketing department seems to have found mathematics of little assistance, and top management may well be wondering whether the reluctance to use it comes as a result of (1) basic inconsistencies between the new tools and the marketing problems or (2) a built-in reluctance on the part of marketing executives. Stated more congently, is there any justification for the skepticism with which marketing executives seem to be greeting the use of mathematical models?[10]

Crawford felt that the main obstacles were the inability of models to handle creativity and the weaknesses in implicit assumptions for problems. His very telling point is in his discussion of the absurdly, abstruse technical language which has been created.

*Current Usage of EDP in Marketing*

Three areas of computer applications were chosen for investigation in the questioning. Companies were asked, "How does EDP information influence decision-making in the areas of:

    Test marketing simulation
    Media selection
    Customer, geographic profitability?"

The tabulation below shows the neglected application of EDP techniques to marketing:

|  |  |  | Profitability |
| --- | --- | --- | --- |
|  | *Simu-* | *Selec-* | *Customer* |
| *Status* | *lation* | *tion* | *Geographic* |
| Used | 0 | 0 | 4 |
| Not Used | 17 | 20 | 16 |
| In Development | 3 | 0 | 0 |
| Total | $\overline{20}$ | $\overline{20}$ | $\overline{20}$ |

Simulation of *test market results* is an exciting concept but unfortunately, it has not yet reached the stage of active business usage. Experience thus far has not proven its practicality. Company P participated in such a project but was quite dissatisfied with the result. Nevertheless, some companies are actively working on programs of a similar nature.

Company J has a program underway to establish pertinent criteria for test market selection. Company T has a program for simulation now under development and expects to have it completed very shortly.

Company A defended its nonuse of test market simulation by saying that they had achieved the same results with panel studies and selected family sampling. Other companies stated that they felt this to be better adapted to use by big advertising agencies with their large resources for gathering information. However, test marketing is time consuming, often irrelevant and expensive. It also provides fine opportunities for competitors to gain an edge through product copying or ruinous pricing tactics. It has been a rare product that had the temerity to go "national" without test marketing (*Fab with Borax* was one). In any event, it would seem that any effort, however small, to identify and classify variables affecting the marketing effort would be a vehicle for large cost savings.

As a topic, *media selection* generated more interest. This occurred despite the fact that none of the twenty companies had any appropriate EDP programs. Some few expressed the thought that this was really an agency function.

Company C replied:

> No program is in existence to simulate or make decisions for media selection. However, after a selection is made on the basis of judgment and selected criteria, products are grouped into ten categories of audience appeal. In a similar manner, messages are also grouped into ten categories of audience appeal. On the basis of these ratings and their correlation with the type of media, product messages and media are matched.

Company J is assisting their agency in such a project:

> Five ad agencies are currently working with the company to use either their facilities or the company's to select spot TV. It has not yet been determined whether it is feasible to use EDP for optimization of network TV. The project completion is about two to three years away.

Company Q was outspoken about its poor experience with EDP media systems:

> The company, a few years ago, had a disastrous experience when the problem of automated media selection was given to (the advertising agency). The problem which they presented was completely nonacceptable and we subsequently learned that they are still having trouble in applying their formulae to business situations.

Questioning in the area of *customer and geographic profitability* produced mixed responses. Sixteen of them did not keep a continuous track of customer and geographic profitability. Within that group, however, five companies looked at it on an exception basis. The remaining four out of the twenty respondents monitored this action continuously.

Company N evaluates the gross profit of each product line by market and family. To do this they apply a standard cost of sales and allocate corporate overhead to product lines, based on sales importance. In addition, interest is charged on budgeted amounts.

Once a year Company I evaluates geographic profitability on the basis of a minimum of standard geographic profit less distribution costs and field sales expense. They claim that receivables by geographic area tend to be fairly constant. They do have difficulty, however, in measuring inventories because regional distribution centers cross district lines.

Company J does not now specifically use EDP for geographic analysis. They perform breakeven studies for shipment sizes on a selected basis. At present they do not comtemplate specific studies of customer profitability. They do plan to have an interesting information-data bank in operation that will enable them to have the flexibility to accomplish much of the above:

> EDP is now being used to establish a basic data bank for marketing information. In addition to this, selected projects are currently being programmed. One of these, MIDAS, is a system by which marketing information will become available for selected two or more step problem solutions on an overnight basis. Other projects underway, include MRD, which is designed to measure advertising effectiveness and computerization of the annual plan model, designed to permit the company to simulate varying conditions. Approximately one-fifth of the systems and programming staff will be engaged in the organization of marketing data at any one time between 1967 to 1969. This encompasses approximately 22 systems people and about 21 programming personnel. A ballpark estimate of the cost of providing this marketing data, including the running time for the incremental system 360 machine, is about $600 thousand.

EDP has come far and fast, perhaps too fast. Ridley Rhind of McKinsey & Company, commented on this:

> In summary, my message is this: The great power of computers has led many of us—in academic circles, in management, and in the computer systems profession—to dream of and speak of ambitious information systems that are not yet designed or proven; some of us have promised a golden future in which lack

of information will no longer pose a problem, and have at times implied, flatteringly but wrongly, that the major obstacle to perfect management today is a lack of information—and that this can be overcome. All these claims are dangerously misleading. To promise what you cannot deliver may win one election but it does not win favor, especially from practical managers. I do not think that systems men can deliver some of the unproven systems that have been talked about and which some managers now expect; yet, I think they can deliver so much that it is a pity for anyone to be guilty of overselling. The responsibility for judging between the possible and impossible rests with management.[11]

# Chapter VII

# Product Life Cycles and Profitability Analysis[1]

*The Concept of Product Life Cycles*

"The concept of product life cycles is today at about the stage that Copernican view of the universe was 300 years ago; a lot of people knew about it, but hardly anybody seemed to use it in any effective or productive way."[2] Since the concept has been presented somewhat differently by different authors for different audiences, it is useful to review it here as background for later discussion.

The product life cycle concept is a simple one. It has three key elements:

1. *Products Have a Limited Life:* Products move through the cycle of introduction, growth, maturity and decline at varying speeds.
2. *Product Profits Tend to Follow a Predictable Course Through the Life Cycle:* Unit profits climb sharply in the growth phase and during the maturity phase start to decline because of competitive pressures as sales volume continues to rise.
3. *Products Require a Different Marketing, Production and Financial Program in each Stage of the Life Cycle:* The functional emphasis required for succesful product exploitation—engineering and research, manufacturing, market-

ing, and financial control—changes from phase to phase in the cycle as shifts occur in the economics of profitability.

The stages of product life cycle can be classified as follows:

1. Development
2. Growth
3. Maturity
4. Saturation
5. Decline

From management's point of view, during each of these stages, a great deal of varied economic activity takes place which goes into making a product's future, as well as that of the corporation. The specific activity within each of the life cycle stages will vary, depending upon the type of the product, the type of market and many other complex factors, but speaking in general, the trend of the cycle is similar for almost all products.

### Development Stage

Bringing a new product to market is full of uncertainty and risk. Demand has to be created in a process termed by Staudt and Taylor "Cultivation of Primary Demand."[3] While it has been demonstrated many times in past that customer-oriented new product development is one of the primary conditions of sales and profit growth, high costs and frequent fatalities associated with launching new products often occur. In deference to the fatality rate associated with launching new products, many companies adopt a "follow the leader" or "me too" policy. Introduction of new products involves breaking customer habits that discourage response to new products. The market for new products is concentrated among the limited consumer group with high income and individualistic tastes, known as "high mobiles."

By definition, new products have no direct competition, but competitors will enter the market quickly if the product gains acceptance. The first to jump in will be those who use the "follow the leader" or "me to" policy, but at this stage, the number will be smaller than in any other stage except decline. Micro-enzyme pre-soak is a very good example of this stage. Within the first few months of the launching of Colgate's "Axion", there were at least five or six other companies with very similar products.

The market development stage is highlighted by frequent product modifications. New products are usually not free of technical. imperfections. Many times modifications must be made to a "perfect" product to gain wider market acceptance. Occasionally, competitors add product modifications because the originator did not have enough time to study the imperfections.

Production costs and prices tend to be quite high. Mortality rates among new products and uncertainties about the chances of success tend to restrict management from making big capital investments. In other words, some assurance that sales will justify the expenditure is needed, before management will decide to go ahead with mass production. Frequent product modifications also serve as limiting factors in such decisions. High costs often present a difficult marketing problem. It is difficult to decide, for example, whether initial prices should be based on pioneering production costs or on the lower production costs anticipated after sales have increased. A choice has to be made between larger market expansion and a shorter payback period. This choice is further complicated by the elements of uncertainty involved. Characteristically, prices will be higher in this period than in those that follow. Prices will typically show a downward trend in the advanced stage of market development, enhancing the chances of the development of a mass market.

Marketing costs are typically high in this period; the major component is the substantial introductory expense. Sometimes high promotional expenses have to be incurred in order to find space in a retail outlet. Product profit margins tend to be quite low; in fact, many companies incur heavy losses during this stage of the life cycle.

Perhaps the most important characteristic of the market development stage is heavy concentration on stimulation of primary demand. This contrasts to selective demand cultivation, where the manufacturer tries to persuade the customer to prefer his brand to others. In this stage the efforts are directed towards persuading the customer to "try" the product. This may mean "educating" the consumer market in the advantages of the product. Enzyme pre-soaks and free-dried coffee are good examples of this type of marketing effort.

In the market development stage, a product's quality and elasticity characteristics play a most important part. The study conducted by Gosta Mickwitz[4] indicates that various marketing devices tend to follow an order of importance, with media efforts following quality factors, and pricing policy and service considerations follow in order of importance.

The high production and marketing costs, and lower margins may force many companies to follow a more conservative policy. Instead of aspiring to be first to see and seize an opportunity, they systematically avoid early entry, and let others do the pioneering. When the product is finally modified and gains acceptance, they jump into the market. Even patent protection means little; the copying firms know that they can enjoy a substantial share of the innovator's market before the lengthy litigation can stop them. By then, the product might have spent its life. In desperation, many companies have found it wise to license these companies before they can copy, hoping at least to collect some royalties.

As viewed by Dr. Robert D. Buzzell,[5] the market developing stage is characterized by a very slow growth in sales, and this is attributed to some combination of four possible causes:

1. Delays in expansion of production capacity
2. Technical problems, i.e., "working out the bugs"
3. Delays in making the product available to the customers, especially in obtaining adequate distribution through retail outlets
4. Customer inertia, arising primarily from reluctance to change established behavior patterns.

### Growth Stage

Having survived the introductory stage and having gained widespread buyer approval, the company faces the problem of producing enough to meet the skyrocketing demand. This is a period of high and sharply rising profits. A rise in consumer demand gives an upward surge to the sales curve. At this point, potential competitors, who have been watching the development, enter the picture. Some enter the market with an exact copy of the originator's product, others add functional and design improvements.

Product and brand differentiation begins to develop. Differentiation attempts to get the customer to "prefer" a particular brand. This calls for an important shift in the marketing strategy. Managerial emphasis is placed on large scale production. Many products have languished in the growth phase because technical research divisions reworked the product designs so extensively that competitors had jumped the market by the time "in-business" production got under way.[6]

In the growth stage, sales rise rapidly and often increase at an accelerating rate. At this point, product sales throughout the industry rise very sharply, a clear indication of a growth market. The product no longer is used by the "mobile" group only. Its exposure becomes so extensive that the use of the product becomes widespread. With the development of a mass market, the manufacturers have to shift their marketing strategy significantly. Acceleration in consumer acceptance is so rapid that it is easy to open new distribution and retail outlets. This rise in market acceptance is attributable to softening prices, major product improvements, greater product reliability, and increased competition.

This stage generates a great influx of competitors. Duplication of the originator's product by competitors is not uncommon. Many manufacturers add design features to make their product more attractive.

Emphasis on production is paramount in this stage. Market growth reduces the risk to a point where management can justify a large investment in mass production. Economies of scale result in a reduction of unit production costs.

Large scale production, fewer product modifications, efficient production techniques and increased pressures from competition tend to force the price level to a more realistic level. With the growth of the market and the increase in the number of producers, the number of distribution outlets rises rapidly and there is a scramble for acquisition of outlets by the producers. At this stage, the manufacturers begin to create a product image, e.g., quality product, price product, etc. Retailers tend to adopt "multiple-lines" policies and may carry many brands of a same product.

With the market acceptance of the product class and the increase in the number of direct competitors, manufacturers begin to emphasize the stimulation of selective demand. Product and brand differentiation trends become evident. This normally requires important changes in marketing strategies and methods.

The product is now best able to resist the adverse effects of a downward trend in the general economy. Sales can weather major economic and other disturbances with relatively little effect on growth; price reductions and product changes may be required to keep the product within the prevailing levels of purchasing power.

A study conducted by Dr. Buzzell in 1966 gives a classical example of a product in the growth stage. Powdered coffee creamers were introduced in the early 1950's. Until 1961, only one brand (Pream) was sold through retail food stores. The growth in demand was very slow until 1962, when a second brand was introduced with aggressive promotion by a major national food processing company. A few other major competitors have since entered the field, and the demand for the product has been rising ever since.

The Mickwitz study indicated that in the growth stage, advertising surpasses quality as a primary influence. Quality moves a step downward in importance followed by pricing policy and service.

### Maturity Stage

This stage, sometimes called the "turbulence" stage, exhibits a peak in sales and profit margins, and the beginning of a *decline* in profit margins. Competition is intense and only the most vigorous enterprises are capable of remaining in the market. The most important characteristics of this stage are a leveling of market growth and a change in product policy. Distribution outlets tend to alter their approaches and the general nature of the marketing effort shifts.

The rate of sales growth gradually levels off and slowly begins to decline, although the aggregate sales may continue to rise at a decreasing rate. All of the market segments at which the product was directed have been reached and the initial demand satisfied. In this stage the product is usually sold to the mass market. Purchases are made primarily by middle and lower income groups. New families dominate the customer base. This creates a cycle within a cycle; there is a sudden product awareness on the part of the new families similar to that of the original consumers in the later part of the development and growth stages.[7]

The forces motivating the purchaser change as well. Price, for example, may be much more important than it was in the earlier stages. At this point, all competitive products are reliable and there is less of a basis for differentiation. The laundry detergent market provides good examples of products at this stage of the life cycle. Practically all products are similar in content, with some very small additive differences. Price competition becomes intense, and attempts to achieve and hold brand preference now involve making increasingly subtle differentiations in the product and in customer service. Promotional practices tend to emphasize psychic distinctions. "Put a Tiger in Your Tank" or the very commonly used "You Get Something Extra" slogans capitalize on this type of differentiation.

In the durable goods market, model changes become more stylized and design-oriented and less oriented to technical improvements. This stage is also characterized by what is known popularly as "planned obsolescence," a strategy which has often been criticized as unfair to the consumer. Nevertheless, it has become a part of our marketing philosophy and does have some advantages if applied diligently and cautiously. This is a strategy often used by automobile manufacturers.

During this period "trade-ins" begin to appear. The increasing age of the earlier products and the introduction of new models promote a growing volume of trade-ins. Manufacturers not only introduce new models, but may broaden their line to more effectively reach various segments of market demand. As the product ages, the requirements for service and parts increase. The policies of some manufacturers demand a large stock of parts, and the variety of brands handled by the dealers make the management of parts inventories more difficult.

Dealer gross margins and profits decline pressures or cost and/or revenue factors begin to squeeze profits. On one hand, the effective price that the dealer can charge for the product declines. This reduction results from increasing price competition on new units and from trade-in allowances. In addition, the introduction of annual models leads to carryovers of year-end inventories, and substantial price discounts for the carryovers. Distribution outlets are often forced to reduce prices without corresponding cost reductions.

To offset the pressures on profits, dealers offer fewer brands and become more selective in manufacturer representation. Institutional brand preference among customers strengthens during this period because as smaller firms are forced out from the market, the larger manufacturers offer more assurance of good service and adequate supplies of spare parts. The strengthening of institutional brand preference, therefore, handicaps smaller firms and gives larger firms a competitive advantage.

The increase in institutional brand preference, the need to provide product services and parts, the pressures to reduce prices during this stage, and inability to distribute the products makes it very difficult for the smaller firms to survive. The decline in the number of competitors is sudden. The position of the small firms shifts dramatically from strength during the development and acceptance stages to struggle for survival during this stage. The altered competitive environment requires many changes in the character of marketing efforts. Only those firms that are willing and able to adjust can hope to survive.

Since most of the products are comparable in form and reliability, price becomes an important key to preference. The Mickwitz study lists, in order of importance, the influences that affect sales during this stage. They are price, advertising, quality and service.

### Saturation Stage

This stage is characterized by the dominance of replacement sales, which creates market conditions altogether different from those of previous stages of the life cycle. This is the beginning of product degeneration. The length of time necessary to reach this stage may vary from product to product. Joel Dean observed that the rate of product degeneration is governed by technical change, the rate of market acceptance, and the ease of competitive entry.[8]

In this stage, the number of first-time purchasers are few, especially for durable goods. The total of first-time purchases may depend upon the numbers of marriages, births, and new housing starts. The decline in initial purchases is relatively slow and stable. In some cases, the trend may be reversed, depending upon the ability of the marketer to promote the idea of multi-purchases of the product. T.V., radios, and a "two-car" family have been promoted in this fashion.

Once the basic demand of customers has been met, they become more discriminating, and the manufacturers have to offer varieties of the same product to satisfy the self-images of the market. Thus, market segmentation and also planned obsolescence become a major strategies. Because the company must manufacture many different product varieties, their unit cost of production rises. In this stage, manufacturers cannot hope to survive if their cost structure does not allow competitive prices.

Profit margins and the rates of return on the investment decline; advertising and promotional expenditures have to be maintained at a high level to keep the product alive in face of the proliferation of competition.

Sales volume, although declining in the aggregate, depends heavily on the strength of distribution outlets. It is important that manufacurers carefully select properly located outlets. A number of manufacturers move their products exclusively on a franchised dealership basis. Many will depart from the traditional outlets and will experiment with new modes of distribution. Television sets, for example, are now sold in channels broadened considerably from the traditional outlets of appliance and department stores.

Since most of the semi-efficient manufacturers have been driven out of the market in an earlier stage of the cycle, this stage consists of only a few efficient manufacturers. These established firms have already achieved the large sales volume and economies of scale that make low unit costs possible. Competition at this stage is stable, and the stability erects very high entry barriers to potential competitors. New entrants are not likely to achieve sufficient sales volume in the mature market to give them competitive cost advantages. Brand preferences are difficult to break, and efficient outlet systems difficult to establish. All of this adds up to a high entry restriction. At this stage, it is incumbent upon the manufacturers to consider alternative investment opportunities in the face of a falling rate of return on the existing product. The Mickwitz study reports that once again various marketing devices are resequenced, as follows: quality, advertising, service and, price.

### Declining Stage

This is also called the obsolescence stage, because competitive innovations render the product obsolete and the market declines. In this stage, there is an absolute drop in the industry sales. The rate of decline is governed by the speed with which new substitutes or improved products gain market acceptance. Technical changes cause a more abrupt decline in sales than is caused by a change in consumer habits.

Perhaps the most important feature in this stage is "demand erosion." Eventually, there is only a small core of customers, and the demand for the product tends to return to original levels. As the product reverts to the "core" market, product lines tend to be greatly simplified and the number of varieties is reduced. Manufacturers tend to rely upon product differentiation for capturing what little market remains.

The market, in this stage, is characterized by conditions similar to those that existed in the market development stage: the industry faces indirect competition, and marketing efforts tend to return to the stimulation of primary demand in an effort to slow down the decline in market size. Advertising and promotional expenses are reduced substantially. Advertising is directed towards the core market instead of mass market, as in the earliest stages. The product is regarded as a specialty by the remaining buyers; its purchase may require some inconvenience.

Manufacturers will manipulate prices to maintain their market position. Prices will decline slightly and then stabilize. Finally, an upward movement may be observed. However, any price decline is only a short-term defensive move on the part of the manufacturer. In the later stages of market obsolescence, the demand is relatively inelastic and hence, price changes have very little effect on sales. This gives manufacturers an opportunity to raise their prices slightly, thus passing on any increases in cost to the consumers without experiencing a negative effect on sales.

The number of producers dwindles to a very few. Even though many manufacturers withdraw, the remaining market can support a limited number of firms. Profit opportunities for surviving firms can be quite attractive in the later phase of this stage because of the inelastic demand. Typically, the surviving companies are often smaller, specialized firms.

The Mickwitz study found that at this stage of the life cycle, advertising exerts the greatest influence on the product market, followed by service, quality and price.

Some companies will introduce new products or attempt to make major technological improvements in the old product. Although recycling or market extension efforts begin to take shape during the maturity or saturation stage, it is often possible to rejuvenate the product even at this stage. Unfortunately, many companies simply struggle to hold on by trying different marketing techniques until they are forced out of business. Only if they have a new product development program, a recycling plan, a product performance review, and a termination program that are all effective, can a firm expect to get the maximum possible return.

## Preplanning the Market Extension Strategy

It is safe to assume that by the end of the decline stage, the product has run its initial course. But it need not be the end of a product's life; it is possible to take further steps to rejuvenate the product. These are termed recycling or regenerating efforts and result from a set of future strategies outlined *before* the introduction of the product; these are implemented as the need for recycling becomes apparent.

The advantages of preplanning the market extension strategies should be obvious. A study conducted by A. C. Nielsen Company[9] recommended incorporating a "ready plan" into a new brand's marketing strategy right from the beginning. Of course, a rigid and inflexible strategy would be of little value. The plan should be sufficiently flexible to incorporate the knowledge gained during the product's initial periods on the market.

Market extension strategies include:

1. Promoting more frequent usage of the product among its current users.
2. Developing a more varied usage of the product among current users.
3. Creating new users for the product by expanding the market.
4. Finding new uses for the basic material.

Planning for new life-extending efforts at the pre-introduction stage can be extremely beneficial:

> . . . *It Results in Active Rather than Reactive Product Policy.* A company's long-term marketing and product development programs are systematically structured under this technique. These preplanned recycling efforts enforce a systematic analysis of strategies that could be used by competition and of possible changes in consumer reaction to the product.
>
> . . . *It Adds Precision to the Total Marketing Plan.* These rejuvenating efforts not only maximize the effectiveness of the total marketing efforts but add a degree of precision. This results in a long-term plan designed to infuse new life in the product with an astonishing degree of accuracy. Many such marketing decisions are made without regard to their relationship to each other, to the timing of optimum consumer readiness, or to the peak competitive effectiveness. Careful advanced planning, long before such plans are put to practice, can help to assure that these activities are appropriate to the situation.
>
> . . . *It Broadens the Scope of a Firm's Activities.* As discussed earlier, enlarging the scope and outlook of the company's area

of activity is of critical importance. Many industries have failed to reach their potential because of a narrow management outlook. Preplanning helps the company to look ahead, and to take into account the future developments in their product field. All possible developments, from one extreme to the other, should be evaluated. Once limited to the cellophane tape business, preplanning made 3M Company an expert in bonding things to other things. This lead to the development of scores of profitable products, including magnetic recording tapes (bonding electron-sensitive materials to polyester tape), and "Thermo-Fax" duplicating equipment and supplies (bonding heat-reactive materials to paper). Currently 3M is developing electro-static copiers (bonding electron sensitive material to paper).

Thus, it should be clear that new product strategy must take into account future possibilities and should try to project the future competitive market environment. While projection is always hazardous and seldom very accurate, it is usually preferable to no prediction attempts at all. Every business decision inescapably involves some degree of prediction about the future. Thus, if preplanning results in offensive rather than defensive or reactive product strategies, such plans will include a provision for a times sequence of conditional moves, flexible enough to incorporate any subsequent developments.

## Recent Research in This Area

In 1968, the *Nielsen Researcher* contained an article which quietly explored the concept and implications of product life cycles. It is an important study because most previous life cycle analyses had been theoretical in nature. In this study, Nielsen approached the problem in terms of market shares instead of physical volume as a measure of a product's velocity. The Researchers studied 275 Lever Brothers brands of consumer products from 37 product classes. All products had been sold through grocery outlets between 1961–1966. New terms introduced to product life cycle analysis by the report included *primary cycles, recycles, prolonged cycles* and *incomplete cycles*. The latter two are defined in the study as follows:

The term *prolonged cycle* was applicable to brands, introduced prior to 1961, that were experiencing protracted trends in the same direction during most of the five years under study. Here, the recycling efforts were not clearly discernible in the long-term improved trend or "upcycles," or long-term declining trends labeled "down-cycles." *Incomplete* life cycles referred to new brands introduced in late 1965 or afterwards, as well as to brands that had entered a recycle phase but had not completed it by mid-1966. Since the data for history was insufficient, these brands were excluded from the study.

The objective of the study was to note and describe the various characteristics of stages of the life cycle, to measure duration, and to observe variations in the life cycle pattern due to type of product.

The whole study was expressed in terms of market share. Amount or size of share achieved were not taken into consideration except in determining outright failures, because of the vast differences in the product classes studied. Bi-monthly share trends of all the products studied was the basic source of data. In addition, the Nielsen Food Index for 35 product categories was used.

## The Findings of the Study

Results showed that almost half of the brands reached their peak and started to weaken in two years or less. Another 37% passed the point of maximum growth in less than 3 years and only 15% of the new brands continued to grow three years after their introduction.

When the length of primary cycle was separated by product type, definite differences in average duration were observed. Health and beauty aids exhibited slightly longer cycles than household products. Food products had the shortest cycle.

Over the five-year period, the number of new brands increased significantly; the introductions in 1965 doubled those of 1961. However, the life expectancy (i.e., primary cycle length) almost halved between 1961 and 1964 from approximately 3 years to 18 months.

The most important factor influencing the closing of the primary cycle was the introduction of new competitive brands. In 12% of the cases, the termination was due to the manufacturer's action, or lack of it. Competitive action in some form ended 72% of the primary cycles.

Attempts to invigorate established brands increased the product's life by a shorter period than that of the primary cycle, averaging slightly more than a year. On a composite basis, recycle length for 62% of the brands ranged from only 10 to 20 months. It was noticed that there were some differences in the length of recycles when segregated by product type, but in terms of an average for all products, the differences were insignificant. In addition, the study found that the average length of a recycle for any product was about 16 months. Even the recycles, however, appeared to be declining in length during the five-year study period.

## Some Practical Conclusions

The practical value of these observations could be startling for many marketing executives. The findings reveal that the primary cycles of 275 brands, within various types, averaged slightly longer than two years. The initial recycling efforts tended to extend the life of the product, but by just over a year. In other words, within the short span of three years, an average consumer product would have run its stage of development, growth, maturity, saturation and decline.

The short life span of new products could be a tribute to the vigor of free competition, but it inevitably means a harder life for concerned marketing executives. Many firms often surrender to price cuts, or even losses on a new product that is quickly copied or improved, and even the copier frequently cannot recover the expense of tooling and production before the product succumbs. The race to get to the consumer first has forced companies to shorten their product development time. In some cases, this has resulted in inefficient use of marketing resources, and research and development funds. These observations should give pause to any executive concerned with not only the efficient use of research and development funds but also with the effectiveness of total marketing efforts.

Recycling is a unique technique that differs from the basic primary cycle strategy. In 60% of the cases studied, recycling efforts were made either in the form of additional advertising expenditures, a change in copy, or some combination of both. In the remaining 40% of the recycles, the advertising effort was keyed to product improvement or innovation. Regardless of the vehicle for the recycle, the length of improvement achieved varied only slightly.

This process invariably required substantial expenditures in time, effort, and money; even then the odds for holding the share of an established brand over a five-year period were found to be only 50–50. As an alternative, in the case of brands in prolonged cycles, where little or no recycling efforts were made, the odds for holding the share of the brand's market were reduced to one chance in eight. This clearly establishes the importance of recycling, in one form or other, as an instrument to increase or at least hold the competitive share of the brand's market.

The conclusions of the Nielsen study may be summarized as follows:

1. It is critical that a "ready plan" be included in brand strategy right from the beginning, to anticipate the infusion effort that will almost certainly be required after the initial two years of the product's life. These plans should include alternatives sufficiently flexible to incorporate the knowledge gained during the brand's initial period on the market. This will enable the product to meet and survive the challenges of the competitive environment.

2. Once past the first cycle, new recycle plans will be needed more frequently and the time available to formulate these plans will become shorter. This imposes an even greater obligation on the planner to establish a follow-up system which sets a "due" date for the next plan or change in marketing strategy at least once each year.

*A Technique for Segregating Product Profits on the Basis of Product Life Cycle Concept*

To illustrate the technique we may take any brand from a general product category, e.g., any brand of food product. The aggregate contribution of any one of these brands to corporate profits can be substantial and may form a major part of total corporate sales. The importance of segregation of the profits into life cycle stages, lies in the area of proper allocation of marketing resources. Often, profit planning tends to disregard many important factors and may be biased by subjective human judgments. A product manager's personal feelings about his product may cause him to overlook the fact that his product is mature or declining, and that it might have a very limited remaining profitable life. He may regard his decision to carry the product in the mix as a measure of loyalty to the brand. Using life cycle concepts in profit planning helps optimum utilization of scarce corporate resources because this technique will not function unless long-term considerations have been integrated in the analysis.

Without questioning the value of the traditional concept of "Net Annual Profits," I think it is important that these "net annual profits" take into account the risk factors involved: What is the weighting in the product mix? . . . . How long can we expect this flow of profits? . . . . How much do growth products contribute to profits? . . . . How much do mature and declining products? . . . . What is the nature of the risk entailed in each life cycle category?

*Weighting the Product Mix*

The consumption of evaporated milk has been declining at approximately 3% per year since 1964, primarily because of the development of substitute products including prepared infant formula, non-fat dry milk and powdered coffee creamers. A major national food processing company like Borden produces evaporated milk; Borden also produces powdered coffee creamers and promotes it aggressively. The demand has been rising rapidly since 1963. Both the volume and profits indicate a very encouraging future. The comparison of the futures of the two products suggests that, today, a dollar of profit derived from the sale of evaporated milk does not have the same value to the company as a dollar of profit derived from the sale of powdered coffee creamer.

The crux of the problem of segregating profits into life cycle stages lies in using aggregate data, i.e., finding a consistent correlative base average for comparison. For example, there is a fairly close statistical co-relation between birth-rates and consumption of prepared infant formulas, or between disposable personal income and consumer spending for food. Similarly, there is a very close relationship between sale of gasoline and rate of new car registrations.

If the growth in the birth rate is 2%, then a manufacturer of prepared infant food can logically assume that his is a growth product if volume increases faster than the birth rate. Similarly, it will be reasonable to consider a product as mature if the growth rate is parallel to the rate of increase in the correlative base. According to the study conducted by Dr. Robert D. Buzzell, packaged dessert mixes fall under this category. Since 1954, there has been virtually no change in sales, price, advertising, etc.

Further, a manufacturer might consider that his product is declining if its growth does not equal or exceed the associated statistical base. The above illustrates, of course, only one of the simplified techniques for establishing the source of profits as expressed in terms of life cycle stages.

Another technique analyzes marketing expenditures and rate per unit of marketing expenditures over the life of a product. Similarly, stability of market share or simple intuition and observation may form a basis for segregating profits into life cycle stages. Again, one might analyze marketing expenditures and identify the product's stage of its life cycle through the use of empirical observations based upon the conclusions reached in the Mickwitz study. Detailed statistical analyses can permit an examination of the intensity of various external forces, such as advertising, quality, price, service, etc., on a product's performance. Comparison of the relative intensity of these factors can help to separate product characteristics into life cycle stages.

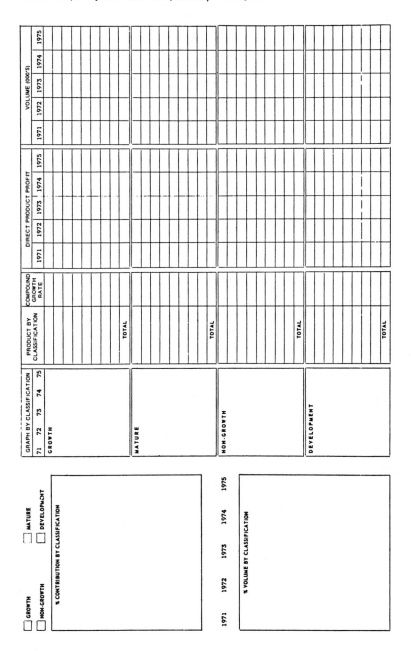

Figure 26.  Product Life Cycle Worksheet

Figure 26 is an illustration of the basic worksheet that can be effectively used to evaluate the quality and the risk factors inherent in profits.

Assume that a hypothetical company, "Pearl Products, Inc.," has a product line which ranges from A to M, and, further assume that it has reached a point where the annual marketing plan, which covers the current and subsequent four years, has been developed. In addition to the regular marketing plan, "Plan A," an alternative plan, "B," has also been developed. The hypothetical profit and volume data in each of the plans is shown in Exhibits E and F. Here, it is necessary to deviate from normal accounting practices and include the concept of relevant costing within the framework of our profit plan. With the inclusion of relevant costing we can derive direct profits. Thus, profit figures in Exhibits E and F are *direct* profits based on direct costing principles. Exhibits G and H show the incremental prospects for each product as contained in the profit plan. It is important to point out the peculiar characteristics of Product J, which shows a tremendous increase in sales from year 1971 to 1972 but suddenly drops off in 1973, and then disappears from view altogether. At this stage, it is also worthwhile to note the different volume performances of the products in Plan A as compared to Plan B. Exhibits I and J build up the concept of life cycle segregation by summarizing some hypothetical product types, together with the relevant bases for comparison of each product type.

Growth rates of the relevant bases form the foundation for segregation of products into life cycle stages. These growth rates are shown, together with the average annual growth rate of the product's volume performance, to facilitate the classification. Here I differ from the Nielsen approach, which classifies life cycle phases on the basis of market share. The market share approach does not take into account the *potential* market but takes into account only the *existing* market share.

To bring our hypothetical example closer to reality, some particular product problems which cause changes in the characterics of performance, have been introduced. Attempts are made to present a wide range of products with real life product performance problems. Product J is worth noting. The volume in-

# EXHIBIT E
## PEARL PRODUCTS, INC., MARKETING PLAN, 1971–1975
### Plan A

| Product | Direct Profits $(000's) | | | | | Volume (000's Units) | | | | |
|---|---|---|---|---|---|---|---|---|---|---|
| | 1971 | 1972 | 1973 | 1974 | 1975 | 1971 | 1972 | 1973 | 1974 | 1975 |
| A | 3,000 | 3,000 | 3,500 | 4,000 | 5,800 | 30,500 | 31,800 | 33,050 | 34,950 | 35,850 |
| B | 4,500 | 3,300 | 4,400 | 8,000 | 8,900 | 15,000 | 22,850 | 28,500 | 32,700 | 39,000 |
| C | 8,500 | 9,400 | 10,800 | 12,000 | 13,000 | 60,000 | 63,830 | 76,710 | 82,150 | 85,200 |
| D | 900 | 1,000 | 950 | 1,100 | 1,400 | 8,000 | 10,650 | 11,630 | 12,100 | 12,800 |
| E | 2,000 | 1,800 | 2,000 | 2,000 | 2,500 | 25,000 | 21,310 | 18,850 | 15,510 | 14,500 |
| F | 250 | 600 | 1,500 | 2,500 | 4,000 | 5,000 | 7,880 | 9,220 | 11,100 | 12,100 |
| G | 1,500 | 1,300 | 1,200 | 1,150 | 1,100 | 8,500 | 7,900 | 7,250 | 7,080 | 6,970 |
| H | 900 | 850 | 810 | 810 | 750 | 12,000 | 11,800 | 11,350 | 10,900 | 10,320 |
| I | 3,000 | 3,000 | 3,100 | 3,500 | 3,900 | 28,000 | 27,950 | 27,800 | 27,520 | 27,440 |
| J | 6,000 | 12,000 | (7,500) | — | — | 7,000 | 17,500 | 6,950 | — | — |
| K | — | (500) | 200 | 250 | 300 | — | 1,100 | 2,500 | 2,500 | 4,900 |
| L | — | — | (1,000) | (500) | 500 | — | — | 900 | 1,600 | 3,000 |
| M | 1,500 | 1,300 | 800 | 1,200 | 1,400 | 11,000 | 11,000 | 14,000 | 16,000 | 18,000 |

# EXHIBIT F
## PEARL PRODUCTS, INC., MARKETING PLAN, 1971–1975
### Plan B

| Product | Direct Profits $(000's) | | | | | Volume (000's Units) | | | | |
|---|---|---|---|---|---|---|---|---|---|---|
| | 1971 | 1972 | 1973 | 1974 | 1975 | 1971 | 1972 | 1973 | 1974 | 1975 |
| A | 3,000 | 3,000 | 3,500 | 4,000 | 6,000 | 30,500 | 32,800 | 35,600 | 37,400 | 38,430 |
| B | 4,500 | 3,300 | 4,500 | 4,300 | 9,300 | 15,000 | 22,850 | 29,500 | 34,500 | 39,000 |
| C | 8,500 | 9,400 | 10,800 | 12,000 | 13,000 | 60,000 | 65,500 | 76,750 | 81,000 | 85,200 |
| D | 1,000 | 1,000 | 1,500 | 1,000 | 1,500 | 8,000 | 9,850 | 11,550 | 12,250 | 12,960 |
| E | 2,250 | 1,800 | 3,000 | 3,000 | 3,500 | 25,000 | 19,900 | 14,850 | 12,000 | 10,000 |
| F | 200 | 700 | 1,500 | 1,600 | 5,000 | 5,000 | 8,850 | 9,670 | 10,500 | 10,000 |
| G | 1,900 | 1,800 | 1,500 | 1,650 | 1,600 | 8,500 | 7,100 | 6,850 | 6,160 | 5,810 |
| H | 900 | 950 | 1,000 | 1,000 | 1,500 | 12,000 | 11,150 | 10,500 | 9,880 | 9,360 |
| I | 3,500 | 4,000 | 3,800 | 5,200 | 5,200 | 28,000 | 27,380 | 26,950 | 26,490 | 26,320 |
| J | 7,000 | 12,000 | (5,000) | (500) | — | 7,000 | 18,500 | 8,900 | 3,500 | — |
| K | — | (500) | 100 | 200 | 300 | — | 1,100 | 2,500 | 2,600 | 4,900 |
| L | — | — | (1,000) | (500) | (50) | — | — | 900 | 1,500 | 3,000 |
| M | 1,500 | 1,450 | 1,700 | 1,900 | 2,100 | 11,000 | 11,100 | 12,000 | 13,000 | 14,000 |

EXHIBIT G

PRODUCT LIFE CYCLE PLANNING DATA

Plan B, 1971–1975

| Product | Type | Relevant Base | Growth Rate of Base (average annual %) | Product Growth (average annual %) | Life Cycle Classification |
|---------|------|---------------|----------------------------------------|-----------------------------------|---------------------------|
| A | Ground coffee | Ground coffee | 1.00 | 6.50 | Growth |
| B | Powdered coffee creamer | Powdered creamers | 18.20 | 40.00 | Growth |
| C | Instant cocoa | Sweetened cocoa | 11.00 | 10.50 | Mature |
| D | Dessert syrup | Sugar syrups | 16.60 | 15.50 | Mature |
| E | Bleaching agents | Laundry aids | (8.70) | (15.00) | Non-growth |
| F | Frozen dessert topping | Dessert topping | 15.00 | 35.00 | Growth |
| G | Gelatin | Gelatin desserts | (3.50) | (8.50) | Non-growth |
| H | Spray starch | Laundry aids | (1.30) | (5.50) | Non-growth |
| I | Bread | Population growth | 1.10 | (1.50) | Non-growth |
| J | Fruit drinks | Retail beverage mkt. | — | — | Growth/Non-growth |
| K | Frozen entrees | Frozen foods | — | — | Development |
| L | Peanut spreads | Jams, jellies | — | — | Development |
| M | Baby foods | Birth rate | .50 | (6.80) | Non-growth |

207

# EXHIBIT H

## PRODUCT LIFE CYCLE PLANNING DATA

### Plan A, 1971–1975

| Product | Type | Relevant Base | Growth Rate of Base (average annual %) | Product Growth (average annual %) | Life Cycle Classification |
|---|---|---|---|---|---|
| A | Ground coffee | Ground coffee | 1.00 | 4.50 | Growth |
| B | Powdered coffee creamer | Powdered creamers | 18.20 | 40.00 | Growth |
| C | Instant cocoa | Sweetened cocoa | 11.00 | 10.50 | Mature |
| D | Dessert syrups | Sugar syrups | 16.60 | 15.00 | Mature |
| E | Bleaching agents | Laundry aids | (8.70) | (10.50) | Non-growth |
| F | Frozen dessert topping | Dessert toppings | 15.00 | 35.50 | Growth |
| G | Gelatins | Gelatin desserts | (3.50) | (5.50) | Non-growth |
| H | Spray starch | Laundry aids | (1.30) | (3.50) | Non-growth |
| I | Bread | Population growth | 1.10 | (0.50) | Non-growth |
| J | Fruit drinks | Retail beverage mkt. | — | — | Growth/Non-growth |
| K | Frozen entrees | Frozen foods | — | — | Development |
| L | Peanut spreads | Jams, jellies | — | — | Development |
| M | Baby foods | Birth rate | .50 | 0.10 to 21.00 | Mature/growth |

208

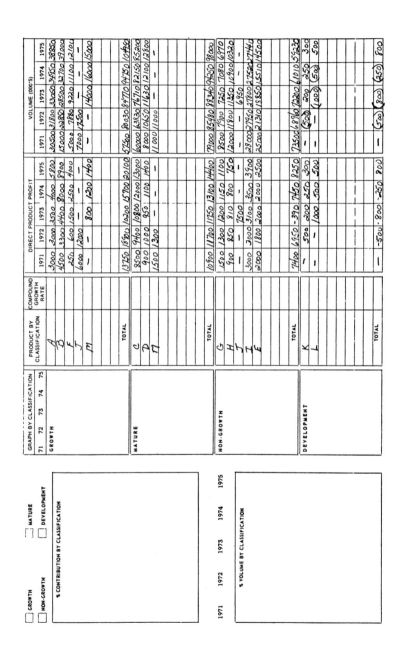

Figure 27. Completed Product Life Cycle Worksheet (Plan A)

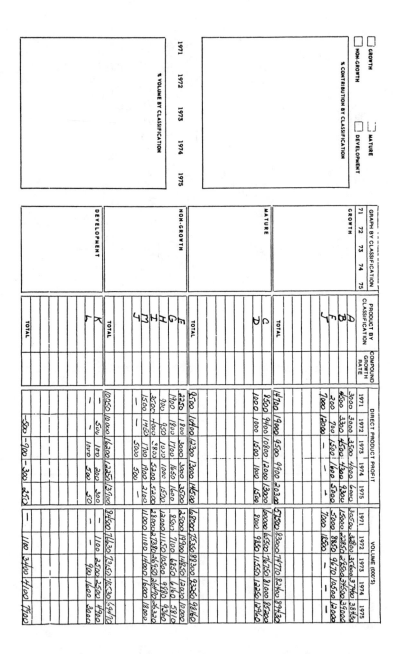

Figure 28.  Completed Product Life Cycle Worksheet (Plan B)

creases from 7,000 units in 1971 to 17,500 units in 1972, then drops markedly back to 6,950 units, and then disappears. This is a classic pattern of new product introduction. A new product frequently requires substantial marketing investment. At a point there may not be sufficient demand to move the product from the shelves after the distribution pipelines have been filled. As a result, companies will be forced to discontinue production. Even when the initial product performance is very encouraging, any subsequent serious decline in that performance might justify a reclassification of the product from growth to nongrowth. This is exactly what has happened to Product J. This example is by no means typical of all products showing similar trends. It may benefit the company to keep the product on the market, as long as it returns at least a marginal contribution. Thus, although the plan is just a forecast based on data available in 1970, the fact that the next two years show a declining trend does not mean that Product J should be dropped immediately. Normally such products, even though declining in *projection* data, deserve a further observation of their *actual* product performance. There may be financial tradeoffs involving inventories, tax benefits, writeoffs, etc.

It is instructive to note the anticipated performance of Product M, which shows a very modest growth between years 1971 and 1972. Based upon that growth rate, it has been classified as a mature product. Remember that technological breakthroughs in areas such as flavoring, packaging and model features may permit the product to be recycled. In certain cases, the product may substantially outpace the growth of the market itself. As a result, in later years the product may be reclassified as a growth product, as in the case of Product M. Further examples are provided in the product movements in Exhibits G and H in conjunction with Exhibits I and J. Exhibits G and H are examples of worksheets showing product performances segregated into life cycle stages.

In our hypothetical example, Product M moves from a mature stage into the growth stage in the year 1973. In addition, Product J clearly moves from growth into non-growth in year 1973. Notice that Exhibits I and J are presented in terms of dollars, under the heading "unadjusted."

On an unadjusted basis, Plan B might seem superior to Plan A in terms of incremental direct profit dollars. On an unadjusted basis, Plan B returns $182,550,000, compared to $182,310,000 from Plan A. So far in our analysis, we have isolated the product lines into life cycle stages on the basis of the incremental profits contained in the profit plan. Profit dollar aggregates from each stage have been summarized without taking into account the quality of these profits, or the risk involved. Quality of profits and the risk factor introduce another element into our analysis, i.e., cost of capital, which needs little further definition. In our analysis, we shall consider the cost of capital as the target rate of return for capital projects.

### Assigning Profit Quality and Risk Factors

The next step of analysis involves a degree of subjective judgment about the use of cost of capital as a factor of profit quality. Definitions of target rate of return and cost of capital may vary from corporation to corporation. For example, some companies distinguish between the target rate of return required from new capital projects, and those involving either established products or cost reduction projects. Many companies, in practice, set a higher target for new products, reflecting the greater risk involved in new products. Our analysis now requires the assignment of weights to profit dollars from products, based on the appropriate stage of the life cycle. These weights should be viewed as multiples of the cost of capital as defined by the company.

In our hypothetical example, we assumed that the dollar of profit derived from a mature product is the base against which all other profit dollars will be measured. Undoubtedly, a dollar of profit from a growth product is preferable to a dollar of profit from a mature product: the stream of profit dollars from the growth product will be longer than those from the mature product. Since the mature product profit dollars serve as our base rate, we may assign them a weight of one or unity, and to growth product profit dollars a weight of two. This implies that a dollar of profit from a mature product is worth one dollar to the company in terms of its future, as compared to a two dollar value assigned to every profit dollar derived from growth product. The converse is also true. The author has therefore, arbitrarily assigned a weight of 0.50 for a non-growth profit dollar, implying that a dollar of profit from non-growth product is worth only 0.50¢ to the company. This recognizes the drain on corporate resources that can result from carrying a sick product.

This brings us to the problem of assigning weights to development products. Development products may realize losses initially, but have a great potential for either evolving into the growth stage or of being dropped quickly. For this reason, the author has assigned a weight of $1.50 to every development product profit dollar. In other words, every dollar derived from development products is worth $1.50 to the company. This recognizes a hoped-for longevity of source. Conversely, in the event that the development product does not attain its anticipated goal and results into losses, loss of every dollar from a development product is actually a loss of $1.50, because of the opportunity cost inherent in losing a growth prospect.

It should be noted here, however, that the weights assigned are arbitrary and subject to argument. As a matter of fact, any valid argument challenging the weights, can only result in further refinements, suited to the individual requirements of a company. Whether the weights assigned absolutely correctly is irrelevant to the technique, since the same weights will be applied to the analysis of both Plans A and B, therefore negating the impact of any imperfection in the weights. The projects will be measured on the basis of their intrinsic worth. Exhibits I, J and K show the transition from the unadjusted results of Plan A and Plan B, to the adjusted results weighted by the profit quality factor. On an adjusted basis, the advantages of Plan A exceed Plan B by $2,330,000, whereas on an unadjusted basis, Plan B was superior.

Our hypothetical example is included to familiarize the reader with the impact of product life cycles and with the utility of this concept in marketing planning. Many aspects of this concept remain relatively unexplored because of a lack of appropriate models, and the rare application of correlation techniques to the actual histories of the product performance data. As promising

## EXHIBIT I
## SUMMARY RESULTS
## PLAN A
(thousands of dollars)

| | 1971 | 1972 | 1973 | 1974 | 1975 | |
|---|---|---|---|---|---|---|
| *Unadjusted* | | | | | | |
| Growth | 13,750 | 18,900 | 10,200 | 15,700 | 20,100 | |
| Mature | 10,900 | 11,700 | 11,750 | 13,100 | 14,400 | |
| Non-Growth | 7,400 | 6,950 | (390) | 7,450 | 8,250 | |
| Development | — | (500) | (800) | (250) | 800 | |
| Total | 32,050 | 37,050 | 20,760 | 36,000 | 43,550 | |
| | | | | | | *Quality Factor* |
| *Adjusted* | | | | | | |
| Growth | 27,500 | 37,800 | 20,400 | 31,400 | 40,200 | 2.00 |
| Mature | 10,900 | 11,700 | 11,750 | 13,100 | 14,400 | 1.00 |
| Non-Growth | 3,700 | 3,475 | (195) | 3,725 | 4,125 | 0.50 |
| Development | — | (750) | (1,200) | (375) | 1,200 | 1.50 |
| Total | 42,100 | 52,225 | 30,755 | 47,850 | 59,925 | |

## EXHIBIT J
## SUMMARY RESULTS
## PLAN B
(thousands of dollars)

| | 1971 | 1972 | 1973 | 1974 | 1975 | |
|---|---|---|---|---|---|---|
| *Unadjusted* | | | | | | |
| Growth | 14,700 | 19,000 | 9,500 | 9,900 | 20,300 | |
| Mature | 9,500 | 10,400 | 12,300 | 13,000 | 14,500 | |
| Non-Growth | 10,050 | 10,000 | 6,200 | 12,250 | 13,900 | |
| Development | — | (500) | (900) | (300) | 250 | |
| Total | 34,250 | 38,900 | 27,100 | 34,850 | 48,950 | |
| | | | | | | *Quality Factor* |
| *Adjusted* | | | | | | |
| Growth | 29,400 | 38,000 | 19,000 | 19,800 | 40,600 | 2.00 |
| Mature | 9,500 | 10,400 | 12,300 | 13,000 | 14,500 | 1.00 |
| Non-Growth | 5,025 | 5,000 | 3,100 | 6,125 | 6,950 | 0.50 |
| Development | — | (750) | (1,350) | (450) | 375 | 1.50 |
| Total | 43,925 | 52,650 | 33,050 | 38,475 | 62,425 | |

## EXHIBIT K
## COMPARISON OF ALTERNATIVE PLAN RESULTS
(thousands of dollars)

| Year | Unadjusted | | Adjusted | |
|---|---|---|---|---|
| | Plan A | Plan B | Plan A | Plan B |
| 1971 | 32,050 | 34,250 | 42,100 | 43,925 |
| 1972 | 37,050 | 38,900 | 52,225 | 52,650 |
| 1973 | 20,760 | 27,100 | 30,755 | 33,050 |
| 1974 | 36,000 | 34,850 | 47,850 | 38,475 |
| 1975 | 43,550 | 48,950 | 59,925 | 62,425 |
| TOTAL | $169,410 | $184,050 | $232,855 | $230,525 |

as the concept is, its true value cannot be realized unless industries actively involve themselves in intensive model building and in the establishment of more consistent correlations between various marketing factors. The product life cycle concept has as brilliant and exciting a future as any one of today's successful marketing techniques.

The proposed market planning and control system is expensive, but this cost must be compared to the greater overt and hidden costs of having an imperfect and unscientific market plan. Furthermore, spurring corporate executives to define standards, gather information, and make decisions in this manner, creates a system which brings the company much closer to the institution of formal long-range product and market planning procedures.

# Chapter VIII

# The Marketing Controller Concept

Much of the data presented so far emphasizes the vast gaps in the network of relationships involved in quantitative marketing and financial decision-making. There is evidence of hesitancy towards the use of sophisticated techniques which could increase the efficiency of the decision maker. Much of the hesitancy stems from older, entrenched management groups, sorely in need of a modern education in quantitative methods. Other causes stem from the inability of personnel to accept a philosophy which states that the variables of consumer behavior can be quantified and expressed in terms of probabilities. The study also revealed a serious lack of formal interdisciplinary exposure, with the result that accountants tend to think only of accounting while their marketing counterparts think mainly in terms of creative marketing. The path of accounting evolution suggests that the time is ripe for the creation of a new corporate entity, the "marketing controller." His task would be the delineation of quantitative relationships and the assignment of decision uses to them. There can be no question that the accounting precept requiring the matching of expense and revenue is often violated in reports of advertising expense that are based on a September through August media year. The constraint of reporting would impose no barrier to the marketing controller who would attempt to identify sales with related media efforts and thus establish results based on a media year.

The marketing controller would also redefine the parameters of traditional accounting input by attempting to measure the *quality* of profit, leaving *quantity* measurement to the traditionalists. Profit should be considered not only in the context of dollars of monetary value, but also in the context of the risk arising from the source of each dollar of earnings in a product life cycle/profit analysis.

Regrettably, all of this is alien to the traditional accountant.

### The Marketing Controller Concept

The study indicated that many participants practice selected elements of the marketing controller concept, if somewhat informally. In decentralized companies especially, division controllers participate, to some degree, in marketing decision-making and planning.

Each of the participants was asked his reaction to the creation of a new corporate position, the "marketing controller." The position required an individual, financially trained, whose primary responsibility would be to the marketing area with decision-making assistance. He would have access to, and work closely with, the conventional controller, whose main responsibility is reporting. The man would be placed within the marketing function in a decentralized organization, and would be a corporate staff man in a centralized organization. Further, he would filter all quantitative input data for the marketing department.

Each participant was asked, "If a marketing controller's position were established in the functional marketing area, but relatively divorced from conventional accounting, how would his role be envisioned?" The most interesting aspect of the research embodied in the study was that *all twenty companies unanimously endorsed the concept* with an enthusiasm that ran the gamut from moderate to strong.

The greatest agreement concerning a marketing controller's primary duties was that he should *maintain a record of adherence to profit plans*. One large company, immediately concerned with diversifying into consumer areas, posited the man in their media area to establish a statistical background for marketing decisions.

Their marketing controller would, in effect, be a media controller. In carrying out his function, the marketing (media) controller would maintain a "track record for adherence to the profit plan" and report variations to responsible parties. The company's attitude is shaped by their centralized financial and marketing operation and by their type of marketing policy (media is heavily emphasized).

Another consensus was that the marketing controller should *advise on optimum timing for strategies.* One respondent felt that the idea of a marketing controller had "great merit." He spoke positively of a marketing controller's position because "in these days of extreme competition, marketing management cannot afford to make decisions relative to pricing, volumes and costs without knowing the profit impact of such decisions. They need a specialized financial advisor." In his estimation, the marketing controller would report to the marketing area and be considered a fully responsive member of the marketing team.

Company M felt that the marketing controller should be a "two-headed man" who could *understand and evaluate the effect on operations of marketing and financial requirements.* He would take the creative approach to these problems and concern himself mainly with:

a. The control of advertising and promotion
b. The evaluation of promotion alternatives
c. The analysis of the production costs of spot media commercials in order to evaluate customer and geographic profitability.

The company felt that the marketing controller position should be filled by its current division controller, who at times becomes deeply involved in the assessment of marketing opportunities. It stated that the need is for future data, and that emphasis should be placed neither upon historical data nor on custodial reporting in conformance with traditional accounting methods. They felt, however, that such a man should work closely with the accounting controller.

Another company, which asserted that the concept is really not new but that nevertheless "it is an exciting idea," indicated that in the four months preceding the study, it had created the position of a division controller. This division controller, however, has responsibilities that are very close to the spirit of the study. He has a mandate to *exercise free form in rendering assistance,* and that is his only charge. He reports directly to the division head, and is not tied to the corporate controller. The man is free from accounting and reporting rigidities, and concentrates solely on decision-making assistance for marketing. Such an individual, they found, can communicate to marketing in its own language and breach the gulf which exists between finance and marketing.

Almost all the respondents indicated that one of the prime responsibilities of the marketing controller should be to educate the marketing area in the financial implications of decisions. One large company indicated that this would be the man's primary responsibility. The company has found over a period of time that (a) by bringing their sales forces and brand management from all over the country into a centralized location and (b) by exposing them to the financial implications of their decisions, it has reaped large benefits in terms of increased efficiency and awareness of corporate considerations contained within its profit plan. As a result, this two-way communication has become a way of life within the company. The problem, however, is in finding a financially trained individual who can speak the marketing language. Too often the speakers or discussion leaders begin to lose the marketing audience through the use of jargon peculiar to the financial area. The object is to find a "two-headed" individual who was born with one heritage but who has become fluent in a new language.

The more aggressive companies indicated that one of the main advantages of such a corporate individual would his assistance in *evaluating the efficiencies of consumer promotions.* They realized that they had too often deluded themselves in rendering the criteria for promotional efficiency in terms of shares of market and volume gains. They conceded that the name of the game is still profit and that they are now beginning to see fallacies in the market share concept. Additionally, they felt that volume gains are becoming a decreasingly important criteria for efficiency;

they have found, over periods of time, that such gains can be achieved easily, but that the cost is high.

An interesting variation came from a company which indicated that they are currently working toward that concept. The top executives viewed the position as one concerned with "consumer values." Their marketing controller would be an individual capable of *rendering assistance to direct accounts* in order to help them automate purchases and optimize inventory levels. In this sense, he was to act as an "on loan" management consultant.

The range of replies concerning the marketing controller's primary duties is itself an indication of the unfulfilled needs of marketing. It is, in essence, an indictment of the financial function.

In summary, this is the lineup of primary duties for the marketing controller:

. . . Maintain record of adherence to profit plans
. . . Closely control media expense
. . . Prepare brand managers' budgets
. . . Advise on optimum timing for strategies
. . . Measure the efficiency of promotions
. . . Analyze media production costs
. . . Evaluate customer and geographic profitability
. . . Present sales-oriented financial reports
. . . Assist direct accounts to optimize purchasing and inventory policy
. . . Educate the marketing area in financial implications of decisions

Guidelines for incorporating these primary duties into a comprehensive job description for a marketing controller are presented in the Position Guide below.

### Recommendations for Implementing the Marketing Controller Concept

Based upon a detailed analysis of the replies, and conversations with the respondents, a practical position guide can be created for the "marketing controller's" position.

This can be considered as a short form position guide, incorporating the basics of the position:

### THE MARKETING CONTROLLER—ABBREVIATED POSITION GUIDE

*Basic Function:*

The Marketing Controller will provide overall financial guidance and analytical services to the Division Manager of the Marketing Division. He will receive assignments *directly from the Marketing Division Manager* or his appointed representative.

*Specific Activities:*

1. Counsel Marketing Division personnel on the profit impact of proposed marketing plans.
2. Participate actively in marketing division meetings relating to product and division planning, both short and long-term.
3. Provide marketing personnel with item/pack profitability statements, and an analysis of the effect of item mix on profitability.
4. Develop any other analytical techniques required to guide marketing personnel towards maximizing product and division profits.
5. Review and monitor, at least monthly, major raw material inventory costs and market prices, and inform marketing management of trends which might affect pricing or other competitive activity.
6. Review analysis of actual vs. planned profit results and underlying justifications.
7. Work with product managers to improve estimating of promotional expenditures, updating of estimates, and improve analysis of promotion results.
8. Control market research and other miscellaneous expenses in relation to budget.
9. Prepare product profitability analyses by item/pack and by geographic area. This should show allocation of advertising, promotions and sales force expenses to geographic area and/or item/pack.
10. Review and analyze division expenses in terms of available alternatives.
11. Analyze and report direct divisional charges resulting from those marketing division activities which reflect on expendi-

tures of other divisions. (For example,—production schedule changes, special equipment purchases, obsolete materials.)

12. Assist marketing management in the evaluation of promotional and volume alternatives within the agreed marketing division objectives.
13. Assist marketing management in the examination of long-term plans for product profit improvement.

## Is the Concept Realistic?

To the extent that so many modern corporations are now beginning to appreciate the need for specialized decision makers, the basic rational behind the marketing controller concept is entirely realistic. Further reinforcing this thought is the reaction to the study by the twenty participating companies. Recall that the entire sampling of twenty companies felt strongly enough to favor the concept, although to varying degrees. Of those twenty companies, at least three have now begun organizational changes which will make room for the marketing controller.

One of these is a large health aids company. The consumer products division has added a marketing controller whose sole responsibility is to assist the consumer products division in optimizing its decisions. Conversations with the corporate controller have revealed that the entire corporate structure has been profoundly affected. The marketing controller of the division reports to the marketing division head, but still maintains a dotted line relationship to the corporate staff controller. One of the most gratifying results of the change was the reaction of the marketing personnel. The financial area is excited that they are finally making inroads into the marketing area in a manner that is *helpful* to the various echelons of marketing personnel. The sales force has also benefited by exposure to the financial personnel. All sales force personnel periodically attend seminars largely prepared and given by the marketing controller's staff. The object of the seminars is to teach the salesmen the value of selling certain product mixes and thereby increase the overall profitability of the division's product line. In addition, the marketing controller has thus far in his short tenure been helpful in assisting the national sales manager to evaluate the efficiency of the sales force.

The concept, of course, is far too new to provide varied results of different case histories. The concept will probably work best in a decentralized consumer products company. There is no reason, however, why the essentials of the concept cannot be applied to centralized companies. At least one company who was not included in the original study sample is now exploring the possibility of creating the position of a *production* controller. His function would be to optimize production levels with inventory policies. He would also interpret sales requirements established by the marketing staff. This company is a manufacturer of heavy equipment for the paper industry.

It is probable that no finite conclusions can be reached as to the type of company to which the concept is most applicable. In reality, the item of paramount importance is the receptivity of finance and marketing to innovation. This receptivity must be born of a long series of cooperative efforts between the two functional areas. It is unlikely that it can be successfully applied on the basis of an abrupt dictum, because there are too many fluid relationships which will be affected by implementation. If the company's game plan is based upon an objective profit maximization, then it follows that the creative financial man who *feels* marketing, can participate in meeting that objective by applying his best efforts to an area which did not previously recognize his talents.

## The Question of Dual Reporting Relationships

Throughout the course of the study it was obvious that the companies participating in the study were conscious of problems which would be posed by the dual reporting relationships of the marketing controller. None, however, felt that this was an insurmountable problem. All agreed that if the position were structured properly and if all parties concerned entered into the implementation of the marketing controller concept with the correct perspective, it would prove to be an entirely viable program. Their optimism gives confirmation to the original findings of the Controllership Foundation Study,[1] which investigated the reporting relationships for plant and staff controllers in decentralized companies. That study concluded that the evidence "indicates that a division of formal authority is entirely workable." The individual who will serve in the capacity of a marketing controller will have to maintain a loose relationship with his fellow financial men. He obviously cannot create numbers in a vacuum. He may have to depend heavily upon the controller, who will be responsible for custodial financial reporting. This, in itself, may construct somewhat of a personality barrier between the two individuals. Financial people naturally tend to shy away from the limelight, but it is inevitable that the position of marketing controller will absorb some of the aura of glamour normally attributed to the marketing area. The relationship between the two men, therefore, must be structured around common goals. The Controllership Foundation study found that if two individuals have a commonality of interest and a commonality of goals, the fact that there may be personality differences or differences in work emphases, should not present a barrier to an effective working relationship.

## Will the Marketing Controller Be the Man in the Middle?

In a sense, any financial man is always in the middle. On one side he is required to report facts to various authorities and, on the other side, to obtain information with which to create the facts. When the financial man obtains information, he is often confronted with situations which give rise to mutual mistrust between the giver and the recipient. One of the more common instances results from the periodic requirement of the financial function to obtain information from the marketing area relative to firm commitments for various types of promotional spending. Marketing rarely appreciates the reasons for the requirements, let alone the importance and impact of the eventual accrual itself. As a result, the financial people are often looked upon as "experts from out-of-town" who are coming to the marketing area to "spy" on their plans and future strategies. If the marketing controller is positioned as a staff member within the marketing function, much of this type of common irritant will be allayed. A great deal of sensitivity to this situation was expressed by one respondent. The controller of one large food processor indicated that he felt the marketing controller should be capable of establishing secret or hidden reserves for strategic marketing purposes. In this way he would thwart the desire of the corporate staff controller to give firm estimates of profits to company management. For this reason, the staff corporate controller of the company was against positioning the marketing controller within the marketing function. He preferred the position to be an adjunct to his own.

There have been far too many instances of friction between the marketing and financial areas of large companies. This situation has been a widely discussed topic for years. One blatant example occurred a few years ago in the consumer products division of a large pharmaceutical and confectionery company. In order to appreciate the import of the situation, it is necessary for the reader to keep in mind that the Securities and Exchange Commission has the power to force corporations to submit financial data for its review. It requires that sales be reported net of promotional payments expended to achieve the sales. As a result, sales are reported on a "net-net" basis. This often masks the true amount of physical turnover which lies behind the various transactions of companies. Nevertheless, in the eyes of the Securities and Exchange Commission, the transaction has included a de facto price decline and as such, should be reported as a deduction from sales. Bearing this in mind, consider then the following situation which arose in the company mentioned above. The head of the consumer products division, in order to increase sales, authorized the use by his salesmen of temporary promotional offers to their direct accounts. One type of promotional offers employed was called an "off-invoice allowance." This device permits the customer to remit the net amount for a purchase after deducting the allowance from an invoice. Thus, if the merchandise has a list selling price of $10.00 and the promotional grant is $2.00, the purchaser remits to the company a total of $8.00. To meet competitive pressures, companies will often employ this device for short, specified periods of time, sometimes in specified areas. In the case at hand, the marketing head of the division wanted his salesmen to be completely aware of the cost of employing such a device; permission had been granted to the request of the sales force. In the past, financial reports had shown promotional allowances as deductions from sales, and had not highlighted them anywhere on the profit and loss statement. The head of the division felt that for decision-making purposes and, more importantly, for control purposes, such an expense should be shown as a marketing expense in the operating statement and that sales should be reported on a gross basis. He took his case to the corporate controller. The controller replied that he was sorry that he could not accommodate the division head because that such a request was contrary to SEC reporting requirements. The answer, of course, displayed a serious lack of understanding of the decision-making requirements of a specific marketing area, and betrayed an ignorance of the function of financial information. The controller, in this particular instance, was overly concerned with his reporting obligation and should have recognized that he has an equal obligation to assist people in the preparation of effective internal financial statements. Certainly he could have retained his reporting statements for conventional use in supplying information to the Securities and Exchange Commission or other agencies.

## The Nestlé Experience

Five years ago, the financial structure of The Nestlé Company was redesigned to provide for a group of specialists who would assist the marketing function in their decision-making. The controller of the company, which is highly centralized except for the marketing function, has reporting to him five major areas: General Accounting, Cost Accounting, Payroll, Special Projects Analysis, and Financial Analysis and Planning. It was decided that a group of specialists called Marketing Services Analysts be formed within the framework of the marketing-oriented financial analysis and planning area. The main responsibility of these analysts would be to assist the marketing function in a creative and innovative manner. These individuals would be free from any routine or recurring financial responsibilities. As the job was defined, the individual would more often than not find himself seated in the marketing area. The original staff was recruited

from a variety of sources. The bulk of the staff was hired from
other consumer product companies where, for the most part, they
had held positions as financial analysts. Each candidate was chosen on the basis of his broad perspective of the uses of finance,
and his exposure to and interests in the marketing function. The
majority were mature individuals in their early thirties.

In the begining the evolution progressed slowly. Their initial
year was mainly devoted to the pursuit of a marketing education.
They attended sales meetings, traveled with salesmen and product
managers, developed marketing plans, and worked closely at
various strategy sessions with the marketing heads of the divisions. Over the course of time, as the individuals became more
proficient and readily accepted in their jobs, their responsibilities
grew. In retrospect, it can be seen that the five year period since
the inception of the program has provided at least two distinct
benefits for the corporation. Firstly, it has demonstrated that such
an area can be an excellent training ground for future managers
of the company. It is unusual to find one position within a
corporation as firmly situated at the vortex of communications
activities, as is the marketing service analyst. The original group
of analysts has long since been absorbed into management positions within the organization and, at this writing, the third generation of analysts has now completed its training. Two of the original analysts became product managers, one went on to become a
marketing research analyst, two have become assistants to national sales managers, one has become manager of inventory
planning, one was absorbed into the manufacturing area and has
become an assistant office manager for a manufacturing plant,
and one is the administrative assistant for the head of a division.

The analysts all report directly to the divisional marketing
heads. Their sole contact with the corporate controller is to establish the correctness of certain technical procedures and for the
routine personnel evaluations which are made by the controller
in conjunction with the marketing chiefs. Because of their quantitative expertise, the analysts work on unique marketing projects.
These range from establishing and designing linear programming
techniques to optimize the product mix of divisions, to demon-

strating to the product managers within the marketing area the benefits of matrix analysis in evaluating the probable outcomes of price changes and changes in media and promotional strategies. Since its inception, the entire program has been eminently successful. The process of acceptance, itself, has been one of evolution. First the talent had to be demonstrated and then the need acknowledged. In the true marketing sense then, the marketing controller concept as employed by The Nestlé Company, is fulfilling that specific need just as marketing fulfills the needs of the customer.

### Implications of The Marketing Controller Concept

The implications in the assessment of the respondents of the marketing controller concept center on the following points:

a. Marketing has a quantitative need which *traditional* accounting cannot fulfill.

b. Finance, for the most part, is reluctant to provide technical assistance to the marketing decision-makers.

c. Reporting relationships under the concept are considered to be quite testy.

d. Decision-making, as a technique, needs greater sophistication and knowledge on the part of both marketing and finance.

I was left with the impression that if finance could not fulfill marketing's needs, then marketing would seek assistance elsewhere, possibly to the exclusion of finance. This may have serious consequences. If finance can take the lead and train "two-headed men" who will utilize creativity for marketing purposes, the problem should be solved. Finance should also work to create an atmosphere of mutual trust. The fear that marketing controllers will set up their own hidden reserves can be ameliorated by proper reporting techniques and close working relationships. In the final analysis, the reporting relationship of the marketing controller is immaterial, if the man and the job are positioned in an atmosphere of trust and shared objectives.

## Ancillary Problems

Serious professional questions and dissatisfactions exist within the marketing and financial spheres. Twenty companies certainly do not constitute a statistical universe; nevertheless, the firms are large enough and sophisticated enough to be pacesetters. It became obvious during the interviews that the dissatisfactions existing between marketing and finance were of a healthy type; each was attempting to find a mutually satisfactory solution. Frequently, an entrenched management unwilling to accept any risk associated with innovation, was the source of the friction. Thus, the following conceptual problems have emerged.

1. Within professional accounting circles, authorities are reticent to recognize that traditionally separated functional lines are being crossed. Consequently, the professional field has been slow to place a man *within* the marketing area to offer quantitative advice and assistance.
2. This profession, in its preoccupation with reporting, has inhibited the growth of alternative decision techniques, such as relevant costing, by frequently stating that relevant costing and direct costing are undesirable.
3. Marketing, as a profession, has not achieved the unanimity of definition. Finance has.
4. Responsibilities under the marketing concept have not been delineated.
5. Rigidities in accounting statements frequently inhibit marketing creativity.
6. Accounting is not sufficiently marketing-oriented. Thus the use of ROI and customer and geographic profitability studies have not moved beyond the embryonic stage.
7. Analysts are a bashful lot. In written analysis, they place themselves in the position of an unassailable devil's advocate. The author believes that analysis might better be accomplished by face to face discussions prior to any written report.
8. Senior entrenched managements do not understand, and

therefore have not sanctioned, the best use of profitability concepts.

9. Management science techniques have failed to assist in marketing decisions because its proponents have not appreciated the nature of the market's day-to-day dynamics.
10. The role of the controller in decision-making has not been adequately defined. He is taken advantage of for his basic auditing training is used, but his quantitative intuition is neglected.
11. The use of data processing has been limited in the area of marketing decision-making.
12. There is insufficient opportunity for marketing and finance to speak out at any formal strategy sessions.

## Possible Remedies

The dynamics which flow from the academic field to the business area and back, must be utilized extensively in any attempt to improve and strengthen marketing and financial relationships. Specifically, the educational area should recognize its responsibility to prepare the student for his *present* working environment and to train him to exercise his imagination in improving it. Specifically, education could:

1. Make accounting education more flexible by emphasizing financial aspects of:
   a. Agency-client relationships
   b. Marketing promotional planning
   c. The marketing mix
   d. Marketing profitability
   e. Sales incentive systems
2. Encourage the participation of prominent marketing leaders in business dialogues about finance. This should take the form of student-executive forums.
3. Orient managerial accounting away from a manufacturing emphasis and concentrate on a "gestalt" approach that emphasizes the total marketing concept.

4. Give more emphasis in basic accounting to the analysis and evaluation of quantitative relationships, and less to the reporting responsibility.
5. Train the finance employee to become less of an accountant and more of a "total quantitative man."
6. Raise the possibility that the departmental boundaries which compartmentalize accounting, corporate finance, marketing, etc., may be ineffective in this quantitative era.
7. Encourage senior management to return to school for reeducation. It is common for the American Medical Association to periodically offer medical men such an opportunity. Business schools can offer the same. Opportunities for reeducation available through professional associations are inadequate—and are prone to encourage the separation of disciplines and current business techniques.
8. Expose analysts to more uses of simulation techniques and Bayesian logic in finance.
9. Bring EDP education into the classroom with an overview that will present the limitations as well as the potentials for the equipment.
10. De-emphasize the reliance on quantitative techniques, until the human is sufficiently trained to wisely use them.
11. Encourage the overhaul of cost accounting systems. Dearden wrote that "far too many firms have the very latest in EDP equipment installed but are still relying on accounting systems—and particularly, I would add, upon cost accounting systems—that are at least twenty years out of date."[3]

# Appendix

*Interview Guide*

STATEMENT OF PURPOSE: The purpose of this interview is to inquire into the nature of financial/marketing relationships that exist in selected large companies. The major objective of the research is to assess the implications inherent in a proposed new concept for a marketing position, that of a "marketing controller." In order to accomplish the objective, an interview program has been designed which will probe:

1. Degree of efficiency of marketing/financial communication links.
2. Degree of financial participation in marketing decision making.
3. Types of marketing/financial people involved in marketing decision making.
4. Sequence and levels of marketing decision making.
5. Extent to which sophisticated decision techniques are used—(relevant costing, PERT, CPM, computerized media selection, etc.)

CONFIDENTIAL: Information obtained in these interviews will be used as primary research data which may be published. Copies will be available to participants in the study. Replies to questions asked in the interview are restricted only to the author. Material appearing in any published report will not be identified in any way with companies or individuals participating in the study.

*General Questions of Background*

A. *Industry*
1. What standard industry classification (SIC) best describes the company?
2. What are the most important five product lines produced by the company?
3. How does your company define the marketing function? The financial function?
4. Would the marketing function best be described as oriented toward industrial or consumer purposes?
5. Is the company generally considered to be conglomerate enterprise, as the term is commonly used?

B. *Size*
1. What is the size of the company in terms of:
   a. Sales volume?
   b. Number of employees (United States only)?
   c. Mainline products (other than flavor, size variants)?
   d. Number of principal marketing divisions?
   e. Number of employees in largest division?

C. *Customers*
1. Does the company (division) sell primarily to direct consumers?
2. If not, does it sell primarily to:
   a. Direct accounts?        %
   b. Jobbers?                %
   c. Wholesalers?            %
   d. Brokers?                %
   e. Distributors?           %
   f. Interdivisional?        %

D. *Organization—General*
1. Is the company (division) marketing function organized on a centralized or decentralized (divisional) basis?
2. If decentralized, do division managers have ultimate authority in marketing decision making?
3. Is the financial area (excluding treasurer's functions)

organized on a centralized or decentralized (divisional) basis?

4. To whom does the controller (or each divisional controller) report?

E. *Organization—Marketing* (To be asked of marketing only)

1. Does the company have a product manager system?
2. Are product managers held responsible for product profits?
3. How adequate are accounting measures of profit to assess marketing profit responsibility? What criteria are used (ROI, volume, profitability)?
4. What types of financial data are required for marketing decision making?
5. Are marketing personnel trained to understand the implications of financial data?
6. Have there been significant instances where closer financial/marketing communication linkage would have improved marketing decision making?
7. What type of organization exists within the marketing function specifically for planning and control?

F. *Organization—Finance* (To be asked of finance only)

1. Does any part of the financial function exist primarily to service the marketing area?
2. If so, what specific training in marketing equip these personnel for their service function?
3. Are any of the following advanced techniques used for marketing decision making?
   a. Return on investment?
   b. Profitability concept?
   c. Relevant costs?
   d. Other management science techniques (operations research, etc.)?
4. Are marketing personnel capable of understanding the implications resulting from answers derived from these techniques?
5. Is financial data supplied to the marketing function adequate to assess profit responsibility? Assist in marketing decision making?

6. Describe the role of the corporate (division) controller in the following functions:
   a. Purchasing policy?
   b. Pricing?
   c. New product ventures?
   d. Acquisitions?
   e. Sales incentive planning?

G. *Decision Making—General*
   1. Which marketing and financial personnel are involved in decisions pertaining to:
      a. Pricing?
      b. New product ventures?
      c. Acquisition policy?
      d. Sales incentive planning?
      e. Purchasing policy?
      f. Return on investment for sales districts?
   2. How does EDP information influence decision making in the areas of:
      a. Test marketing (prior to selection of test market)?
      b. Media selection?
      c. Customer, geographic profitability?
   3. Are there standing committees which meet regularly and possess authority to evaluate marketing strategies and longer term decision implications? Are both marketing and finance represented on the committee?

H. *Training and Learning*
   1. Do formal programs exist to provide:
      a. In-house seminars by outside experts?
      b. Off-location education?
      c. Interdepartmental training?
   2. Is it desirable for marketing and financial personnel to be formally trained in each other's respective functional area?

I. *Marketing Controller*
   1. If a marketing controller's position were established in the functional marketing area, but relatively divorced from conventional accounting, how would his role be envisioned?

2. Do you feel that a "different" type of reporting system for marketing decision making is needed? Different from accounting reports now received?
3. Would you be concerned about a possible duplication of staff if a marketing controller were appointed? Might the benefits outweigh the disadvantages?

J. *Additional Data Requested*
  1. Position descriptions for:
     a. Controller-corporate, division
     b. Product manager
     c. Financial (product) analysts

The last major section probed the ramifications of the "marketing controller" concept, chiefly the opinions of those interviewed and their concepts of the position.

## Profile of the Companies Interviewed

Twenty of the largest companies in the United States were seen and interviewed. All companies (or divisions of companies) had annual revenues which exceeded $30 million. The distribution is set forth below:

| Amount of Annual Revenue | Number of Firms | % of Total |
|---|---|---|
| Over $1 billion | 5 | 25 |
| $500–$999.9 million | 6 | 30 |
| $100–$499.9 million | 7 | 35 |
| $ 50–$ 99.9 million | 1 | 5 |
| $ 30–$ 49.9 million | 1 | 5 |
| Total | 20 | 100% |

It should be remembered in the above tabulation instances where a segment of a company was interviewed only the sales of that segment were included in the tabulation. For example, the segment showing revenues of $30 million is a part of a $600 million company. From a *total* company point of view, none of the companies interviewed would have ranked lower than 480 in the *Fortune 500* listing for 1966. Aggregate sales for all companies or divisions interviewed were about $16 billion, approximately 5% of the *Fortune* listing.

Another interesting positioning of the respondents is shown by the scope of the product interests for the specific consumer items covered in the report:

### Beverages and Food

Beer

Coffee

Tea

Chocolate

Milk

Nutritionals

Soup

Margarine

Vegetable juices

Processed foods

Pet foods

Spaghetti

Baby foods

Frozen bakery products

Cereals

Confectionery products

Desserts

Alcoholic beverages

Beans

### Health and Beauty Care Products

Hospital products

Spray antiseptics

Analgesics

Antacids

Cardiac medicinals

Gynecological products

Breath sweeteners

Soaps

Cosmetics

Dentifrices

Dental products

Detergents

Fragrances

Prescription drugs

### Miscellaneous

Air transportation

Electric blankets

Broadcast equipment

Television sets

Cigarettes

Cigars

Tobacco

Cup and container products

Household paper products

Floor finishes

Electric clocks

Cement repair products

Hair dryers

Reproduction papers

In terms of SIC codes, the companies are classified as shown below. The one caution in viewing the tabulation is that in instances where a particular consumer segment was interviewed, it may have little bearing on the overall company classification.

### *Distribution of Respondents by SIC Code*

| SIC Code, Description | | Number of Companies | % of Total |
|---|---|---|---|
| 202 | Dairy products | 1 | 5 |
| 203 | Canning and preserving | 1 | 5 |
| 207 | Confectionery and related products | 1 | 5 |
| 208 | Beverages | 2 | 10 |
| 209 | Miscellaneous and kindred food preparative products | 2 | 10 |
| 211–214 | Cigarettes, cigars, tobacco and snuff | 1 | 5 |
| 241–261 | Paper, lumber and wood products | 1 | 5 |
| 284 | Cosmetics, soap and other toilet preparations | 6 | 30 |
| 286, 289 | Industrial chemicals, synthetics, plastics | 1 | 5 |
| 366–367 | Communications equipment, components and accessories | 1 | 5 |
| 361–362 | Electrical transmission apparatus | 1 | 5 |
| 383–365 | Optical, surgical and ophthalmic goods | 1 | 5 |
| 451–452 | Air transportation | 1 | 5 |
| Total | | 20 | 100% |

Another interesting characteristic of the sample is shown by the number of mainline products (other than flavor or size variants) in the respondent companies. These results are consonant with the number of firms which reported they employed the product manager concept. The mainline product summary is shown below:

*Distribution of Respondents by Number of Mainline Products*

| Number of Mainline Products | Number of Companies | % of Total |
|---|---|---|
| Over 100 | 4 | 20 |
| 75–99 | 3 | 15 |
| 50–74 | 2 | 10 |
| 25–49 | 5 | 25 |
| Under 25 | 6 | 30 |
| Total | 20 | 100% |

All respondents were entirely cooperative and intensely interested in the subject of the research. They volunteered valuable additional material in the form of operating statement formats, organization charts and position descriptions.

# Notes and Bibliography

### AUTHOR'S PREFACE

1. The Interview Guide is reproduced in the Appendix.

### CHAPTER I

1. Sam R. Goodman, *Techniques of Profitability Analysis,* New York, John Wiley & Sons, Inc., 1970.
2. Clarence E. Eldridge, "The Management of the Marketing Function; No. 1—Marketing." New York, Association of National Advertisers, Inc., 1966, p. 2.
3. John Howard and Jagdesh Sheth, *The Theory of Buying Behavior,* John Wiley & Sons, Inc., 1970.
4. Michael Schiff and Martin Mellman, *Financial Management of the Marketing Function,* New York, Financial Executives Research Foundation, 1962, p. 146.

### CHAPTER II

1. Marketing Definitions: A Glossary of Marketing Terms, compiled by The Committee on Definitions of the American Marketing Association, Ralph S. Alexander, Chairman, Chicago; American Marketing Association, 1960, p. 15.
2. T. A. Staudt and D. A. Taylor, *A Managerial Introduction to Marketing,* Englewood Cliffs, N.J., Prentice-Hall, 1965, p. 10.
3. H. Lazo and A. Corbin, *Management in Marketing,* New York, McGraw Hill Book Company, Inc., 1961, p. xii, Preface.
4. Remus Harris, "New Product Marketing Instituted by Agency V.P.," *Advertising Age,* December 27, 1965, p. 39.
5. H. Jackson Hendricks, "Marketing—The Accountant's New Frontier," *The National Public Accountant,* April 1963, pp. 21–24.
6. Clark Sloat, "What the Accountant Can Do for the Marketing Executive," *The Price Waterhouse Review,* Winter, 1963, pp. 2–8.
7. Ibid, p. 3.
8. Ibid, p. 3.
9. A dialogue between Professors Jack Schiff and Michael Schiff, "The Role of Accounting in Marketing," *Sales Management,* December 3, 1965, pp. 36–45.

241

10. Robert Clewett, "Marketing Opportunity and Corporate Management," Proceedings, American Marketing Association, September 1965, p. 188.
11. Ibid, p. 194.
12. Bruce E. Mallon and Stephen D. Silver, "Modern Marketing and the Accountant," *Cost and Management,* February, 1964, pp. 75–85.
13. Robert E. Weigand, "The Accountant and Marketing Channels," *The Accounting Review,* July, 1963, pp. 584–590.
14. Remarks by Lynn Townsend, "How Chrysler Restyled Its Top," *Business Week,* December 10, 1966, pp. 71–81.
15. Schiff and Mellman, op. cit., p. 34.

## CHAPTER III

1. Schiff, Michael, op. cit., p. 42.
2. Thomas C. Kelley, Jr., "The Marketing-Accounting Partnership in Business," *Journal of Marketing,* July, 1966, Vol. 30, pp. 9–11.
3. John W. Barry, "Accounting's Role in Marketing," *Management Services,* January-February, 1967, pp. 43–50.
4. Sam R. Goodman, "Management Accounting and the New Marketing Concept," *Budgeting,* January/February, 1968, Vol. 16, No. 4, pp. 20–22, 27.
5. Sam R. Goodman, "Controller in the New Marketing Concept,"— Correspondence, *Financial Executive,* August, 1967, Vol. 35, No. 8, p. 4.
6. Richard A. Feder, "How to Measure Marketing Performance," *Harvard Business Review,* May-June, 1965, Vol. 43, No. 3, pp. 132–142.
7. Kenneth Ford, "Decisions: Can Science Take Out the Guesswork," *Printers' Ink,* March 12, 1965, Vol. 292, No. 5.
8. The précis by *Sales Management* in its December 15, 1967 issue of the report by the Sales Executive Club entitled, "Adoption of the Marketing Concept—Fact or Fiction," commented that most companies have a marketing attitude and believe that the product should be shaped to consumer wants. The same précis, though, also noted that only 9 of the 464 companies studied have a "fully implemented marketing program."
9. Clarence Eldridge, op. cit., p. 1.
10. See, for example, Pearson Hunt, Charles M. Williams and Gordon Donaldson, *Basic Business Finance,* Homewood, Ill., Richard D. Irwin, Inc., Third Edition, 1966, p. 171.
11. "Centralization vs. Decentralization in Organizing the Controller's Department," Controllership Foundation, August, 1954.
12. Ibid, p. 11.
13. Neal J. Dean, "The Computer Comes of Age," *Harvard Business Review,* January-February 1968 Vol. 46, No. 1, p. 84.
14. Sam R. Goodman, "Improved Marketing Analysis of Profitability, Relevant Costs, and Life Cycles," *Financial Executive,* June, 1967, Vol. 35, No. 6, p. 28.

## CHAPTER IV

1. Schiff and Mellman, op. cit., pp. 136–137.
2. Harold W. Jasper, "Future Role of the Accountant," *Management Services,* January-February, 1966, Vol., No. 1, 1.52.
3. Eldridge, op. cit., Essay 16, p. 5.
4. Ibid, p. 11.
5. Sam R. Goodman, "Management Accounting and the New Marketing Concept," *Budgeting,* January-February 1968, Vol. 16, No. 4, p. 22.
6. Robert Beyer, "Profitability Accounting for Planning and Control," New York, Ronald Press, 1966, p. 4.
7. Sam R. Goodman, "Improved Marketing Analysis of Profitability, Relevant Costs and Life Cycles," *Financial Executive,* June, 1967, p. 29.
8. Beyer, op. cit., p. 6.
9. Ibid, p. 11.
10. The Product Manager System; Experiences in Marketing Management No. 8, New York, National Industrial Conference Board, 1965, p. 50.
11. Michael Schiff, "The Use of ROI in Sales Management," *The Journal of Marketing,* July, 1963, p. 72.
12. The Product Manager System—A Symposium, National Industrial Conference Board, New York, 1965.
13. Controllership Foundation, op. cit., p. 13.
14. Controllership Foundation, op. cit., p. 83.
15. Buchin, Stanley I., "The Harbets Simulation Exercise and Management Control," Bonini, Jaedicke and Wagner (Eds.), Management Controls: New Directions in Basic Research, New York, McGraw Hill, 1964, p. 135.
16. Peter Drucker, "Controls, Control and Management," Management Controls: New Directions in Basic Research, Charles Bonini, Robert Jaedicke and Harvey Wagner (Eds.), New York, McGraw Hill, 1954, p. 286.

## CHAPTER V

1. Michael Schiff, op. cit., p. 70.
2. Bruce D. Henderson and John Dearden, "New System for Divisional Control," *Harvard Business Review,* September-October 1966, Vol. 42, No. 6, p. 111.
3. Philip A. Scheuble, Jr., "ROI for New Product Policy," *Harvard Business Review,* November-December 1964, Vol. 42, No. 6, p. 111.
4. Robert Beyer, "Meaningful Costs for Management Action," *Harvard Business Review,* September-October 1960, Vol. 38, No. 5, p. 63.
5. Feder, op. cit., pp. 132–133.
6. Edward B. Roberts, "Industrial Dynamics and the Design of Management Control Systems," Management Controls: New Directions in Basic Research, Charles Bonini, Robert Jaedicke and Harvey Wagner (Eds.), New York, McGraw Hill, 1954, p. 124.

7. Michael Schiff and J. S. Schiff, "New Sales Management Tool: ROAM," *Harvard Business Review,* July-August, 1967, Vol. 45, No. 4, p. 59.
8. Based on ideas expressed in "Expanded Uses of the ROI Concept," *Financial Executive,* March, 1968, Vol. 36, No. 3, p. 30, by Sam R. Goodman. Certain passages are reproduced with permission.
9. Sam R. Goodman, "Improved Marketing Analysis of Profitability, Relevant Costs and Life Cycles," *Financial Executive,* June, 1967, Vol. 35, No. 6, p. 29.
10. This Exhibit was originally contained in an article in the *Financial Executive,* entitled "Improved Marketing Analysis of Profitability, Relevant Costs and Life Cycles," June 1967 by the author.

CHAPTER VI

1. Charles T. Horngren, Cost Accounting: A Managerial Emphasis, Englewood Cliffs, N.J., Prentice-Hall, Inc., 1965, p. 375.
2. Sam R. Goodman, "Management Accounting and the New Marketing Concept," *Budgeting,* January-February, 1968, Vol. 16, No. 4, p. 22.
3. Ibid., p. 30.
4. Robert D. Buzzell, *Mathematical Models and Marketing Management,* Harvard University Press, 1964.
5. Arthur B. Toan, Jr., "Management Science. . . . Its Impact on Management Thinking," *Price Waterhouse Review,* Winter, 1964, p. 3.
6. William J. Vatter, "The Use of Operations Research in American Companies," *The Accounting Review,* October, 1967, Vol. 42, No. 4, p. 727.
7. Peter Drucker, op. cit., p. 294.
8. Dean, op. cit., p. 89.
9. Joseph N. Froomkin, "Marketing Management and the Computer," Sales Management, Vol. 95, No. 4, August 20, 1965, p. 50.
10. C. Merle Crawford, "A Shotgun Marriage of Mathematics and Marketing," Business Horizons, Summer, 1966, Vol. 9, No. 2, pp. 37–38.
11. Ridley Rhind, "Management Information Systems," *Business Horizons,* June, 1968, Vol. 11, No. 3, p. 37.

CHAPTER VII

1. The subject of product life cycles is intensely complex. A fine exposition of the subject can be found in an unpublished masters thesis by one of my graduate students, Ashok Gupta. His thesis entitled, "Product Life Cycles: A New Dimension to Marketing Strategy," is on file in the library at the Iona College, Graduate School of Business Administration. I am indebted to him for many of his stimulating thoughts.
2. Theodore Levitt, "Exploit the Product Life Cycles," *Harvard Business Review,* Nov.-Dec., 1965, p. 81.
3. Thomas A. Staudt and Donald A. Taylor, *A Managerial Introduction to Marketing,* (Prentice-Hall, Inc., Englewood Cliffs, N.J., 1965), p. 147.

4. Gosta Mickwitz, *Marketing and Competition,* (Helsingfors, Finland, Centraltryckeriet, 1959), p. 88.

5. Robert D. Buzzell, "Competitive Behavior and Product Life Cycles," *New Ideas for Successful Marketing,* (American Marketing Association, Chicago, Ill., 1966), pp. 46–67.

6. Arch Patton, "Top Management's Stake in the Product Life Cycles," *Management Review,* June 1959, p. 12.

7. Sam R. Goodman, *Techniques of Profitability Analysis,* John Wiley & Sons, Inc., New York, 1970, p. 79.

8. Joel Dean, "Pricing Policies for New Products," *Harvard Business Review,* Nov.-Dec., 1950, p. 28.

9. *The Nielsen Researcher,* (A. C. Nielsen & Co., Nov., 1968, New York).

10. This Exhibit was originally contained in an article in the *Financial Executive* entitled, "Improved Marketing Analysis of Profitability, Relevant Costs and Life Cycles," June 1967 by the author.

11. The basic format for solving product life cycle analyses was originally set forth by the author in his book, *Techniques of Profitability Analysis,* John Wiley & Sons, Inc., New York, 1970. Schedules E through H follow that format but are original and created especially for this volume.

## CHAPTER VIII

1. Controllership Foundation, Idem.

2. Eldridge, op. cit., Essay No. 16.

3. Rhind, op. cit., p. 39. He is referring to the Dearden article titled, "Can Management Information be Automated," which appeared in the March/April 1964 issue of *Harvard Business Review.*